NEGOTIATING THE NAZI OCCUPATION OF FRANCE

Basque Conference Papers Series No. 19

NEGOTIATING THE NAZI OCCUPATION OF FRANCE

Gender, Power, and Memory

Edited by Sandra Ott

This book was published with generous financial support from the Basque Government.

Center for Basque Studies
University of Nevada, Reno
1664 North Virginia St.
Reno, Nevada 89557 usa
http://basque.unr.edu

Copyright © 2022 by the Center for Basque Studies and the University of Nevada, Reno
Series: Basque Conference Papers Series No. 19
Series Editor: Sandra Ott
Paperback 978-1-949805-52-9
Hardcover 978-1-949805-53-6
All rights reserved.

Cover image credit: From the collections of the E. Ringelblum Jewish Historical Institute

Library of Congress Cataloging-in-Publication Data:
Names: Ott, Sandra, editor.
Title: Negotiating the Nazi occupation of France : gender, power and memory
   / edited by Sandra Ott.
Description: [Reno, Nevada] : Center for Basque Studies Press, 2022. |
   Series: [Basque Conference Papers] | Includes bibliographical references and
   index. | Summary: "The history of the Nazi occupation in France in the
   lens of power and gender"-- Provided by publisher.
Identifiers: LCCN 2022009488 | ISBN 9781949805529 (paperback)
Subjects: LCSH: France--History--German occupation, 1940-1945.
Classification: LCC D802.F8 .N44 2021 | DDC 944.081/6--dc23/eng/20220225
LC record available at https://lccn.loc.gov/2022009488

Printed in the United States of America

Contents

Acknowledgments	vii
Introduction *by Sandra Ott*	1
1. Human Photography: Julia Pirotte's Portraits of Life in Occupied Marseille *by Abigail E. Lewis*	14
2. The Effects of the German "Occupation" on Relief Work in Unoccupied France *by Shannon L. Fogg*	41
3. A Women's Occupation? Female Wehrmacht Auxiliaries in France and Europe, 1940–1944 *by Julia S. Torrie*	62
4. The "Wild East" and the "Soft West": Alcohol, Masculinity, and Geographies of Sexual Violence *by Edward B. Westermann*	86
5. Otto Doberschütz: A Nazi Officer's Unlikely Relationship with a Basque Double Agent *by Sandra Ott*	108
6. Dining at the Tour d'Argent: Ernst Jünger, Power and the Othering of Paris *by Bertram M. Gordon*	137
7. "Millions of men in Germany and elsewhere have more than one reason to be ashamed": Franco-German Commemorative Scripts and the Gurs Camp *by Scott Soo*	164
Contributors	193
Index	197

Acknowledgments

This book is the result of a two-day conference in early March 2020 at the William A. Douglass Center for Basque Studies at the University of Nevada, Reno. The conference convened just days before the COVID-19 pandemic began to alter the lives of millions of people around the world. In our correspondence during the past year and a half, conference participants have often noted how fortunate we were to have had the opportunity to meet for what proved to be an intellectual and social highlight of 2020. We look back upon our small gathering as a very special privilege. The conference gave scholars of Nazi Germany and occupied France a rare opportunity to explore multiple transnational perspectives on the war and genocide in both the East and the West, rather than through a solely German or French lens.

My sincere thanks go to those historians who contributed chapters to this book, as well as to Julie Schweitzer, archivist at the National Institute for Holocaust Documentation at the United States Holocaust Memorial Museum in Washington, DC. Julie presented a paper at the conference on "Collections Documenting Gurs at the United States Holocaust Memorial Museum," based mainly upon collections of personal papers held at the USHMM, as well as the digital copies of collections received from international repositories. Her presence at the conference gave us a rare chance to learn about an archivist's perspective on our research. I also wish to thank Xabier Irujo, director of the William A. Douglass Center for Basque Studies, for his presentation on the bombing of Gernika by Hitler's Condor Legion in 1937. The horrific destruction of that Basque market town and thousands of human lives highlights the importance of analyzing Nazi atrocities against innocent civilians before World War II under an avowed "neutral" dictatorship, complicit with Hitler.

The contributors and I are also grateful to the two anonymous peer reviewers who graciously commented on an earlier version of this book. We appreciated their valuable comments and suggestions for improvement. One reviewer lamented that this book contains little information about the Basques during the Occupation of France, especially given that it is published by the Center for Basque Studies Press. I take full responsibility. As the organizer of the conference, I wanted to widen the lens of intellectual inquiry beyond Basque Studies, while also providing a transnational framework within which to place the wartime and postwar experiences of one particular (and rather unusual) French Basque double agent, Jean Laborde. Chapter 5, "Otto Doberschütz: A Nazi Officer's Unlikely Relationship with a Basque Double Agent," explores the relationship established by Laborde and Doberschütz in occupied Pau. I explore the "Basque side" of this curious friendship in depth in chapter 12 ("Duplicitous Accommodation: A Basque Double Agent and a Nazi Officer") of *Living with the Enemy: German Occupation, Collaboration and Justice in the Western Pyrenees, 1940–1948* (Cambridge University Press, 2017). Basques' experiences in negotiating the Nazi Occupation and the Vichy regime, their experiences of internment at Gurs, and their involvement in resistance activities and in the liberation of France constitute important topics covered by numerous secondary sources, to which I refer readers with a special interest in this area.[1]

The conference would not have been possible without the generous financial assistance of the Autonomous Basque Government, the Center for Basque Studies at UNR, and the Hilliard Foundation, which funded travel and accommodation for Professor Scott Soo. In addition to presenting a conference paper, Soo gave a Hilliard Endowment Lecture on "Mass Internment: The Complexities of Commemorating France's 'Concentration' Camps." My sincere thanks are also due to Kate Camino, our administrative assistant at the Center, who handled all travel, accommodation, and meals for conference participants; to our doctoral students in Basque studies (Edurne Arostegui, Nerea Eizagirre, Callie Greenhaw, and Eneko Tuduri), who kindly helped with logistical arrangements; to our student assistant at the Center for Basque Studies Press, Carly Sauvageau, for her much-appreciated technical help with the manuscript; and to my colleagues at the Center (Larraitz Ariznabarreta, Xabier Irujo, and Mariann Vaczi) for their participation in our conference and post-conference conversations. Finally, I extend my warm thanks to Marie-Louise Lekumberry at J. T.'s Basque Restaurant in Gardnerville, Nevada, for having provided a memorable, family-style Basque dinner for conference participants, who now know that Basques take commensality and camaraderie very seriously indeed.

—Sandra Ott
William A. Douglass Center for Basque Studies
University of Nevada, Reno
Reno, NV

Notes

1. My monograph, *War, Judgment, and Memory in the Basque Borderlands, 1914–1945* (University of Nevada Press, 2008), examines the impact of war and foreign occupation on four French Basque communities and provides a bibliography on the Basques under the German Occupation. The principal French language references include, among others, works by Isabelle Bilbao, *Jean Ybarnegaray: Entre "petite patrie et grande patrie"* (Baiona: Elkar, 2013); Mixel Esteban, *Regards sur la Seconde Guerre Mondiale en Pays Basque* (Baiona: Elkar, 2007); Gisèle Lougarot, *Dans l'ombre des passeurs* (Donosti: Elkar, 2004); Laurent Jalabert and Stéphane Le Bras (eds.), *Vichy et la collaboration dans les Basses-Pyrénées* (Pau: Cairn, 2015); Laurent Jalabert (ed.), *Exodes, Exils et Internements dans les Basses-Pyrénées (1936–1945)* (Pau: Cairn, 2014; Laurent Jalabert (ed.), *Les Basses-Pyrénées pendant la Seconde Guerre Mondiale 1939–1945: Bilan et perspectives de recherche* (Pau: Presses de l'Université de Pau et des pays de l'Adour, 2013; Jean-Claude Larronde, *Le bataillon Gernika; les combats de le Point-de-Grave (Avril 1945)* (Bayonne: Bidasoa, 1995); and Louis Poullenot, *Basses-Pyrénées, occupation, libération 1940–1945* (Biarritz: Éditions J&D, 1995). For Gurs, see Josu Chueca, *Gurs: El campo vasco* (Tafalla: Txalaparta, 2007) and Claude Laharie, *Le camp de Gurs, 1939–1945: un aspect méconnu de l'histoire du Béarn* (Pau: Infocompo, 1985).

Introduction

Sandra Ott

The French and the myriad of foreigners who lived in wartime France often developed clever strategies for negotiating the Nazi Occupation of 1940–1944. As the excellent work of Robert Gildea shows, many ordinary citizens learned how to cope with their circumstances, "demonstrating imagination, resourcefulness, and Gallic cunning in order to make the Occupation liveable."[1] As several studies reveal, the French and minority groups such as the Basques often figured out how to live with the Germans in their midst.[2] This sometimes entailed living in harmony and cooperating with the "enemy," accommodating to the Germans' presence, or rejecting them through various modes of resistance and hostility, among other responses. A wide range of factors motivated people's choices: the possibility of economic gain; a desire to protect and to provide for loved ones; a humanitarian and/or ideologically driven urge to help people whose lives the German and Vichy authorities threatened; an opportunity to take revenge against personal enemies and rivals; sexual desire and sometimes love; and, among others, an ideological commitment to rid France of the German occupiers. People so often simply tried to survive the Occupation as best as they could; and contrary to early perceptions of the French people, most were neither "bad" nor "good" in a murky moral universe that was decidedly not black and white. As this book argues, that murky universe needs to be explored beyond the solely French or German experience.

The contributors to this collection of essays take an innovative approach to the ways in which various French, German, Jewish, American, and Basque individuals experienced and negotiated the Occupation at a grassroots level. By largely focusing on daily experience, the authors create a space in which to explore relations among people of varying ethnic, religious, regional, and national identities who lived in France at that time. The authors also engage with multiple disciplines: anthropology, history, visual studies, genocide studies, transnational studies, memory studies, and gender studies.[3] Their interdisciplinarity and differing national perspectives help them break down barriers that have so often led historians to take a one-sided approach to the German Occupation of France.

The chapters that follow are geographically and temporally broad. They raise important questions about the nature of foreign occupation itself, especially in relation to gender roles, values, and expectations; agency, violence, and power; transnational networks; humanitarian aid; spaces of exception, commemoration, and memory; and human sociability; among others. Tensions figure prominently in many of the chapters: tensions in personal and institutional relationships, tensions generated by power struggles and by contradictions between ideology and practice, and tensions over gender and identity, to name a few. The stories told in these chapters take the reader not only to occupied France and Nazi Germany, but also to Austria, Eastern Europe, the Soviet Union, and the United States. The transnational connections people and institutions made before, during, and after the Second World War are another recurring theme of this book, which also highlights the importance of widening the timeframe of our analyses to the decades preceding and following the Occupation. As several chapters reveal, prewar, wartime, and postwar experiences all shaped the choices and strategies of individuals and groups in their negotiations at macro- and micro-historical levels. Thus, this book modestly seeks to build upon developments in the historiography of occupied France; and while it fits in with a growing current of scholarship that emphasizes the complexity of that period, this volume is also innovative in its exploration of the transnational, multi-cultural nature of human interactions during a "long" Second World War, one other striking feature of this collection.

In 1972, the publication of Robert O. Paxton's *Vichy France: Old Guard and New Order, 1940–1944* had a longstanding impact on studies of France under the German Occupation, shaping much of the scholarship that has followed. Drawing upon German archives yet retaining a focus on Franco-French relations from a "top-down" perspective, Paxton argued controversially that the Vichy regime had actively pursued its own authoritarian and racist agenda under the "National Revolution" and had "established a voluntary (though militarily neutral) collaboration within Hitler's Europe."[4] Since then and until the 1990s, most historians of occupied France mainly focused on the French and on Vichy's agency during the Second World War. Scholars tended to compartmentalize themselves into specialists on Vichy, on French-focused collaboration, or on the Resistance, and they developed a rich literature with a largely Franco-French perspective.

In the late 1990s and early twenty-first century, historians of the German Occupation and Liberation of France, such as Philippe Burrin, Robert Gildea, Richard Vinen, and Hilary Footitt, addressed the problematic categories of resistance and collaboration, as well as the "good" versus the "bad" French, by introducing concepts such as accommodation and cohabitation.[5] These new categories enabled them and other scholars to explore more effectively the strategies employed by the French as they negotiated their relationships with one another and with the Germans in their midst.[6]

Until recently, most historians who have taken a social, cultural-historical approach to the French experience of the Occupation have tended to leave German soldiers as "a faint shadow in the background." Some historians shifted their gaze from "high politics" to everyday life yet often retained a quite one-sided, French perspective.[7] While there is now an increased emphasis in the literature on Germans' experiences in wartime France, all too often scholars replaced a Franco-French perspective with a German-centric approach. (Both perspectives were probably a function of scholarly training that was discipline and nation-specific.) As Julia S. Torrie points out, historians who have studied the Occupation from a German point of view have tended to take a top-down approach and to focus on German high policy and the military commander in France (*Militärbefehlshaber in Frankreich* or MBF) in Paris.[8] In the late 1960s, one of the earliest historians to focus on a German perspective, Hans Umbreit, analyzed the strategies of the

German military commander in *Der Militärbefehlshaber in Frankreich 1940–1944* (Boppard am Rhein: H. Boldt, 1968). More recently, Thomas J. Laub made a thorough top-down analysis of MBF policies. The experiences of German occupiers at a grassroots level were not their focus.[9]

In his 2016 review of recent scholarship on the Occupation of France, Talbot Imlay emphasized the need for studying the intertwined experiences of both the French and the Germans, rather than focusing solely or mainly on "one side" of the experience at the expense of the other.[10] He invited further exploration of the "interactive dynamics" between the occupied and occupiers and closer examination of the extent to which French and German agency took place. Rather than taking a Germano-German or Franco-French perspective, he argued, the historian can make the most valuable contribution by writing a history of the Occupation that is Franco-German. One masterful exception that predated Imlay's critique is Robert Gildea's regional study of the Occupation, *Marianne in Chains: In Search of the German Occupation*.[11] Gildea's innovative study of Franco-German interactions in the Loire inspired me to focus on relations among the French, the Basques, and the Germans during the Occupation of the Basses-Pyrénées.[12]

Julia S. Torrie's monograph, *German Soldiers and the Occupation of France, 1940–1944* (2018), firmly placed German soldiers in the foreground as she explored their experiences in France at a grassroots level through their diverse modes of consumption, tourism, and leisure. Bertram Gordon likewise made a significant contribution to our understanding of German experiences in occupied France with his monograph, *War Tourism: Second World War France from Defeat and Occupation to the Creation of Heritage* (Cornell University Press, 2018), which focuses on the links between tourism by German personnel and French citizens and war-related memory tourism. I also tried to bring German soldiers "out of the shadows" in *Living with the Enemy* (2017), where I explore the agency of specific German officers in their interactions with local Basque, French, and Spanish citizens in the occupied French Basque Country and Béarn.[13]

The works of Gildea, Gordon, and Torrie, alongside Imlay's call for deepening our approach to Franco-German relations in occupied

France, led me to bring together the contributors to this edited volume for a conference that offered multiple lenses through which to broaden the scope of our inquiries into the Occupation of France. The task proved to be much more complicated than developing a deeper "Franco-German" approach to the period; it also had broader implications than Imlay suggested. Many more than two "sides" were involved in our transnational explorations of prewar, wartime, and postwar human and institutional interactions.

In her chapter on "The Effects of the German 'Occupation' on Relief Work in Unoccupied France," Shannon Fogg uses the activities of the American Friends Service Committee in the southern, unoccupied zone as a lens through which to explore the complex politics of humanitarian aid and the limits imposed upon it or implied during the war. What factors enabled the American Friends to provide aid to children and other victims of Vichy and Nazi oppression? As one of the principal foreign agencies involved in providing wartime aid, the American Friends Service Committee operated in a complex web of relationships. As Americans, Quakers (unlike their British counterparts) were able to work in France until its total occupation in November 1942. As an example of Burrin's structural accommodation, the American Friends worked closely with the collaborationist Vichy authorities and with the Germans; they also liaised with the British (whose blockade they strongly opposed) and American governments.[14] The neutrality of the American Friends and its long history of nonpartisan aid in Europe (especially to Germans during and after the First World War) proved to be instrumental to its humanitarian efforts, through institutional and governmental connections as well as through grassroots-level actions (legal and illegal) by individual Quakers during the German Occupation.

Several authors follow the paths of specific individuals as they variously moved in or between the "soft" occupied West and the "hard" occupied East. In her chapter on "Human Photography: Julia Pirotte's Portrait of Life in Occupied Marseille," Abigail Lewis focuses on the wartime and postwar experiences of Pirotte, a Jewish photographer of Polish descent who was active in Communist and Jewish resistance groups. Pirotte used her camera as "an instrument of struggle" with which to document what the Occupation looked like in Nazi-occupied Marseille at a grassroots level for women, children, workers, the homeless, and for those active in the Resistance. In her moving photographs of women in Marseille, Pirotte often focused on their faces and hands. Her female Jewish subjects frequently looked away from the camera, giving the observer a sense of their physical and emotional discomfort. Her striking photos of children, taken in the Hôtel Bompard internment camp in late summer 1942 (several of which are reproduced in this volume), chillingly shift her gaze to scenes of apparent joy, normalcy, and play. Although told that the internees awaited visas, Pirotte later learned that the women and children she had photographed were deported to Drancy and on to Auschwitz. As Lewis observes, Pirotte wrestled with the "moral weight" of participating in events at Bompard. Returning to her native Poland in 1946, Pirotte also documented violence in her photos of the Kielce pogrom, one of the deadliest episodes of postwar violence against Jews. As a Polish Jew, she had an intimate sense of her own danger in being there. Never fully removed from the violent scenes she encountered, she shared in her subjects' suffering to some extent.

Pirotte's artistic gaze, close observations, and the moral weight of responsibility she felt for documenting the important events she witnessed provide an interesting contrast to the distant and very different gaze of the well-known German officer, Ernst Jünger, whose prewar, wartime, and postwar experiences are the focus of the chapter by Bertram Gordon, "Dining at the Tour d'Argent: Ernst Jünger, Power, and the Othering of Paris." In July 1942, after having dined on *suprême* of sole and the famous duck at the Tour d'Argent in occupied Paris, Jünger described his fellow diners "looking down from their demonic comfort upon the gray sea of roofs at their feet, beneath which the starving eke out their living. In times like this—eating well and much— brings a feeling of power."[15] Power and agency are other recurring themes in this book. As Gordon observes, the quotidian bureaucratic activities of Germans such as Jünger, his privileged position, and the attractions (as well as distractions) of Paris enabled him to avert his gaze from Vichy and Nazi German policies that sent millions of Jews to their deaths and caused severe privations and suffering for most French citizens. In a rare comment about the plight of the Jews, his entry for June 7, 1942, records Jünger's purported embarrassment "to be in uniform" in Paris when he first encountered Jews wearing the yellow star.[16]

Specific individuals are also followed in "Otto Doberschütz: A Nazi Officer's Unlikely Relationship with a Basque Double Agent," which reconstructs the unusual bond forged by Doberschütz and a Basque double agent, Jean Laborde, in Pau. Focusing on "the German side" of this peculiar friendship, I use a gendered analysis to examine manifestations of male camaraderie between these two "frenemies." Both men engaged in acts of performative masculinity through excessive drinking and extramarital liaisons. Resonating with Thomas Kühne's analysis of the "hard" and "soft" sides of masculinity in the Wehrmacht, their relationship also allowed for "femininely coded affection, tenderness, empathy, caring, and moments of weakness."[17] Both men also had extensive, transnational military networks and elite social connections that intersected in Bordeaux and led to their close ties in occupied Pau. Their social interactions with each other and with their French, Basque, and German companions (male and female) show how eating and drinking interacted with ideas about masculinity and its relationship to specific spaces, such as the kitchen.[18] This chapter also offers insight into female complicity with the Third Reich through documents about Otto Doberschütz's Nazi German wife that his American stepdaughter and step-nephew kindly provided. Their attempts to find out about the wartime experiences of their mother/aunt led them to me and add a poignant postscript about silence, memory, and contradictory family desires to reveal and to conceal the truth.

Notions of masculinity and femininity also figure prominently in two chapters that complement each other, as well as my analysis of the Doberschütz/Laborde relationship: Torrie's contribution in "A Women's Occupation? Female Wehrmacht Auxiliaries in France and Europe, 1940–1944," and Edward Westermann's chapter, "The 'Wild East' and the 'Soft West': Alcohol, Masculinity, and Geographies of Sexual Violence." Torrie's chapter shows how Hitler's regime struggled to reconcile its emphasis on the role of German women as nurturing mothers with its need to exploit female labor in occupied territories and with the "hard" masculinity required of a brutal foreign occupation. Torrie explores the impact that female auxiliaries had on the character of the Occupation. Their deployment behind the lines in both France and Eastern occupied territories posed potential problems concerning their safety and military logistics and the more complicated issues relating to their roles as women under National Socialism and what constituted appropriate female behavior in the military. The Nazi regime sought both to avoid the militarization and "masculinization" of German women serving as auxiliaries in the Wehrmacht and to manage the "softness" that female benevolence brought to occupied countries. National Socialism sought to resolve these issues by turning German motherhood into an ideal for the postwar years and elaborated a model of femininity that permitted the large-scale, wartime mobilization of young women in largely service-oriented jobs.

In his chapter, Edward Westermann argues that even as ideals and standards of masculinity and femininity exist only in relation to one another, Nazi perceptions of the East and the West were both imagined areas that, nevertheless, existed in a very real sense primarily in relation to one another. Westermann compares the actions of SS, police, and Wehrmacht forces in occupied Eastern territories of the "hard Wild East" and in the "soft West" of occupied France. Focusing on the role of excessive alcohol consumption, perceptions of masculinity, male camaraderie, and sexual violence, he argues that the double standard for German troops based in the East and West was primarily a manifestation of Nazi racial ideology. A martial masculine mentality justified National Socialist colonization of both geographical spaces and female bodies. However, Nazi ideology, the glorification of hypermasculinity, excessive alcohol consumption, German perceptions of gender and of Eastern populations as racially inferior led to a higher incidence of sexual aggression and violence against "conquered" women in the East—a violence that senior members of the German military regularly chose to ignore or even to encourage as a "right of the victors."

In this book's final chapter, "'Millions of Men in Germany and Elsewhere Have More Than One reason to be Ashamed': Franco-German Commemorative Scripts and the Gurs Camp," Scott Soo explores Gurs as an early site of transnational, Franco-German commemoration associated with the repression and genocide of Jews. On the eastern border of the French Basque Country in Béarn, the former internment camp at Gurs contains the largest cemetery of its kind in France. In October 1940, Vichy authorities interned 6,500 Jews from the Baden and Saarland regions at Gurs. By November 1943, more than 1,000 men and women had perished there. Vichy deported almost 4,000 other Jewish internees at Gurs to Auschwitz from August 1942 to March 1943. French neglect of the cemetery after the camp's closure in 1945 attracted the attention of French Jewish organizations and spurred efforts to create the first commemorative focus of its kind at a former concentration camp. The inscription on the monument erected in 1948 made no reference to the involvement of the French state in the deportations and deaths of Jewish internees. The commemorative narrative crystallized around the transnational inauguration of the Gurs cemetery in 1963, made possible by the collaborative efforts of a German Jewish organization (the Baden Jewish Consistory), German authorities from the Baden region, and a French delegation that included a former French consul who had served in the Palatinate region of Germany during the 1930s. The German and German Jewish speeches of March 1963 acknowledged but also sought to deterritorialize racial discrimination and resistance to Nazi Germany by focusing on common struggles that bound together the people of Karlsruhe and those associated with Gurs. This discourse, however, stood in sharp contrast to the prefect's patriotic framing of the camp as a site that symbolized French opposition and resistance to Nazism, while neatly skirting French culpability for the tragedy of Gurs, specifically, and for the Holocaust in general.

Soo's chapter challenges postwar myths and the silences that surround them. Silences "appear" in other parts of this book, too. They frame many of Pirotte's photographs: silence speaks through the averted gazes and folded hands of Jewish women in Marseille and in the funerary image of the solitary vehicle she photographed in the Old Port of Marseille in early 1943, following the mass deportation of its Jewish residents. Selective silences punctuate the idiosyncratic memoir of Ernst Jünger. Silences have long surrounded the competing human need to remember and the desire to forget what happened in Nazi Germany and occupied France, as found in the family narrative of Otto Doberschütz. As historians of Nazi Germany and occupied France, we all seek to understand why such silences occur and what these silences mean.[19] This volume tries to fill in some of the silences and, by examining relationships that are often overlooked, give voice to those multicultural individuals who "lived" and negotiated their way through the German Occupation of France.

Bibliography

Broch, Ludivine. *Ordinary Workers, Vichy and the Holocaust: French Railwaymen and the Second World War.* Cambridge: Cambridge University Press, 2016.

Broch, Ludivine & Alison Carrol (eds.). *France in an Era of Global War, 1914–1945.* London: Palgrave Macmillan, 2014, pp. 231–240.

Burrin, Philippe. *La France à l'heure allemande, 1940–1944.* Paris: Éditions de Seuil, 1995.

———. *France under the Germans: Collaboration and Compromise.* New York: The New York Press, 1996.

———. "Writing the History of Military Occupations," *France at War: Vichy and the Historians.* Oxford: Berg, 2000, pp. 77–90.

Diamond, Hanna. *Women and the Second World War in France, 1939–1948: Choices and Constraints.* Abingdon, UK: Routledge, 2nd edition, 2013.

Dodd, Lindsey and David Lees (eds.), *Vichy France and Everyday Life: Confronting the Challenges of Wartime, 1939–1945.* London: Bloomsbury Academic, 2018.

Fishman, Sarah. *We Will Wait: Wives of French Prisoners of War, 1940–1945.* New Haven, CN: Yale University Press, 1991.

Fogg, Shannon. *The Politics of Everyday Life in Vichy France: Foreigners, Undesirables, and Strangers.* Cambridge and New York: Cambridge University Press, 2009.

Footitt, Hilary. *War and Liberation in France. Living with the Liberators.* Basingstoke, UK: Palgrave Macmillan, 2004.

Gildea, Robert. *Marianne in Chains: In Search of the German Occupation, 1940–1945.* London: Pan Macmillan, 2002.

———. "Epilogue: A Historiographical Overview," in Ludivine Broch & Alison Carrol (eds.), *France in an Era of Global War, 1914–1945.* London: Palgrave Macmillan, 2014, pp. 231–240.

Imlay, Talbot. "The German Side of Things: Recent Scholarship on the German Occupation of France," *French Historical Studies,* Vol. 39 (No. 1), February 2016, pp. 183–215.

Jackson, Julian. *France: The Dark Years, 1940–1944.* Oxford: Oxford University Press, 2001.

Jünger, Ernst. *A German Officer in Occupied Paris: The War Journals, 1941–1945.* New York: Columbia University Press, translated into English by Thomas S. Hansen and Abby J. Hansen, 2019.

Kühne, Thomas. *The Rise and Fall of Comradeship: Hitler's Soldiers, Male Bonding and Mass Violence in the Twentieth Century*. Cambridge: Cambridge University Press, 2017.

Laub, Thomas J. *After the Fall: German Policy in Occupied France, 1940–1944*. New York: Oxford University Press, 2010.

Ott, Sandra. "The Informer, the Lover and the Gift Giver," *French History*, Vol. 22 (No. 1), (March) 2008, 94–114.

———. *War, Judgment, and Memory in the Basque Borderlands, 1914–1945*. Reno: University of Nevada Press, 2008.

———. *Living with the Enemy: German Occupation, Collaboration and Justice in the Western Pyrenees, 1940–1948*. Cambridge: Cambridge University Press, 2017.

Paxton, Robert O. *Vichy France: Old Guard and New Order, 1940–1944* New York: Columbia University Press, 2nd edition, 2001.

Pollard, Miranda. *Reign of Virtue: Mobilizing Gender in Vichy France*. Chicago: University of Chicago Press, 1998.

Scheck, Raffael. *Love between Enemies: Western Prisoners of War and German Women in World War II*. Cambridge: Cambridge University Press, 2021.

Sweets, John F. *Choices in Vichy France*. New York: Oxford University Press, 1986.

Torrie, Julia S. *German Soldiers and the Occupation of France, 1940–1944*. Cambridge: Cambridge University Press, 2018.

Vinen, Richard. *The Unfree French. Life under the Occupation*. London: Allen Lane, 2006.

Virgili, Fabrice. *Shorn Women: Gender and Punishment in Liberation France*. Oxford: Berg, 2002.

Winter, Jay. *Sites of Memory, Sites of Mourning: The Great War in European Cultural History*. Cambridge: Cambridge University Press, 1995.

Winter, Jay and Emmanuel Sivan (eds.), *War and Remembrance in the Twentieth Century*. Cambridge: Cambridge University Press, 1999.

Notes

1. Robert Gildea, *Marianne in Chains: In Search of the German Occupation, 1940–1945* (London: Pan Macmillan, 2002), 419.
2. In addition to Gildea 2002, see Ludivine Broch, *Ordinary Workers, Vichy and the Holocaust: French Railwaymen and the Second World War* (Cambridge: Cambridge University Press, 2016); Lindsey Dodd and David Lees (eds.), *Vichy France and Everyday Life: Confronting the Challenges of Wartime, 1939–1945* (London: Bloomsbury Academic, 2018); Shannon Fogg, *The Politics of Everyday Life in Vichy France: Foreigners, Undesirables, and Strangers* (Cambridge and New York: Cambridge University Press, 2009); Sandra Ott, *War, Judgment, and Memory in the Basque Borderlands, 1914–1945* (Reno: University of Nevada Press, 2008).
3. Several contributors build upon the work of historians who developed new perspectives on gender in wartime France, including Hanna Diamond, *Women and the Second World War in France, 1939–1948: Choices and Constraints* (Abingdon, UK: Routledge, 2nd ed., 2013); Miranda Pollard, *Reign of Virtue: Mobilizing Gender in Vichy France* (Chicago: University of Chicago Press,

1998); Fabrice Virgili, *Shorn Women: Gender and Punishment in Liberation France* (Oxford: Berg, 2002); and Sarah Fishman, *We Will Wait: Wives of French Prisoners of War, 1940–1945* (New Haven, CT: Yale University Press, 1991). Memory studies relating to both world wars burgeoned in the 1990s, largely through the works of Jay Winter in *Sites of Memory, Sites of Mourning: The Great War in European Cultural History* (Cambridge: Cambridge University Press, 1995). See also Jay Winter and Emmanuel Sivan (eds.), *War and Remembrance in the Twentieth Century* (Cambridge: Cambridge University Press, 1999).

4. Robert O. Paxton, *Vichy France: Old Guard and New Order, 1940–1944* New York: Columbia University Press, 2nd ed., 2001), xviii.
5. Gildea, 233. See Philippe Burrin, *France under the Germans: Collaboration and Compromise* (New York: The New York Press, 1996); Hilary Footitt, *War and Liberation in France. Living with the Liberators* (Basingstoke, UK: Palgrave Macmillan, 2004); Robert Gildea, *Marianne in Chains: In Search of the German Occupation, 1940–1945* (London: Pan Macmillan, 2002), Richard Vinen, *The Unfree French* (London: Allen Lane, 2006).
6. I utilize both concepts in my own work. See Sandra Ott, "The Informer, the Lover and the Gift Giver," *French History*, Vol. 22 (No. 1), (March) 2008, 94–114; *War, Judgment, and Memory in the Basque Borderlands, 1914–1945* (Reno: University of Nevada Press, 2008); and *Living with the Enemy: German Occupation, Collaboration and Justice in the Western Pyrenees, 1940–1948* (Cambridge: Cambridge University Press, 2017).
7. Philippe Burrin observes that German soldiers are often treated as a "faint shadow," in his chapter on "Writing the History of Military Occupations," *France at War: Vichy and the Historians* (Oxford: Berg, 2000), 77–78. Works that do so include Julian Jackson, *France: The Dark Years, 1940–1944* (Oxford: Oxford University Press, 2001); John F. Sweets, *Choices in Vichy France* (New York: Oxford University Press, 1986).
8. Julia S. Torrie, *German Soldiers and the Occupation of France, 1940–1944* (Cambridge: Cambridge University Press, 2018), 9.
9. Thomas J. Laub, *After the Fall: German Policy in Occupied France, 1940–1944* (New York: Oxford University Press, 2010). In my review of the literature, I draw upon the chapter by Robert Gildea, "Epilogue: A Historiographical Overview," in Ludivine Broch and Alison Carrol (eds.), *France in an Era of Global War, 1914–1945* (London: Palgrave Macmillan, 2014), 232. I also use the Introduction to Julia S. Torrie's *German Soldiers and the Occupation of France, 1940–1944* (Cambridge and New York: Cambridge University Press, 2018).
10. Talbot Imlay, "The German Side of Things: Recent Scholarship on the German Occupation of France," *French Historical Studies*, Vol. 39 (No. 1), February 2016, 183–215.
11. Robert Gildea, *Marianne in Chains: In Search of the German Occupation, 1940–1945* (London: Pan Macmillan, 2002).

12. Sandra Ott, *Living with the Enemy: German Occupation, Collaboration and Justice in the Western Pyrenees, 1940–1948* (Cambridge: Cambridge University Press, 2017).
13. More recently, in *Love between Enemies: Western Prisoners of War and German Women in World War II* (Cambridge University Press, 2021), Raffael Scheck provides a rare, comprehensive examination of transnational "forbidden relations" between German women and prisoners of war in Germany.
14. Philippe Burrin, *La France à l'heure allemande, 1940–1944* (Paris: Éditions de Seuil, 1995).
15. Ernst Jünger, *A German Officer in Occupied Paris: The War Journals, 1941–1945* (New York: Columbia University Press), translated into English by Thomas S. Hansen and Abby J. Hansen, 2019, 73.
16. Ibid., 69.
17. Thomas Kühne, *The Rise and Fall of Comradeship: Hitler's Soldiers, Male Bonding and Mass Violence in the Twentieth Century*. Cambridge: Cambridge University Press, 2017.
18. I am very grateful to Ed Westermann for this and other observations made about the version of this chapter presented at the conference in March 2020.
19. I am grateful to Shannon Fogg and Julia Torrie for their correspondence with me about silence. I also thank Fogg for her helpful critique of an earlier draft of this introduction.

CHAPTER 1

Human Photography: Julia Pirotte's Portraits of Life in Occupied Marseille

ABIGAIL E. LEWIS

In 1986, Julia Pirotte, a Jewish photographer of Polish descent, told her life story of photography and political resistance in occupied Marseille for Yale University's Fortunoff Video Archive.[1] Speaking about her motivations for photographing officially and clandestinely during the Nazi Occupation of France, Pirotte stated: "I wanted to leave a little bit of history—what is war, what is occupation, what is Nazism.[2] And my camera helped me in this. I always had it with me."[3] As she told her story, Pirotte showed her interviewers her camera, a Leica Elmar III, she had used her entire career. Pirotte received the camera as a gift for completing photojournalism school in 1938 from Suzanne Spaak, a Belgian resister whom the Nazis executed in August 1944 for helping Jewish children escape France.[4] Throughout her career, Pirotte wielded her camera, a material object she termed her "instrument of struggle," to document the human toll of state violence, racism, and social inequity in wartime France and postwar Poland. Pirotte's photographs of occupied Marseille provide access to two subjective portraits of wartime life: the deeper emotional experiences of occupied society and her own position as she witnessed the destruction of her communities.

This chapter analyzes the relationship between Pirotte's life experiences as a Communist, Jew, artist, and witness, and her aesthetic focus on affect and embodiment as techniques to visualize and record the human impact of violence in her Marseille photographs. Pirotte's methodology invoked her political investment in fighting social inequity and anti-Semitism and her own direct experiences of the same violence to which she bore witness. I offer her photographs as a particular kind of historical record with the ability to display the inner fabric of occupied life and experience: human subjectivity in the face of social displacement, state violence, and political resistance. Deploying techniques of realism and portraiture, Pirotte's wartime photographs display human bodies and emotions to capture the subjective depths of these individuals' experiences and struggles. The potential material survival of the photographs also informed how and why Pirotte photographed. Pirotte intended her images to remind viewers of the lives lost in the fight against fascism, including those of Jews and non-Jews.

My focus on Pirotte's story through her photographs lends insight into the complex experiences of photographers and Jewish refugees in Nazi-occupied France. The history of Pirotte's photographs provides a visual record of life in occupied Marseille for Jews, resisters, and others living on the margins of French society. These portraits also reflect Pirotte's own experiences photographing as a Jew living under occupation in France and fighting in the French Resistance. Her ability to photograph hinged on her own life experiences and human contingencies: Pirotte's choices, her access to a camera, her networks—and also luck—all rendered her artistic pursuits possible. Paying attention to both the visual story that the photographs tell and their material history engages with Pirotte's experiences, her political activism, and her precarity in occupied Marseille. Pirotte returned to her native Poland in 1946, and her experiences living under occupation in France altered how she understood her return to Poland as a Jewish resister and survivor. Pirotte's activities in Marseille as a photographer and resister, her encounters with mass violence, and her personal loss conditioned her response to postwar anti-Semitism and poverty in Poland.

Pirotte's perspective as a Jewish photographer in occupied France is rare. During the Holocaust, photography became a form of power often denied to Jewish practitioners. In France, Jews were denied press passes, professional credentials, and access to cameras. Moreover, the act of documenting anti-Semitic violence came with significant risk. As a result, most photographs of the Holocaust in France are tinged by the politics and power structures of the Occupation and anti-Semitism. French authorities banned all outdoor photography in wartime France beginning in April and May 1940, and German authorities extended this ban in newly occupied France in September 1940.[5] This system of authorization resulted in the exclusion of Jewish photographers from the industry. Only photographers authorized to work by the German and Vichy authorities could photograph in public. In a few cases, Jewish photojournalists continued to work in the press and contributed images that documented political and social life in France. A focus on Pirotte's photographs, as a part of a larger story of photography and resistance during the Holocaust, highlights the opportunities that photography offered as a mode of documentation and the agonies of survival.[6] Her portraits also highlight how photography can visualize human stories on film that are not represented in other kinds of historical records.

Pirotte's photographs of the liberation of Marseille from August and September 1944 and the activities of the French Resistance in the city are well known and remain key documents in French collective memory. However, little attention has been paid to her experiences as a Jewish *émigré* in Marseille and its impact on her photographic work.[7] As Pirotte herself later stated in an essay penned after her return to Poland, these occupation images were "made spontaneously, born out of an inner need" and not just out of political resistance.[8] Her inner need extended from the intersections of her identity, politics, and her historical position as a female Jewish photojournalist living under occupation. Speaking about her motivations, Pirotte reflected that:

> As a human being and a photographer, I couldn't ignore the important events I was witnessing. Could I just pass by without capturing the concerned faces of the miners' wives in Gardanne? The sad distrustful faces of the kids I met in the narrow, winding streets around the Old Port? The weary gazes of women queuing up for hours in front of a butcher shop or bakery? *Could I not have photographed scenes that formed an integral totality of wartime life?*

Here, Pirotte described her motivation and, in turn, her aesthetic approach when she was recording the emotional responses that defined wartime life. By photographing the sad faces and weary gazes of those she encountered, Pirotte captured emotion and embodiment to visualize the traumas of occupation.

Photographs as "Sites of Aesthetic Investment"

This chapter argues for the capabilities of photographs as material and visual sources that allow access to the more subjective experiences of photographers documenting crisis and their pictured subjects. Photography, as a particular medium of documentation and art, allowed Pirotte to visualize stories often impossible to represent in the traditional historical record. Moreover, her personal experiences with political violence, poverty, and anti-Semitism made the photographs not only possible, but necessary. I, thus, am inspired by scholarship that has demonstrated the interpretative potential of photographs as both historical and subjective sources that can raise questions about the complex positionality of artists.[9] As Susan Sontag writes in *Regarding the Pain of Others*: "Photographs had the advantage of two contradictory features. Their credentials of objectivity were inbuilt. Yet they always had, necessarily, a point of view. They were a record of the real ... And they bore witness to the real—since a person had been there to take them."[10] Sontag's take on photography turns attention to an aspect of the medium that historians often overlook: the human behind the camera. Although Sontag's point here begs for scholarly attention to the often-problematic positionality of the photographer documenting violence, the same point underscores how photographs are visual records open to an analysis of experience and intention that goes beyond the surface. Historian Leora Auslander adds that the production of material objects represents a nonverbal medium for individuals to create meaning, represent the world, and express emotions. Auslander sees photographs as the material result of a photographer's "aesthetic investment" that then become affective objects connected to the past.[11] I view Pirotte's photographs at a nexus between the human and the historical and as a revelation of her aesthetic investment into her community—a community defined by particular experiences with violence.

Pirotte's life experiences and Jewish identity framed her approach to photography and resonate within her emphasis on the embodied responses to trauma. On the question of Jewishness and photography, David Shneer, in *Through Soviet Jewish Eyes*, insists:

> There is something unsatisfying in simply saying, This is a Jewish story because Jews took the pictures. One wants to ask, Did Jews take different pictures from non-Jews?... The question of "what's Jewish" in these photographs, or for that matter what's Jewish about these photographers, presumes a reified definition of Jewish identity and a static image of the Jew.[12]

Paying heed to Schneer, I untangle the various threads of Pirotte's identity, including her Jewishness, and their impact on her photographic methodology.[13] Pirotte's perspective stemmed from her personal experience with poverty and political persecution that were both entangled with her Jewish identity. Pirotte grew up in an impoverished Jewish shtetl and her first language was Yiddish. She became an avowed Communist and activist while working in a factory in Warsaw and carried her passion for social activism throughout her life. After World War II, she twice visited Palestine to photograph Jewish life on the kibbutz but was disappointed with the social inequities that she still witnessed.[14] These are just a few of the ways that Pirotte's Jewish identity and activism left traces within her photographs.[15]

Although Pirotte's body of work is one of the most extensive of any Jewish photographer active in France at the time, her story seldom appears in the French press and state archives. Her photographs, however, not only fill in the blanks; they offer their own narrative of her experience, choices, and struggles, as well as those of the communities she photographed. This chapter draws on sources produced during Pirotte's postwar reemergence: a 1986 oral testimony given to Yale University's Fortunoff Video Archive and a 2012 photographic exhibition of her personal collection organized by the Jewish Historical Institute in Warsaw. Both the interview and the photographs demonstrate how Pirotte succeeded at producing snapshots that would survive and tell stories that may not otherwise have been recorded, including hers.

Julia Pirotte: a Jewish Photographer and Resister in Marseille

Pirotte was a novice photojournalist when war broke out, and she experimented with the possibilities of her craft in this context of warfare and displacement. Pirotte was born Julia Diament in 1908 in Końskowola, a shtetl then part of the Russian Empire, where anti-Semitism defined much of her young life.[16] Pirotte remembered growing up hearing rumors of pogroms in surrounding villages. After her mother's death, the family moved to Warsaw and as a young girl, Pirotte went to work in a factory with other Polish Jews. In Warsaw and in the factory, Pirotte and her two siblings—a younger sister and an older brother—began to engage in communist politics. At only eighteen years old, Pirotte was arrested for her involvement in the Polish Communist Party and spent four years in prison. In 1934, Pirotte fled Poland for Belgium, where she married Jean Pirotte, a Belgian factory worker and labor activist, and continued to participate in political activism. Following the encouragement of Belgian activist Suzanne Spaak, Pirotte attended journalism and photography school in Belgium and published her work in communist newspapers. Thus, from the beginning of her career, Pirotte understood her photography as historical and political; she used the tools of visualization to expose inequality and to support her ideals. However, as an artist, she was also drawn to human emotion and the embodied reflections of trauma, such as hand gestures and facial expressions. She found human sadness an emotion "more photogenic than joy." Pirotte used her camera to record historical events and political violence through inner human experience and emotional response. This project required her to go beyond the surface of a moment and bring into sharp relief the traumas of wartime life.[17]

In 1940, Pirotte fled to southern France after the fall of Belgium to German troops. On her journey, she quickly learned the power of her camera and the danger of her position as a foreign female photographer. Pirotte stopped in a small French village to photograph an old Jewish woman running after a goat. While taking the photograph, she was spotted by local townspeople. As a foreigner with her expensive camera in hand, a rare commodity, Pirotte was accused of being a German spy by the townspeople, who threatened to shave her hair.

A local policeman intervened but warned her to never take her camera out again. Pirotte recounted that the policeman cautioned her that the camera might cost Pirotte her head rather than her hair next time. Reflecting on the episode in 1986, she remarked, "The story taught me that the camera is a formidable weapon. From then on, the Leica became my instrument of struggle."[18] This episode was not the last time Pirotte garnered suspicion of espionage as a foreigner with a camera. Pirotte related that by 1944 she had been threatened with having her head shaved three additional times. These threats show that the French people had come to view cameras as tools of surveillance in the hands of a foreign occupying power. The punishment for her suspected espionage and later resistance—head shaving—was the very same faced by French women accused of sleeping with German soldiers after the liberation of France in 1944.[19]

Pirotte settled in Marseille and found employment in an airplane factory. Her time in the factory, however, was short lived. Pirotte had to quit her job when France signed the June 1940 armistice and the factory converted to serving, rather than fighting, the German war effort. To make money, Pirotte produced and sold photographs on a private beach. She lived in a brothel in the Old Port near a photography shop where she could obtain film. Her living quarters, perhaps open to her as a place of refuge as a woman, provided proximity to the material resources needed to carry out her craft. At night, she secretly developed the film at the apartment of a friend from the factory. However, acquiring photographic materials and photographing publicly became much more difficult as the Occupation dragged on.[20] Pirotte was forced to abandon her beach photography when the Gestapo began looking for the woman with the camera.[21]

As soon as she arrived in Marseille, Pirotte became involved with several Resistance groups. She joined the Jewish National Front and provided aid to Jewish refugees. As a native Yiddish speaker, she produced and distributed Yiddish language newspapers to the newly arrived refugees to inform them of the political situation in France. Pirotte stated that she often went into camps for Jewish refugees and warned them not to register with the Préfecture de Police or trust the Vichy regime. Recognizing the peril that Jews faced in France, her group also tried to hide lists of Jewish refugees from French officials. She recounted that her group of Jewish youths could not sit around and do nothing because "we knew that the Jews would not survive. Other Jews did not believe this. But we knew."[22] Pirotte also devoted her energy to the more militant communist network for foreign workers: the Francs-tireurs et partisans-main d'oeuvre immigrée (FTP-MOI). Pirotte smuggled clandestine newspapers and weapons for the FTP-MOI, and she used her photographic skills to make fake identity paperwork, a role that photographers often filled for the Resistance.

Pirotte's employment with the newspaper *Dimanche Illustré* (hereafter *DI*) facilitated her clandestine photographic work and her resistance activities. After the German invasion of Marseille in November 1942, Pirotte accepted a position as a photojournalist with *DI*. When she attained the job, Pirotte believed that the editor knew that she was both Jewish and in the French Resistance. The editor "winked his eye" when he hired her, a sign that she believed indicated his support for her cause.[23] In her work for the paper, she made portraits of celebrities who visited Marseille, including Édith Piaf. Pirotte's position at *DI* and her photojournalist credentials came with important benefits that aided in her resistance and her survival. She received a press pass that afforded her mobility and a cover for her travels as a courier between Marseille, Arles, and Nîmes. These documents potentially saved her life on a trip to deliver illicit materials for the Resistance. She once arrived late in Arles, well after curfew, with a suitcase of illicit items. She and others on the train were supposed to be held overnight in the station. Pirotte showed the German soldiers her press pass and said she was in town reporting for *DI*. The soldiers let her go and did not search her suitcase.

Pirotte's permission to photograph and her access to film materials thus opened the possibility for her documentation of social life and human experience in Marseille. These images reflect her desire to create a photographic record of daily life of her various communities: resisters, workers, and displaced families all living in Marseille and all impacted in different ways by occupation. Pirotte focused closely on the embodiment, emotions, and identity of her subjects through portraiture. Her portrayal of trauma, particularly of working-class women and impoverished families, reflects her larger support for communism and her political investment in fighting social inequality. This focus permeated all the photos she took and underscored her aesthetic investment in the people she documented. Her subjects often cover their faces with their hands, bite their nails, look away, and display other signs of emotional anguish. In her oral testimony, Pirotte recounted her struggle to get an authentic and subjective portrait of Piaf. She remembered that Piaf wanted to look like a "Hollywood beauty," but Pirotte found it disingenuous. Instead, Pirotte draped Piaf in a dramatic black shawl and framed the portrait tightly on Piaf's facial expressions. Remembering these photographs, Pirotte recounted to her interviewers that "I explained to her that it was much better to act naturally and felt a lot of satisfaction because the resulting pictures managed to convey some of the dramatic tensions of her life."[24] Even as a photographer of celebrities for the newspaper, Pirotte engaged with her subjects' experiences to render visible the inner aspects of their lives and personalities, including their hidden turmoil.

Viewed as a collage of the "integral totality of wartime life," Pirotte's photographs carefully document what occupation looked like for a range of people: Jews and non-Jews, women and children, workers and the homeless, and resisters. Pirotte photographed to expose their social conditions with empathy and sensitivity to their suffering, for she also knew the trauma of displacement, poverty, and loss of family. A photograph of a woman and a young boy in a refugee camp underscores this artistic approach. The woman deliberately looks away both from the camera and from the boy. She stares downward, deep in thought or sorrow while the boy appears to try to get her attention. Pirotte framed the pair on opposite sides of the image, centering the photograph on their inhumane living conditions and their surroundings. The bed pictured in the corner of the frame tells the viewer that this was their home, heightening the intimacy of the image.

In a series depicting the miners' wives in Gardanne, Pirotte captured the realities of working-class family life in poverty. One image displays two older women crossing their arms, biting their nails, and again, looking away from Pirotte's camera. Pirotte's perspective does not give the viewer access to their eyes, a window into emotional affect,

FIGURE 1. Woman and Boy, Marseille 1942. From the collections of the E. Ringelblum Jewish Historical Institute.

or their full experiences. The photo rather lets us feel their physical and emotional discomfort through their body language. Some of Pirotte's subjects are just barely visible on her photographic film. An image of an old woman sitting in the dark displays Pirotte's portrayal of marginality. Pirotte only barely captures the woman on her film, rendering her almost invisible, a powerful comment on the woman's position on the margins of society. The perspective and framing of the shot place the woman off center in the upper right quadrant of the image. Playing with perspective and darkness, Pirotte presents the woman as a shadow in the background. The image reveals, or rather, conceals half of the woman's face. These photos encapsulate how Pirotte used aesthetic representation and realism to document how ideology and warfare impacted the daily lives of the most vulnerable in Marseille, who were not subjects of public concern. In these portraits, Pirotte played with concepts of visibility and invisibility resulting in images that both force viewers to look closer to try to understand the scene and also comment on these individuals' forgotten place in French society.

FIGURE 2. Two Elderly Women, Wives of Polish Miners, Gardanne, 1942. From the collections of the E. Ringelblum Jewish Historical Institute.

Pirotte's photographs, focused so closely on women and embodiment, also provide a gendered look into trauma and the brutalization of Nazism. As a woman, Pirotte was given access to spaces otherwise inaccessible to others; she once photographed a cloister of nuns for the German authorities because their male photographers were not permitted to enter. Many of her images depict mothers and the families of workers who may have been shared connections through her communist circles or at the very least an important social group in which Pirotte was invested. These photographs also impart a sense of intimacy only possible with an established level of trust between the photographer and subject. These women may have trusted Pirotte to photograph them in highly intimate settings because of her gender, her ability to empathize, and her shared connections to their community. As a photographer with her own experiences of the social issues she photographed, Pirotte's empathic presence leaves powerful resonances within the images. Her shared experiences shaped how she photographed and the stories she

FIGURE 3. Elderly woman among fruit crates, Marseille, 1943. From the collections of the E. Ringelblum Jewish Historical Institute.

FIGURE 4. Children playing, Hotel Bompard, Marseille 1942. From the collections of the E. Ringelblum Jewish Historical Institute.

recorded as part of her personal narrative and sociopolitical commentary. Her photographs thus offer a personal testimony as much as a historical record of occupation.

Pirotte's Jewish Photography

Neither Jewish life nor the Holocaust are main themes of Pirotte's wartime photographs. In this regard, a series of photographs from the Hôtel Bompard internment camp in late summer 1942 stands out as a striking exception.[25] The Hôtel Bompard camp housed Jewish women and children awaiting entry and exit visas to emigrate, often to the United States. Their husbands, fathers, and sons were held at the adjacent camp Les Milles. Unlike other internment camps in France, those held at Bompard were allowed to come and go while humanitarian organizations, including the Joint Distribution Committee (JDC), provided aid within the camp. Pirotte's photographs of the camp and portraits of the Jewish captives show women and children laughing, playing, and eating; they reveal a glimpse of happiness and normalcy within an internment camp.

Explaining the story of the photos, Pirotte remembered that she was stopped on the street by a camp commandant, someone she identified as a "liberal" Frenchman. The commandant told her to show up at Bompard the next day to photograph a banquet organized by the JDC. Pirotte recalled documenting the banquet and the happiness that she witnessed before her—a scene that was perhaps staged for her benefit—and giving the photographs to the camp authorities.[26] Pirotte later learned the women and children were deported a few days after her visit. Most of the Bompard internees were deported first to Drancy and then to Auschwitz.

This story and the resulting photographs raise questions about access, gender, and complicity that linger in the background of the images. With knowledge of their fate, any aesthetic emphasis on joy appears to be an obfuscation of Holocaust realities. However, read in retrospect, the children's joy becomes Barthes' punctum—the element of the photograph that pricks the viewer.[27] These photographs of play become a jolting reminder of these lives lost to Nazi oppression. Pirotte's camera makes this violence visual in its wake. In her oral testimony, Pirotte wrestled with the moral weight of participating in the events at the camp in even the most tangential way. With full knowledge of the tragic fate of the pictured subjects, the photographs' emphasis on normalcy, joy, and play appears unsettling and haunting. Pirotte only learned of the deportations after the fact. This moment was one of her traumas of the Occupation; Pirotte was instrumentalized in ways she did not fully realize in the moment. With attention paid to these deeper layers of contingency and access, the photos can reveal the moral ambiguities of survival and the trauma of the Nazi system.

Pirotte claimed agency in saving and publicizing these photographs; they became an unintended record of the final days of this camp and the now missing lives. The photographs exist today because she protected her copies and made them available to museums and archives as a record of these likely lost Jewish women and children. The photographs' conservation and subsequent display help render them into critical evidence of France's involvement in the deportation of Jews.

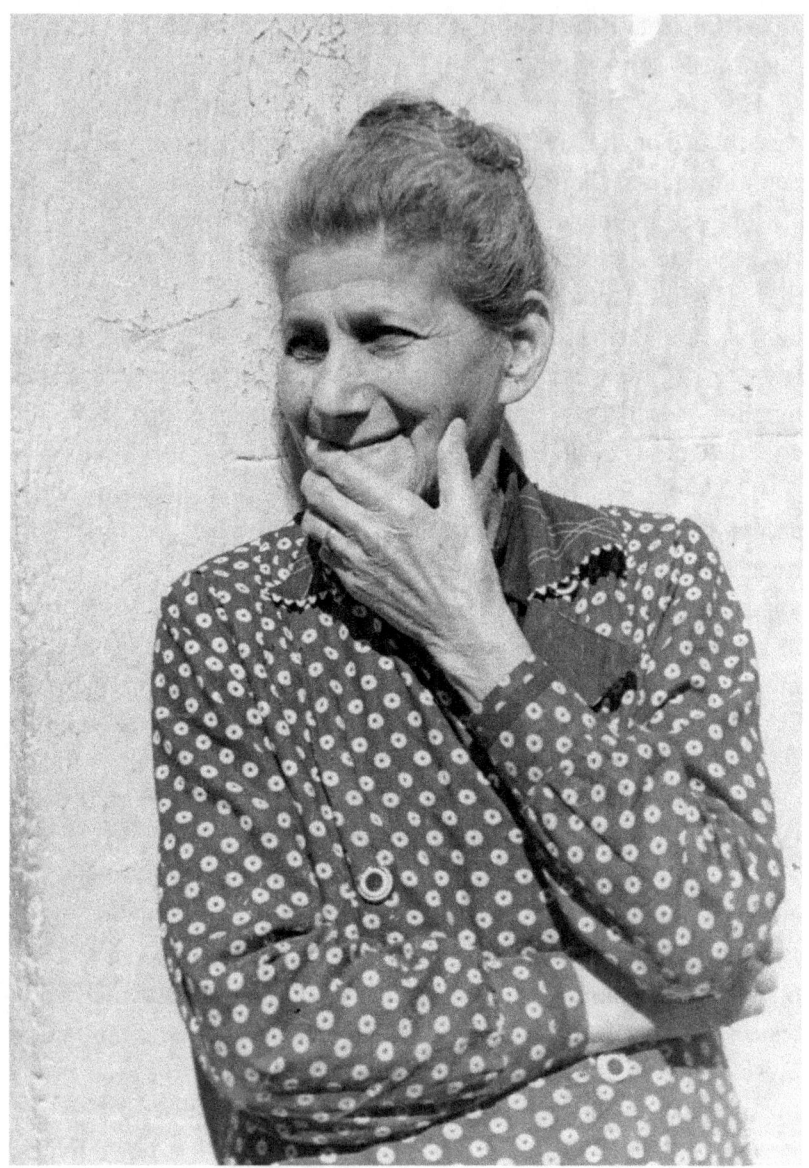

FIGURE 5. Portrait of an older woman, Hotel Bompard, Marseille, 1942. From the collections of the E. Ringelblum Jewish Historical Institute

The Bompard photos are some of the few from Pirotte that depict the Holocaust in France or the deportations, but they only do so directly with full knowledge of the fate of the victims. Only one photograph, taken months after the Bompard deportation, bears witness to the Shoah directly. Her personal collection, as exhibited by the Jewish Historical Institute in Warsaw, contains a single image of the Old Port of Marseille in early 1943, in the aftermath of the mass deportation of its Jewish residents and the leveling of the neighborhood. The photograph is one of the few without people and reveals a dark, empty, and rainy street. In the middle of the photograph stands a transfer vehicle that resembles the silhouette of a hearse, a visual symbol that sets the tone of the photograph as funerary. The emptiness of the photograph makes absence present and visually represents the eradication of the quarter's two thousand Jewish residents and its almost complete architectural destruction.

The force of Pirotte's focus in this image stands out in comparison to her larger body of work and a mass of state administrative photographs produced within the Old Port about the same time. Pirotte was not the only photographer on the scene in January and February 1943. German soldiers and French authorities extensively photographed the Old Port as they planned and documented its destruction. The German authorities depicted the Old Port, says historian Donna Ryan, "as a nest of criminals and brothels" which had to be cleared for hygienic reasons.[28] The Old Port's leveling would allow municipal authorities to clean and modernize the quarter. The administrative and municipal photos picture the Old Port's iconic narrow winding streets—a layout German authorities argued was dangerous—and the presumably Jewish residents of the depressed quarter.[29] Taken before Pirotte's post-deportation shot, the administrative photographs show the Jewish residents and the density of their surroundings to justify the violent destruction the authorities had in mind for the neighborhood. In comparison to the administrative shots, Pirotte's emphasis on absence—a reality that she witnessed with her own eyes—and her aesthetic rendering of the vehicle into a symbol of death, makes her image capable of providing an alternative perspective on what had occurred there. Unable to photograph the deportations themselves,

FIGURE 6. Girl with a metal cup, Hotel Bompard, Marseille, 1942. From the collections of the E. Ringelblum Jewish Historical Institute.

Pirotte used absence in its aftermath to speak out against the episode of mass violence.

Pirotte's Jewish identity and her other positions of marginality—as a woman, a Communist, an *émigré*, among others—framed her aesthetic choices and marked the social world in which she lived. As someone who had twice seen the aftermath of the deportations of Jews from the city, her precarity shaped her every action even in implicit ways. She related that as someone who experienced head shaving during the war, she refused to photograph women shaved at the liberation for their collaboration with the Nazis.[30] Pirotte's vantage point as a foreign Jew in hiding is expressed most clearly in the lone Old Port photograph, which out of necessity breaks from her typical visual emphasis on humanity and embodiment. Her position as a Jewish refugee, looking at the disembodying aftermath of violence, allows her to pointedly portray the loss of an entire community.

Toward the end of the Occupation, Pirotte began to devote most of her time to photographing the actions of the Resistance. As violence mounted against the partisans, she realized that they, especially the Jewish resisters, might not survive the war. She hoped her photographs could survive to tell their stories. Many of these photographs of the Resistance are more journalistic and dynamic than her other shots. These photographs capture movement and activity rather than embodiment, emotion, and stasis. Several of her images depict young male and female resistance fighters, sometimes identified as Jewish, posing with their guns, navigating through the forest, or planning their next offensive. A few are uncharacteristically blurry owing to the hasty work of capturing history as it happened and the movements of her resistance group. Then, in the midst of the city's liberation in August and September 1944, Pirotte was ready to document and publicize the liberation of Marseille as it unfolded. Pirotte not only took part in the liberation—she even described taking pictures while being shot at—she helped to record events for posterity.[31] The blurriness of these photographs, taken as Pirotte participated in the action, reflect the very real experience of witnessing and photographing during a time of war.

Historians Hanna Diamond and Claire Gorarra have shown that it was precisely Pirotte's act of photographing the Resistance and the

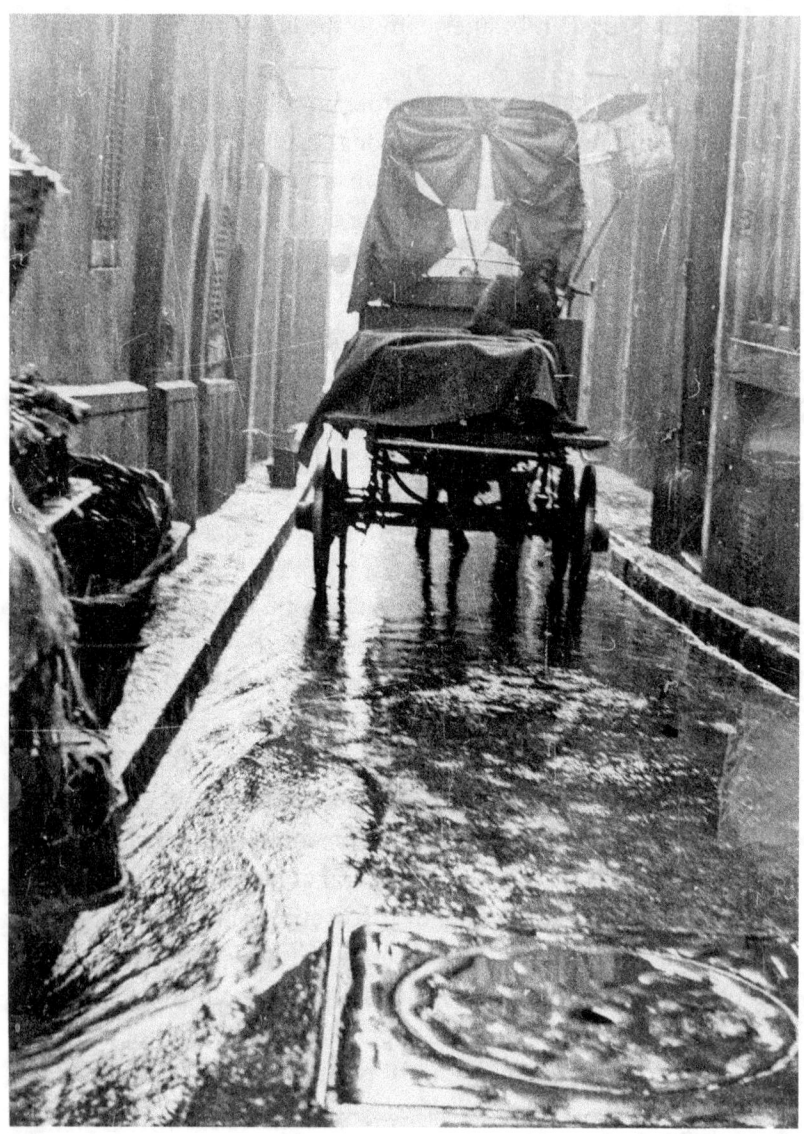

Figure 7. Horse cab on a wet street, Marseille, 1943. From the collections of the E. Ringelblum Jewish Historical Institute.

liberation of Marseille that brought her images into French collective memory.[32] It is for these images that Pirotte is primarily known, but, as this chapter has shown, this series comprised only a small part of her photographic opus. Pirotte's resistance and liberation photographs began to appear in the left-wing press as the city fought for its freedom and have been accorded a place within France's lasting memory of a universal resistance and popular uprising. However, their emergence into France's visual canon of the Resistance clouds a fuller understanding of Pirotte's art and experiences. Pirotte's photographs, as Diamond and Gorrara argue, have "been appropriated at different historical junctures to tell very different war stories" across France and Europe.[33] Part of what makes these photographs so powerful and culturally enduring was her aesthetic focus on people and their bodies in action. Diamond and Gorrara write, "The 'spirit' of liberation is captured in facial expression and gestures which emphasize the fraternity and equality of the collective struggle, whilst the subjects themselves are photographed often in motion as if caught in the moment of history or immediacy of action."[34] Thus, the aesthetic framing that rendered Pirotte's photographs so culturally latent was her same fixation on human embodiment and emotion, now portrayed in action. Beyond their importance as historical documents of the liberation of Marseille, Pirotte's sustained emphasis on depicting history through people and her sharp eye for subjectivity propelled her liberation photographs from the status of documentary sources to that of indelible cultural icons.

For Pirotte, the end of the war in Europe in May 1945 was not a jubilant moment of victory. On May 13, 1945, Pirotte penned an article for *Dimanche* that described her feelings of loss and ambivalence, rather than joy. In the article, entitled, "Ils Étaient Là" [They were here], Pirotte imagined the liberation as a ghostly procession of the dead: the resisters, Jewish women and children, and political prisoners, all murdered by the Nazis. In this way, her photographs attest to the humanity of the victims of Nazism; they record the identities and sacrifices of those who were once here. She concluded the essay with a vow to her deceased sister, who was murdered by the Nazis: "I promise you Marie, never again."[35]

In 1946, Pirotte returned to her native Poland with only a sack of belongings and a collection of five hundred photographs. Despite producing an important record of persecution, resistance, and sacrifice in Marseille, Pirotte admitted that she kept her photographs in a drawer for more than thirty years. She explained that she did not see these photographs as historically significant documents nor did she believe that the Poles, who had suffered their own tragedies and engaged in their own uprisings, would be interested in her snapshots of occupied France.[36] While her Marseille photos remained concealed, Pirotte once again became a witness to and documentarian of anti-Semitic violence. In 1946, she photographed the Kielce pogrom, one of the deadliest episodes of postwar violence against Jews returning to Poland. While working as a photojournalist in Warsaw, Pirotte received word of violence taking place in Kielce. Her newspaper editor sent her on the dangerous assignment to try to get some photographs. Recognizing her own danger as a Jew at a site of anti-Semitic violence, Pirotte traveled and photographed with a bodyguard. Pirotte was the only photographer on the scene and snapped as many photographs as she could of the victims and violence she encountered—118 photos in all. Unlike the Marseille photos, only a handful of these images survived and only in poor quality. Her aesthetic approach in these shots followed a different visual logic: the need to get as many photographs as possible. Like the liberation photographs, these images' quality—their graininess—portray her difficult and dangerous position of trying to photograph in the midst of crisis. Recognizing the photographs' historical importance, she attempted to hide and protect them, but they still went missing, likely destroyed by the political police. Pirotte did what she could to re-create thirteen of the photographs from her test negatives, which resulted in the images' graininess, to ensure the survival of photographic proof.

These two collections highlight Pirotte's positions as a Jewish photographer and her varied approaches to documenting historical violence. Her sharp focus in those Marseille photos on affect, gender, embodiment, and social class, and her techniques of realism and portraiture, reflect her goal of capturing what she saw as the totality of wartime life. When witnessing another episode of mass violence in postwar Poland, Pirotte again wielded her camera in an effort to collect as much documentation as possible. These critical snapshots were not the result of her longer aesthetic engagements with various communities living for years under two repressive regimes, but rather her direct and immediate encounter with mass violence in her home country. However, Pirotte's aesthetic eye and her response to violence, conditioned from her time in Marseille, are still present within the Kielce photographs. Witnessing the aftermath of two deportations in Marseille propelled her impulse to collect as much documentation as possible. As a Jew also returning to her native Poland, Pirotte photographed the pogrom with an intimate sense of her own danger in being there. Never fully removed from the violent scenes she encountered, she shared to an extent in her subjects' suffering. She also recognized the necessity to collect as many photos as possible and to do what she could to safeguard her work. Like the Bompard photographs, their material existence defined the historical work they could do as evidence, while her aesthetic approach heightened her images' impact. At Bompard, Pirotte photographed the chillingly normal scene she encountered. She printed the smiling faces of the children on her film, a now lasting reminder of their identities and their tragic fate. At Kielce, Pirotte's photographs— blurry and grainy—mirrored her position as photographer in the midst of crisis and her fight to preserve evidence.

Pirotte encountered an additional barrier in returning to Polish society. Pirotte stated that she believed that she would not have a receptive audience because Polish Jews and Poles had suffered so severely during the war. Although Pirotte lost both her sister and her brother (who died in a Stalinist gulag), her sufferings and those of her communities in Marseille paled in comparison. For the time being, she kept the images of her own trauma concealed. Pirotte's perspective shifted when she visited Paris for the first time in 1979 and she discovered that her photographs of the Resistance already had an immense audience in France. She encountered her photos in a film about the French Resistance. Pirotte returned to Poland and began copying the photographs in a makeshift studio, now with her copyright stamp. She sent the copies to institutions across France and Europe and launched her public emergence as a photographer of the Resistance in Western Europe.

Conclusion

In the 1986 interview, Pirotte insisted that we should not make a heroine of her; she believed that we only know about her thanks to her camera.[37] In part, she positions her story and its historical significance in relation to the many Jewish and non-Jewish lives lost as a part of the Holocaust and as a consequence of the Resistance. However, her actions to produce and preserve photographic evidence from Marseille and Poland have allowed historians and an international public alike to remember the vicissitudes of Nazi and anti-Semitic violence in Europe during the twentieth century. Her photographs offer a lens into a more subjective and emotional picture of wartime life for particular communities, while also forming a personal testimony to Pirotte's experiences, sacrifices, and commitments. Pirotte's photographs emerged from the human, historical, and material contingencies of her story. These conditions included her ability to gain photographic credentials, access to film and other photographic materials, her acceptance within particular spaces, including Bompard, and moreover her survival. For these reasons, Pirotte's photographs, as snapshots from a Jewish photojournalist, are rare because their material existence hinged on her opportunities, networks, cunning decisions, and also a bit of luck.

Explicit considerations regarding the material value and historicity of photographs also influenced Pirotte's activities and the form of her resistance. Pirotte understood her task as always political and historical, whether humanizing her friends and her community members or recording the Jewish victims of the pogrom. In this way, she photographed for posterity to memorialize those who did not survive the war and to expose violence and social inequity. Even if she initially concealed those Marseille images, one of her key motivations was to ensure that these individuals' identities and stories were recorded in history. Although Pirotte did not think of herself as more than a documentarian of these victims and heroes, it is her perspective in these powerful, intimate shots that renders her photographs an emotional and lasting visual record of daily life, state violence, and resistance in occupied Marseille and postwar Europe.

Finally, Pirotte's story turns attention to several important aspects of Jewish experience in Marseille and the impact of the Holocaust in

France on other parts of Europe. As the postwar context indicates, Pirotte's story was not confined to the French borders, and aspects of her story were transferrable to Eastern and Western Europe. When Pirotte returned to Poland, she carried her experiences in France and her photographs with her. Accordingly, her life, resistance, and persecution in Western Europe impacted her approach to photographing Poland and later Israel. Pirotte's experiences photographing persecution in Marseille and the memories of Bompard influenced her reaction in 1946 to gather as much evidence as possible of another example of anti-Semitic violence. Pirotte's photographs stand at the nexus of the human and the historical. They were the visual and material products of her own human story: her empathy, identity, political commitments, gender, communities, and her migrations from the Polish shtetl, to the urban factory, to Marseille, and back again.

Bibliography

Auslander, Leora. "Beyond Words." *American Historical Review*, Volume 110, Number 4 (October 2005). 1014–1045.

Barthes, Roland. *Camera Lucida: Reflections on Photography*. New York: Hill and Wang, 1981.

Berkowitz, Michael. *Jews and Photography in Britain*. Austin: University of Texas Press, 2016.

Clark, Catherine E. "Capturing the Moment: Picturing History: Photographs of the Liberation of Paris." *American Historical Review* (June 2016), 824–860.

———. *Paris and the Cliché of History: The City and Photographs, 1860–1970*. London: Oxford University Press, 2018.

Denoyelle, Françoise. *La photographie d'actualité et de propagande sous le Régime de Vichy*. Paris: CNRS, 2001.

Diamond, Hanna and Claire Gorrara, "Reframing War: Histories and Memories of the Second World War in the Photography of Julia Pirotte." *Modern and Contemporary France*, Volume 20, Issue 4 (2012), 453–471.

Finkel, Evgeny. *Ordinary Jews: Choice and Survival during the Holocaust*. Princeton, NJ: Princeton University Press, 2017.

Julia Pirotte: Faces and Hands. Warsaw: Jewish Historical Institute, 2012.

Langer, Lawrence. *Versions of Survival: The Holocaust and the Human Spirit*. Albany: State University of New York Press, 1982.

Lee, Daniel. *Pétain's Jewish Children: French Jewish Youth and the Vichy Regime, 1940–1942*. Oxford: Oxford University Press, 2014.

Nelson, Anne. *Suzanne's Children: A Daring Rescue in Nazi Paris*. New York: Simon and Schuster, 2017.

Poznanski, Renée. *Jews in France after World War II*. Translated by Nathan Bracher. Hanover, NH: University Press of New England for Brandeis University Press, 2001.

Ryan, Donna. *The Holocaust and the Jews of Marseille: The Enforcement of Anti-Semitic Policies in Vichy France*. Champaign: University of Illinois Press, 1996.

Schneer, David. *Through Soviet Jewish Eyes: War, Photography, and the Holocaust*. New Brunswick, NJ: Rutgers University Press, 2012.

Sontag, Susan. *Regarding the Pain of Others*. New York: Farrar, Strauss, and Giroux, 2013.

Thébaud, Françoise. *Julia Pirotte: une photographe dans la Résistance*. Chaleroi, Belgium: Musée de la photographie, 1994.

Underwood, Nick. "Glimpses of a Puzzling Phenomenon: Robert Capa and Jewish History." *Images: A Journal of Jewish Art and Visual Culture* (2012), 132–135.

Virgili, Fabrice. *La France virile: des femmes tondues à la liberation*. Paris: Fayard, 2000.

Notes

1. This book chapter is the result of research conducted at the United States Holocaust Memorial Museum as the J. B. and Maurice C. Shapiro Fellow from 2018 to 2019. I am grateful for the generous funding and fellowship from USHMM that allowed me to examine Pirotte's story. This chapter was also the result of a seminar on Jews and Photography conducted at the Association for Jewish Studies 2019 conference and a talk I gave at the Jewish History Seminar at Institute of Historical Research in London and at the Western Society for French History 2019 conference. I thank Rebekka Grossmann, Michael Berkowitz, and Sandra Ott for inviting me to present this work, Daniel Lee for his helpful comments at the WSFH conference, and the participants of the AJS seminar for their ideas on how to move this work forward. I also thank the Jewish Historical Institute in Warsaw for permission to use Pirotte's photographs in this article.
2. HVT-774, Testimony of Julia P., Fortunoff Video Archive, Yale University, October 25, 1986, New Haven, CT.
3. Testimony of Julia P., Fortunoff Video Archive, Segment 13.
4. Spaak's life was the subject of a biography by Anne Nelson entitled *Suzanne's Children: A Daring Rescue in Nazi Paris* (New York: Simon and Schuster, 2017).
5. The French began to levy restrictions against public photography months before the fall of France and the beginnings of the Occupation. Laws passed on April 26, 1940, and May 8, 1940, made unauthorized photography illegal across all of France. See Françoise Denoyelle, *La photographie d'actualité et de propagande sous le régime de Vichy* (Paris: CNRS, 2001), 39. Also see Catherine E. Clark, "Capturing the Moment: Picturing History: Photographs of the Liberation of Paris," *American Historical Review* (June 2016), 824–860; here 839–840, cit. 57.
6. In the preface to *Versions of Survival: The Holocaust and the Human Spirit*, Lawrence Langer describes Holocaust survival as an "essential moral agony" in which "each move one made in the 'game' of survival included a gesture that insured, for another if not for oneself, a form of human defeat." Langer, *Versions of Survival: The Holocaust and the Human Spirit* (Albany: State University of

New York Press, 1982), ix. Also see Evgeny Finkel, *Ordinary Jews: Choice and Survival During the Holocaust* (Princeton, NJ: Princeton University Press, 2017).
7. For an analysis of the place of Pirotte's liberation photos in French collective memory see Hanna Diamond and Claire Gorrara, "Reframing War: Histories and Memories of the Second World War in the Photography of Julia Pirotte," *Modern and Contemporary France*, Vol. 20 Issue 4: Gender, Politics, and the Social in the Historical Perspective: Essays in Honour of Sian Reynolds (2012), 453–471.
8. Quoted by Krystyna Dabrowska, "Faces and Hands," in *Julia Pirotte: Faces and Hands* (Warsaw, Poland: Jewish Historical Institute, 2012), 9–10.
9. Catherine E. Clark's work on the historicity of photographs of the Liberation of Paris has since offered an expanded methodological toolbox to the study of photography and has demonstrated the benefits for viewing photographic meaning at once from various levels, especially the material. Clark, "Capturing the Moment: Picturing History." Also see Clark, *Paris and the Cliché of History: The City and Photographs, 1860–1970* (London: Oxford University Press, 2018).
10. Susan Sontag, *Regarding the Pain of Others* (New York: Farrar, Strauss, and Giroux, 2013), 26.
11. Leora Auslander, "Beyond Words," *American Historical Review* 110. No. 4 (October 2005), 1015–1045, here 1016.
12. David Shneer, *Through Soviet Jewish Eyes: War, Photography, and the Holocaust* (New Brunswick, NJ: Rutgers University Press, 2012), 3–5.
13. In his study of Jewish photographers in Great Britain, Michael Berkowitz admits that the subjects as his own study were not terribly "Jewish." Instead, Berkowitz inscribes their Jewishness as socioeconomic and cultural; their Jewish origins "helped to determine the content, limits, and possibilities of their social and socioeconomic opportunities." Michael Berkowitz, *Jews and Photography in Britain* (Austin: University of Texas Press, 2016), 9.
14. Pirotte's photographs in and response to Israel are discussed in the Jewish Historical Institute exhibition, *Julia Pirotte: Faces and Hands* (Warsaw, Poland: Jewish Historical Institute, 2012).
15. Nick Underwood observes that Robert Capa's Jewish identity has been overlooked as a part of his photography. Underwood writes, "His colleagues and viewers have long read Jewishness into Friedmann/Capa, affecting his personal and professional paths, and it is time for scholars to weave these threads of identity into his extraordinary images of humanity and war." See Nick Underwood, "Glimpses of a Puzzling Phenomenon: Robert Capa and Jewish History," *Images: A Journal of Jewish Art and Visual Culture* (2012), 132–135, here 135.
16. I have seen her birthdate listed as both 1907 and 1908. I am using the birth date provided in the Fortunoff interview.
17. Quoted by Teresa Śmiechowska and Jan Jagielski, "Forward," in *Julia Pirotte: Faces and Hands*, 7.
18. Quoted by Krystyna Dabrowska, "Chronology and Life and Work," in *Julia Pirotte: Faces and Hands*, 33.

19. For information on head shaving after the Liberation of France, see Fabrice Virgili, *La France Virile: des femmes tondues à la liberation* (Paris: Payot, 2000).
20. By 1942, the Vichy regime extended the outdoor photography ban to the southern zone of France, thus preventing activities such as Pirotte's beach photography to take place.
21. Testimony of Julia P., Yale Fortunoff Video Archive, Segment 8.
22. Testimony of Julia P., Yale Fortunoff Video Archive, Segment 9.
23. Ibid, Segment 9.
24. Dabrowska, "Chronology of Life and Work," in *Julia Pirotte Faces and Hands*, 33.
25. The United States Holocaust Memorial Museum and the Jewish Historical Institute both record the photographs as July 1942. The residents of the Hôtel Bompard were sent to Les Milles and then deported to Auschwitz in August 1942.
26. Testimony of Julia P., Yale Fortunoff Video Archive, Segment 20.
27. Roland Barthes, *Camera Lucida: Reflections on Photography* (New York: Hill and Wang, 1981).
28. Ryan, *The Holocaust and the Jews of Marseille*, 180.
29. The Bundesarchiv holds a collection of photographs produced by the Wehrmacht in January 1943, in the lead-up to the deportations. The photographs document the conditions of the quarter and its predominantly Jewish residents. Photographs in the same collection from January 24, 1943, document the deportation of Jews. See Bild 101-1 Propagandakompanien der Wehrmacht—Heer und Luftwaffen.
30. Testimony of Julia P., Fortunoff Video Archive, Segment 17.
31. For work on photographers and photography during France's Liberation, see Clark, "Capturing the Moment: Picturing History: Photographs of the Liberation of Paris," *American Historical Review* (June 2016), 824–860; Hanna Diamond, "The Return of the Republic: Crowd Photography and the Liberation of Toulouse, 1944–1945," *French Politics, Culture & Society*, Vol. 37. No. 1, (Spring 2019), 90–116.
32. Diamond and Gorrara, "Reframing War: Histories and Memories of the Second World War in the Photography of Julia Pirotte," 453–471.
33. Ibid., 454.
34. Ibid., 456.
35. Julia Pirotte, "Ils Étaient Là," *Dimanche*, May 13, 1945. See Laetitia Vion, "Article de Julia Pirotte intitulè 'Ils Étaient Là,' *Journal Dimanche*. 13 Mai 1945," La Musée de la Résistance, http://museedelaresistanceenligne.org/media8932-Article-de-Julia-Pirotte-intitulA#fiche-tab.
36. Testimony of Julia P., Yale Fortunoff Video Archive, Segments 15–16.
37. Testimony of Julia P., Yale Fortunoff Video Archive, Segment 18.

CHAPTER 2

The Effects of the German "Occupation" on Relief Work in Unoccupied France

SHANNON L. FOGG

An article appearing in the *New York Times* on July 7, 1940, asked, "If Britain can hold out on land will she permit charitably minded America to feed Europe for Adolf Hitler? If she does permit it will the United States Government deem it expedient to avert famine from a Europe which General Professor Karl Haushofer, the Karl Marx of National Socialism, says Germany must first conquer, then mobilize against the United States?" The author went on to speculate, "It is anticipated in Washington that a Britain resolute enough to capture or sink the navy of her former ally might not consent to allow her chief remaining offensive weapon against Germany, the blockade, to be pierced even in the interest of mercy."[1] The highly politicized nature of "neutral" humanitarian material aid is thus evident from the earliest days of the Nazi Occupation. Would aid agencies be allowed to function in countries defeated by the Nazis? If so, under what conditions? What would the German Occupation mean for humanitarian missions? How influential would outside considerations be on the activities of groups working to improve the daily lives of civilians facing the tragedy of war?

As one of the principal foreign agencies involved in providing wartime aid, the American Friends Service Committee (AFSC)'s work in France allows us to explore these questions. In some ways, this chapter focuses on what appears to be a series of paradoxes: first, the seeming oxymoron of occupation in an unoccupied zone and second, the apparent inconsistency of allowing humanitarian aid under an exclusionary, authoritarian regime. It reveals, however, the key role political considerations—both real and perceived—played in the ability of the AFSC to provide services in wartime France. The aid organization emphasized its neutrality, especially in its public-facing discourse, but its actions on the ground reveal the tensions inherent in humanitarian activity in occupied foreign countries.

The extent and nature of German influence on the Vichy regime has been a consistent theme in the historiography of the period. After the war, some wartime leaders asserted that German pressure had forced the French to collaborate, and they blamed the Nazis for the imposition of exclusionary laws. These same men argued that through their reluctant collaboration, they had protected the French people from harsher treatment under direct Nazi rule. Robert O. Paxton persuasively countered this interpretation of Vichy and collaboration as either imposed or as a protective "shield" against the Germans in *Vichy France: Old Guard and New Order*. Instead, Paxton's study demonstrated the Vichy regime's active pursuit of collaboration and outlined the autonomous nature of many of Vichy's laws and policies.[2] Paxton continued this discussion in *Vichy France and the Jews*, written with Michael Marrus. The two historians placed Vichy's anti-Jewish policies within the broader context of collaboration and argued that "Without direct German prompting, a local and indigenous French anti-Semitism was at work in Vichy."[3] More recent scholarship continues to debate both the "direct" and "indirect" nature of German wartime influence.[4] Many of these studies have focused on occupied France where the physical presence of the Germans and the Nazi political apparatus were both visible and active. Examining what the Nazi Occupation meant in the southern zone of France, especially before the Germans extended their occupation into the area following the Allied landings in North Africa, presents an opportunity to examine the indirect or invisible influence of the Germans from a different perspective. The existence of the so-called Free Zone afforded aid organizations, including the AFSC, with some additional space to function, but the perceived threat of German intervention led to "self-policing" that ultimately limited the extent of relief work. The AFSC also employed its own direct and indirect tactics to achieve its goals of providing life-saving aid to war victims in France.

A History of Nonpartisan Aid

The American Friends Service Committee's work in France began long before the outbreak of hostilities in 1939, and this earlier history contributed to its ability to work in the country after the defeat. When the United States entered the Great War in 1917, the Quakers sought to create alternatives for conscientious objectors who wanted to avoid military service because of their belief in "the unity of all men in God."[5] Rather than joining with the British Friends, the American Quakers initiated their own relief measures and created the AFSC in April 1917. By July, one hundred carefully selected men began to prepare themselves for service in France to tend to "the spiritual as well as the material needs of the victims of war."[6] The AFSC also provided volunteer opportunities to women, and the organization's relief work included nursing, food and clothing distribution, and rebuilding war-ravaged villages in France. Around Verdun, German prisoners of war significantly aided the AFSC in its reconstruction projects, but French authorities would not allow the Quakers to pay the Germans for their time. Instead, the AFSC photographed the prisoners and kept records of their work. After the war, a team of volunteers delivered the money the prisoners had "earned" to the relatives of more than three hundred men. These visits introduced the AFSC to postwar conditions in defeated Germany. An investigative team sent to examine the situation further found widespread malnutrition, especially among children.

This would influence the AFSC's work in Europe during the interwar period. After wrapping up much of its reconstruction efforts in France, the AFSC saw a great need for relief in Germany. With the support of Herbert Hoover, the AFSC instituted a feeding program that, at its height, provided food to more than a million German children per day.[7] Although many opposed the idea of providing aid to the former "enemy," Quaker tenets rest on the belief that "there is that of God in everyone," and the AFSC's mission is to help others regardless of race, religion, nationality, or political affiliation. When war broke out again in the 1930s, the AFSC worked with the British Friends to provide food to children on both sides of the Spanish Civil War. They also supplied clothing, funded hospitals, and established children's colonies. When half a million Republican refugees fled Franco's Spain into France in

1939, the Quakers went with them, initially providing cultural programs and establishing schools in the overcrowded refugee camps hastily built along the Mediterranean coast. The AFSC's work soon expanded to include aid to civilians displaced by the German invasion of Western Europe in May 1940.[8]

Following the armistice in June, British Quakers were forced to leave France as Germany's wartime enemies, but the Americans were allowed to stay because of US neutrality. Establishing headquarters in Marseille in August 1940, the AFSC's work soon shifted from emergency refugee services to meeting ongoing needs in France with a focus on feeding and caring for children, emigration advice and help, and material aid to individuals in French internment camps.[9] During the war, the Quakers provided fifty thousand schoolchildren with additional rations every day; ten thousand babies received daily milk distributions; and one thousand children lived in Quaker-run colonies. In addition, more than four thousand children in concentration camps needed support. Although much of the AFSC's relief work focused on children as the most innocent of war victims, volunteers also worked to release inmates of all ages from the camps and helped refugees with paperwork associated with emigration.

While US neutrality initially made it possible for the AFSC to remain in France, other factors further facilitated the organization's war work. Since its creation, the AFSC consistently emphasized the nonpartisan nature of its relief, regularly asserting that "poverty has no politics nor country."[10] Its interwar work across Europe further demonstrated its willingness to help those in need—no matter the political regime in place. The Service Committee's previous work in Germany also helped pave the way for aid in World War II. For example, in July 1940, the AFSC received permission to circulate within France after visiting German army headquarters. One volunteer noted, "Two German boys whom the Quakers helped feed in 1919 welcomed us and helped us expedite matters. That gratitude over two decades is something to treasure these hard days."[11] A report from Paris in August 1940 described the attitude of German officials as "Cordial, aware of the work of the Quakers in Germany during the last war and disposed to help us get on with as much relief work as we wish to do in France."[12] In unoccupied France, the Quakers in Toulouse were the only organization granted permission to visit camps by the German military governor who remembered the AFSC's post-Great War aid to starving Germans.[13] However, the humanitarian organization also had to contend with the limits imposed or implied by the German Occupation of France.

AFSC Neutrality, Material Aid, and World War II

One of the first and most pressing needs facing many in France was food supply, and during times of extreme shortage, the material becomes explicitly political.[14] With alleviating the daily material hardships of the French population as one of its primary goals, the AFSC immediately entered the political realm of shortages and had to deal with international considerations. Financial support from abroad was essential to the AFSC's work in France, adding another dimension to political concerns. From early in the war, France was prepared "to take care of her own poor and disloged [sic] people but would certainly welcome any international help in taking care of the tens of thousands of foreigners who were unable to leave France."[15] The AFSC launched fundraising campaigns for its various projects, but some Americans believed that money or goods purchased for those in need would instead provide "indirect assistance to the non-democratic governments."[16] From the beginning, the AFSC recognized the importance of emphasizing its "purely humanitarian motives in improving conditions in the various camps."[17]

The food situation was immediately desperate in France during the war. Early reports from AFSC representatives indicated that almost 80 percent of children were already suffering from undernourishment and unbalanced diets.[18] The British blockade of Europe exacerbated shortages and represented a major impediment to material aid. Britain's strategy for defeating the Nazis included stopping the import of *all* commodities to areas under German control, including food. The British argued that the nature of modern warfare, which erased or blurred the lines between armed enemies and civilians, justified including food in the blockade.[19] The AFSC, on the other hand, argued that "never had 'the starvation of populations been proved to be a permanent instrument of peace.'"²⁰ Clarence E. Pickett, executive secretary of the AFSC, regularly called on the British to relax the blockade. At one meeting, "Mr. Pickett, stressing the Quaker belief that human and divine values were at the core of the movement and were inseparable, said the group would continue to work for feeding of all the hungry, regardless of the argument that one partisan nation might thereby be helped at the expense of the other. 'We can't build a workable peace on the dead bones of mothers and babies,' he said."²¹

The British responded to such criticism from humanitarians by placing responsibility for food shortages on the Germans rather than on the blockade. Citing the Hague Convention of 1907, which obligated Germany as an occupying power to "refrain from pillage and to limit its demands on the resources of the countries it occupied," the British asserted that there were adequate supplies in continental Europe to feed all the occupied countries. As a result, Prime Minister Winston Churchill declared, "the only agencies which can create famine in any part of Europe now and during the coming winter, will be German exactions or German failure to distribute the supplies which they command."²² But humanitarian aid agencies were not the only ones calling for exceptions to the blockade, and the fact that the southern portion of France remained unoccupied further complicated matters. President Franklin D. Roosevelt called on the British to allow food into Vichy France to help "bolster the authority of the Vichy government and, it was hoped, to increase its resistance to German demands by offering economic aid and relief."²³ Limited supplies, including milk, clothing, and wheat, were eventually allowed into unoccupied France on American navicerts.²⁴ In addition to the official goods arriving from abroad, the AFSC purchased critical food supplies from neutral countries in Europe; however, these items were to remain in the unoccupied zone in a further attempt to keep them out of German hands.²⁵ The British allowed this exception specifically because the unoccupied zone existed.

Despite the Hague Convention's stipulations, other countries had every reason to assume that the Nazis would confiscate goods in occupied territories. The terms of the Franco-German armistice made it clear that the economic exploitation of France would be a central feature of the Occupation. Article 17 obligated the Vichy regime to prevent the transfer of "economic valuables and provisions" into unoccupied France or abroad. Furthermore, these valuable items could "be disposed of only in agreement with the German Government." Although the armistice stated, "the German Government will consider the necessities of life of the population in unoccupied territory," the French were also responsible for the costs associated with the Occupation, which were calculated to be 20 million Reichsmarks per day.[26] In addition, with their occupation of the northern and coastal portions of France, the Nazis had direct access to territory that produced the majority of the country's coal, steel, textiles, cereals, milk, sugar, and meat.[27] German requisitions of industrial and agricultural products contributed to shortages of basic necessities throughout France, and 55 percent of the French population found provisioning difficult or almost impossible during the war years.[28] Supporters of the British blockade argued that enough food existed in Europe to prevent starvation without imported goods, but would require the unlikely scenario of continent-wide rationing, a quota system, and the "full measure of collaboration of conqueror and conquered."[29] In this context of shortages precipitated by occupation, exacerbated by requisitions, and worsened by the British blockade of Europe, the Vichy regime willingly accepted foreign aid. The question was whether foreign entities would be allowed to provide it.

Direct Actions: The AFSC's Public Face

The AFSC attempted both to counter concerns about relief supplies aiding the Nazi war machine and to raise funds to support its work abroad through the press. Appealing to the public for support was not new to the Second World War. The First World War had created "a thorough restructuring and professionalization of charitable organizations," with groups hiring professional fundraisers and engaging in coordinated press campaigns.[30] The AFSC, recognizing the importance of monetary support, participated fully in propaganda creation from its first days in France. Beginning with colonies created for Spanish refugee children, Quakers in the United States advised the AFSC in France, "The more you can dramatize the situation in France, the better they will understand it and assist."³¹ The need to supply a continual stream of human-interest stories for fundraising led the AFSC to hire Margaret Frawley. With "10 years of newspaper experience and [. . .] publicity work for many social agencies," but no previous experience as a humanitarian aid worker in the field, Frawley arrived in Paris in March 1940 and immediately began sending stories about poor refugee children in France back to the United States.³² The AFSC clearly recognized that the plight of children could be used as propaganda for fundraising. As "the very symbol of innocence and vulnerability," children clearly represented political neutrality.³³ As one group noted in the *New York Times*, "there's no politics in the suffering of children."³⁴

In addition to focusing on neutrality, the AFSC tried to counter prevailing concerns about German requisitions. In December 1940, an article entitled "Friends to Ignore British Blockade" appeared in the *New York Times*. Pickett addressed the issue of the Germans confiscating goods directly:

> Despite the British Government's foreboding that the furnishing of foods to Europe might be a military advantage to the Germans, the American Friends' Service Committee cannot express too strongly the complete independence with which it works in France and the absolute control which it has over its supplies from the moment of arrival to the point of consumption.
>
> Insofar as the American Friends' Service Committee is concerned, there is no debate and there is no controversy. We can assert categorically that there is no danger of seizure of our supplies by military authorities or interference with our administration. We have worked with complete accord with all governments concerned in Poland and France.³⁵

Beyond trying to influence public opinion through the press, the Quakers worked directly with the German and British governments. In January and February 1941, the AFSC sent two representatives to both Berlin and London to discuss the possibility of expanding relief operations in German-occupied countries, including northern France. The Germans agreed that they would not divert imported food, that any food would be used to supplement rations, and that an AFSC commission would be free to inspect any food distribution in the field. They did not agree, however, to contribute a thousand calories of bread for each thousand calories of imported milk, which the AFSC believed would help convince Americans that Germany would not take the food to support its military effort. The AFSC delegates in Britain, however, were not able to convince the UK's Ministry of Economic Warfare to relax the blockade for feeding children or to expand distribution from unoccupied to occupied France.[36]

The absence of Germans in the unoccupied zone, then, was the major factor in allowing any material aid to be delivered to France. As one British official asserted in 1943 when the British again rejected plans for allowing additional food into Europe, "the American Quakers operated only in Vichy France while it was unoccupied and never extended their operations to occupied territory. The Germans did not interfere in that work [...] because they were not there."[37] In response, Howard Kershner, the former director of the AFSC in France, wrote,

> Of course, plenty of Germans were in Southern France in connection with carrying out the terms of the armistice. There was a delegation in every important city. In Marseille, the delegation was housed in the building next to our office. They knew of our work and could have made difficulty for us had it been in their interest to do so. It is, however, no use to speculate on whether or not the Germans would interfere. The chances are they would not, but if they did the entire operation would immediately stop and great psychological advantage would accrue to the Allies as a result of having shown that we were ready to send food but the Germans took it. We would still have the gratitude of the people of the occupied countries for having made every possible effort to assist them.[38]

While the British correctly noted that the American Friends Service Committee did not work in occupied France, the French Quakers in Paris did have an active aid program that functioned with the knowledge and support of the Germans.[39]

Indirect Effects: Ideology of Neutrality versus the Practice of Humanitarianism

In the southern zone of France, the absence of German troops did not imply a lack of influence or minimal effects on the population. In addition to the substantial material effects created by the war and the limits imposed by the Allied governments, AFSC volunteers also had to contend with their own self-imposed limits influenced by the Occupation. Scholar Renée Poznanski has argued that during the war humanitarian aid agencies "unthinkingly accommodated themselves to the existing political structure as long as they were able to carry out their mission."[40] The AFSC was no exception. It worked closely with the Vichy regime, and the Vichy regime actively collaborated with Germany. For aid workers on the ground, working with Vichy was in some ways an extension of working with the Germans. The AFSC sought support from the Germans at the same time that it worked to counter the effects of the German Occupation through its activities. Its work included feeding refugees; working to free "undesirable" inmates from concentration camps; and providing emigration advice to Jews fleeing persecution. In addition to working directly with Vichy and the Germans, the AFSC also engaged in "self-policing" that ultimately limited its actions in favor of the persecuted. However, as persecution increased so did the gap between the discourse of neutrality and humanitarian actions on the ground.

The Service Committee deliberately worked to maintain its neutrality and refrained from making partisan statements. Kershner, working in France, reminded his colleagues in the United States,

> Those of us who are here are much concerned that in publicity nothing should be said that might make it more difficult to carry on our work in cooperation with the many authorities of different nationalities with whom we have to deal. For instance, not a can of milk comes from Switzerland without the approval of the German control. Without going into details, I think you will see, therefore, the necessity for preserving strict neutrality and speaking most respectfully for all.[41]

Access to food supplies was contingent on remaining in the occupiers' good graces. Concerns about German reactions also influenced decisions made in France. The AFSC continually searched for qualified people who could help with its work. One of the greatest barriers to providing aid was language. Office personnel needed strong skills in English and French, and knowing German was also helpful. Most AFSC volunteers from the US spoke only English, so the agency was reliant on additional hired support. AFSC workers noted that the refugees who came to the Marseille office seeking material aid or emigration help were often well equipped to help with humanitarian aid, as were "some of the French Jews who became increasingly available as anti-Semitic prejudice and decrees appeared." Despite the AFSC's desire to help all needy people regardless of their background, political considerations affected hiring decisions. A retrospective report noted, "While it was never definitely determined whether or not AFSC as a charitable organization was subject to the decrees drastically regulating the employment of foreigners and Jews, it was left that as a foreign organization it was better policy not to deviate too far from the restrictions imposed on domestic organizations."[42] The Americans running the AFSC chose to follow the French employment laws, which increasingly excluded Jews.

Rarely testing the boundaries of German limits, the AFSC worked within the system to deliver aid. This was true even of its work in Vichy's internment camps. While the camps were not a direct imposition of the Nazis, the Occupation would have a clear impact in this area. By the beginning of 1941, forty thousand Jews had already been arrested and interned. The AFSC provided supplemental rations and distributed clothing in the major camps in the unoccupied zone. Representatives visited the camps several times a week, but did not generally live on site.[43] Relations with the camp and departmental authorities were often described as cordial and cooperative. In addition to working in the camps, AFSC volunteers tried to remove as many people as they could from the deplorable conditions. The Quakers moved children from the camps into colonies where they would stay just long enough to "build up [the children's] strength, give them a new chance, and remedy a difficult situation caused by the war."[44] They also hired adults to staff the colonies, which facilitated additional releases.[45] They also identified individuals who they felt would be appropriate candidates for emigration.

In keeping with the nonpartisan nature of its mission, the AFSC did not limit its aid to persecuted Jews. In fact, it often emphasized that the majority of its work supported French war victims and not foreigners. However, when the situation shifted from persecution to deportation in the summer of 1942, AFSC tactics also shifted. The August 1942 deportations provide perhaps the starkest example of the effects of the German Occupation on the unoccupied zone. To meet German demands to deport 32,000 Jews from France before the end of the summer of 1942, the Vichy government agreed to deliver Jews living in the southern zone into SS hands.[46] Even without the participation of any German troops, approximately 7,100 Jews from the unoccupied zone were seized and deported during the late summer of 1942. Yet the German influence was felt in more than just setting the quotas for arrests. When asked for secondhand clothing for the Jews selected for deportation, the AFSC could not fulfill the request because "the Committee's hands were rigidly tied by the bureaucratic strictures laid down by the American 'Trading With the Enemy Act' and parallel rulings of the Ministry of Economic Warfare in England."[47] Representatives of the AFSC as well as other aid organizations traveled to Vichy to lodge a protest upon hearing of the impending deportations. They hoped to stop the deportations or to be granted exemptions for internees younger than sixteen or holding valid immigration visas for the United States. Tracy Strong, working with the YMCA, met with Marshal Pétain, but found the meeting to be "unsatisfactory since the old man seemed largely unaware of what was happening, [. . .] and the mention of the deportation measures elicited only the repeated observation from him: 'Les Allemands sont durs' [The Germans are tough]!"[48] In the end, the AFSC was only able to provide some food supplies for the trains as they departed from the southern zone.

The deportations in the fall of 1942 created internal debates about how best to respond to Vichy's actions to meet Nazi quotas, exposing rifts within the AFSC. Volunteers closest to the deportations worked to save as many people as they could, taking both legal and illegal actions.

When rumors of an impending deportation began to circulate in early August 1942, AFSC representatives working directly in the camps began to take action. Mary Elmes, an Irish woman running the AFSC delegation in Perpignan, used all the vacant spots in children's colonies under her direction to house Jewish children liberated from Rivesaltes. This included nine places in a colony that had been designated to house Spanish children. AFSC delegates at the Marseille headquarters noticed that many of the new children on the list of residents in August "were not Spanish but German or Polish Israelites." Still attempting to stay on the right side of authorities, the AFSC in Marseille noted, "I can guess the reasons why you admitted them but since the funds for the Vernet children are paid by the Mexican Consulate and they require a detailed list of names, this puts us in a difficult situation."[49] Elmes responded immediately, saying there was nowhere else to place them and supposed that given the "special circumstances," the Mexican Consulate would understand why non-Spanish children had been placed in the colony.[50] A few days later, Marseille responded: "You know that we have the greatest desire to help Israelite children." They suggested quickly opening a home for a group of Spanish children with a few French children included that could serve as a "cover" so as not to create an "exclusively Israelite home."[51] In addition to these "legal" separations that spared children from deportation, Elmes smuggled children out of Rivesaltes and hid others in the other Quaker colonies around Perpignan.[52] By September, the Vichy regime agreed not to deport the children under Quaker care and hundreds would be saved with the aid of the AFSC.

AFSC leadership, however, was often more cautious. After meeting with Vichy's chief of police, the head of the AFSC warned relief workers in the field not to "'irritate' Vichy with requests for individual exemptions from deportation orders, as that might jeopardize requests for large-scale exemptions."[53] This tension between aiding those in greatest need and jeopardizing larger relief efforts by angering either Vichy or the Germans was never fully resolved. However, within weeks of the large-scale deportations from the unoccupied zone, the AFSC would no longer be able to operate in France. With the Allied landings in North Africa in November 1942, Vichy severed diplomatic ties with the United States and the Germans occupied all of France. The nine Americans still working with the AFSC were arrested and interned at Baden-Baden.[54] Prepared for this eventuality, the AFSC transferred its humanitarian work to a French organization, the Secours Quaker, and aid workers formerly associated with the AFSC with citizenship from neutral countries continued to provide financial, material, and moral support in France.

Conclusion

Shortly after the Germans extended occupation into the previously "Free" Zone, the Friends in France produced a document in French, English, and German that described the Quaker organizations that were currently working in Greater Germany and in occupied countries. The document stated, "The German Authorities have always recognized the non-partisan attitude of Quakers be they German, French, Dutch, etc., and be they engaged directly or indirectly in relieving suffering without regard to nationality, politics, creed, or race."[55] Highlighting both the German acceptance of Quaker aid to those in need and the nonpartisan nature of their work, these documents were clearly preparing for the potential implications of the German Occupation on the Quakers' relief work. Yet, as I hope this chapter has shown, the Friends already had experience in navigating the effects of the German Occupation even before the Germans' arrival. Certain changes did occur in the Quakers' ability to provide humanitarian aid, but many things remained the same. The AFSC and its supporters abroad continued to advocate for the relaxation of the British blockade; aid workers in France continued to provide food to children through school canteens, run children's colonies, manage workshops, and distribute food and clothing to those in need. Further study is needed to understand how dynamics changed for humanitarian aid agencies and the people they were trying to help after the Germans' arrival, but there does not seem to be a drastic shift in aid or tactics.[56]

During the Second World War, the American Friends Service Committee was in a delicate position in a complex web of relationships. Officially, the AFSC was allowed to work in France as an American organization, but it had an international team of volunteers. It also had to work with the collaborationist Vichy regime, the German occupiers, the American government, and other aid agencies within the constraints of the British blockade. The organization's previous work in Europe facilitated its ability to provide aid during the war, but other aid organizations also worked in France. Neutrality, or at least the appearance of nonpartisanship, was key. Even without the presence of German troops in Vichy France, the indirect and invisible influence of the Nazis was clearly felt in decisions being made and the limits placed on aid. Although it might appear contradictory, humanitarian agencies were able to provide aid to the persecuted as well as to refugees and anyone facing the hardships of war, but only in unoccupied territory. External aid meant that the French and the German occupiers could devote less domestic funds and goods to meeting those needs, a fact that did not go unnoticed by the British government intent on waging an economic war against the Nazis. As Vichy's commissioner general for Jewish affairs, Xavier Vallat, explained in response to Quaker protests of actions against the Jews, "I naturally pass over all that would lead us to a useless discussion on the grounds of the governemental [sic] decisions against Jews," he wrote. "I limit myself to retain the feeling of Christian charity which has inspired you, and to confirm to you that I shall gladly accept your offer of voluntary services to help particular distresses endured by unhappy Jewish families."[57] But is it possible for aid organizations to remain apolitical when that aid is politicized and is quite literally a matter of life or death? Exploring the work of the AFSC in unoccupied France during the Nazi Occupation allows us to begin to explore the complex politics of humanitarian aid and the limits imposed or implied during the war.

Bibliography

Barnes, Gregory A. *A Centennial History of the American Friends Service Committee.* Philadelphia: Friends Press, 2016.

Beaumont, Joan. "Starving for Democracy: Britain's Blockade of and Relief for Occupied Europe, 1939–1945." *War & Society* 8:2 (October 1990): 57–82.

Cabanes, Bruno. *The Great War and the Origins of Humanitarianism, 1918–1924.* Cambridge: Cambridge University Press, 2014.

Cépède, Michel. *Agriculture et Alimentation en France durant la IIe Guerre Mondiale.* Paris: Editions M-Th. Génin, 1961.

Finn, Clodagh. *A Time to Risk All: The incredible untold story of Mary Elmes, the Irish woman who saved children from Nazi concentration camps.* Dublin: Gill Books, 2017.

Fogg, Shannon L. "The American Friends Service Committee and Wartime Aid to Families." *Vichy France and Everyday Life: Confronting the Challenges of Wartime, 1939–1945*, edited by Lindsey Dodd and David Lees. London: Bloomsbury Academic, 2018.

———. "The Politics of Penury: Shortages as an Exclusionary Tool in Wartime France." *Beiträge zur Geschichte des Nationalsozialismus*, Vol. 30 (2015): 210–226.

———. *The Politics of Everyday Life in Vichy France: Foreigners, Undesirables, and Strangers.* Cambridge and New York: Cambridge University Press, 2009.

Jackson, Julian. *France: The Dark Years 1940–1944.* Oxford and New York: Oxford University Press, 2001.

Joly, Laurent. "The Genesis of Vichy's Jewish Statute of October 1940." *Holocaust and Genocide Studies* 27:2 (Fall 2013): 276–98.

Keren, Célia. "Autobiographies of Spanish Refugee Children at the Quaker Home in La Rouvière (France, 1940): Humanitarian Communication and Children's Writings." *Les Cahiers de Framespa* Vol. 5 (2010).

Kershner, Howard E. *Quaker Service in Modern War: Spain and France, 1939–1940.* New York: Prentice Hall, 1950.

Mayer, Michael. "The French Jewish Statute of October 3, 1940: A Reevaluation of Continuities and Discontinuities of French Antisemitism." *Holocaust and Genocide Studies* 33:1 (Spring 2019): 4–22.

Marrus, Michael R. and Robert O. Paxton. *Vichy France and the Jews.* Stanford, CA: Stanford University Press, 1981, 2019.

Medlicott, W. N. *The Economic Blockade* (2 vols.) London: His Majesty's Stationery Office and Longmans, Green and Co, 1952.

Moore, Bob. *Survivors: Jewish Self-Help and Rescue in Nazi-Occupied Western Europe.* Oxford and New York: Oxford University Press, 2010.

Moorehead, Caroline. *Village of Secrets: Defying the Nazis in Vichy France.* New York: HarperCollins Publishers, 2014.

Paxton, Robert O. *Vichy France: Old Guard and New Order, 1940–1944.* New York: Knopf, 1972.

Pickett, Clarence E. *For More than Bread: An autobiographical account of twenty-two years' work with the American Friends Service Committee.* Boston: Little, Brown, 1953.

Poznanski, Renée. "Rescue of the Jews and the Resistance in France: From History to Historiography." *French Politics, Culture & Society* 30:2 (Summer 2012): 8–32.

Ryan, Donna F. *The Holocaust and the Jews of Marseille: The Enforcement of Anti-Semitic Policies in Vichy France.* Urbana: University of Illinois Press, 1996.

Sutters, Jack. "Warmth and sweetness: the beginnings of a postwar feeding program in Germany." https://www.afsc.org/story/warmth-and-sweetness-beginnings-postwar-feeding-program-germany (March 29, 2010).

———. ed. *Archives of the Holocaust Vol. 2. American Friends Service Committee, Philadelphia. Pt. 2, 1940–1945*. New York: Garland, 1990.

Trueblood, D. Elton. *The People Called Quakers*. New York: Harper & Row Publishers, 1966.

Under the Red and Black Star: A Brief Account of the American Friends Service Committee. Philadelphia: Society of Friends, 1949.

Voglis, Polymeris. "Surviving Hunger: Life in the Cities and Countryside during the Occupation." *Surviving Hitler and Mussolini: Daily Life in Occupied Europe*, edited by Robert Gildea, Olivier Wieviorka, and Anette Warring. Oxford and New York: Berg, 2006.

Notes

1. John MacCormac, "Agencies Here Give $20,000,000 Abroad." *New York Times* (July 7, 1940). The allusion to the sinking of an ally's navy is a reference to the British attack on the French fleet at Mers-el-Kébir on July 3, 1940. The French refused to accept a British ultimatum, and the British opened fire on French sailors, killing almost 1,300.
2. Robert O. Paxton, *Vichy France: Old Guard and New Order, 1940–1944* (New York: Knopf, 1972). For a discussion of other scholars who challenged the immediate postwar interpretation, see Julian Jackson, *France: The Dark Years 1940–1944* (Oxford and New York: Oxford University Press, 2001), 1–20.
3. Michael R. Marrus and Robert O. Paxton, *Vichy France and the Jews* (Stanford, CA: Stanford University Press, 1981), xvi. The autonomous nature of Vichy's anti-Jewish policies is more strongly emphasized in Marrus and Paxton's second edition of *Vichy France and the Jews* (Stanford, CA: Stanford University Press, 2019).
4. See, for example, Laurent Joly, "The Genesis of Vichy's Jewish Statute of October 1940," *Holocaust and Genocide Studies* 27:2 (Fall 2013), 276–98 and Michael Mayer, "The French Jewish Statute of October 3, 1940: A Reevaluation of Continuities and Discontinuities of French Antisemitism," *Holocaust and Genocide Studies* 33:1 (Spring 2019), 4–22.
5. *Under the Red and Black Star: A Brief Account of the American Friends Service Committee* (Philadelphia: Society of Friends, 1949), 2.
6. Ibid., 4. See also D. Elton Trueblood, *The People Called Quakers* (New York: Harper & Row Publishers, 1966).
7. For the history of the AFSC, see Gregory A. Barnes, *A Centennial History of the American Friends Service Committee* (Philadelphia: Friends Press, 2016). The German feeding program functioned from 1920 to 1922 with some additional aid in 1923–24. See also Jack Sutters, "Warmth and sweetness: the beginnings of a postwar feeding program in Germany." https://www.afsc.org/story/warmth-and-sweetness-beginnings-postwar-feeding-program-germany (March 29, 2010). [Accessed January 17, 2020.]
8. A brief overview of the Quakers' work in France is found in its Annual Report for 1940. See American Friends Service Committee, *Annual Report 1940*, 9–13. For

an account focusing on aid to Spanish refugees, see Howard E. Kershner, *Quaker Service in Modern War: Spain and France, 1939–1940* (New York: Prentice Hall, 1950). See also Clarence E. Pickett, *For More than Bread: An autobiographical account of twenty-two years' work with the American Friends Service Committee* (Boston: Little, Brown, 1953). For one woman's experiences with the AFSC in Spain and France, see Clodagh Finn, *A Time to Risk All: The incredible untold story of Mary Elmes, the Irish woman who saved children from Nazi concentration camps* (Dublin: Gill Books, 2017).

9. Margaret Frawley, "Summary." *Bulletin on Relief in France* No. 6 (September 18, 1940), 3. The bulletin suggested providing food and clothing to internees at Vernet, Rieucros, and Gurs.

10. Henry van Etten, "Le Secours Quaker: Rapport 1944" (Paris: Society of Friends, 1944), 11. Held at Library of the Society of Friends, London.

11. "Refugee Aid Now Urged by Friends: Service Committee Issues Call for Release of Funds Held for Relief in France." *New York Times* (August 4, 1940), 14.

12. Letter from Howard Kershner to Clarence E. Pickett (August 2, 1940) in Jack Sutters, ed. *Archives of the Holocaust Vol. 2. American Friends Service Committee, Philadelphia. Pt. 2, 1940–1945* (New York: Garland, 1990), 63.

13. Bob Moore, *Survivors: Jewish Self-Help and Rescue in Nazi-Occupied Western Europe* (Oxford and New York: Oxford University Press, 2010), 139–140. On German support for the AFSC in France see also Caroline Moorehead, *Village of Secrets: Defying the Nazis in Vichy France* (New York: HarperCollins Publishers, 2014), 124 and Donna F. Ryan, *The Holocaust and the Jews of Marseille: The Enforcement of Anti-Semitic Policies in Vichy France* (Urbana: University of Illinois Press, 1996), 155. For examples of documents addressing the AFSC's work in Germany, see United States Holocaust Memorial Museum (USHMM) RG 67.007M Box 25 Folder 14.

14. See Shannon L. Fogg, "The Politics of Penury: Shortages as an Exclusionary Tool in Wartime France" in *Beiträge zur Geschichte des Nationalsozialismus*, Vol. 30 (2015): 210–226 and Fogg, *The Politics of Everyday Life in Vichy France: Foreigners, Undesirables, and Strangers* (Cambridge and New York: Cambridge University Press, 2009).

15. Extract of Report on Camps in General, Marseille (December 20, 1940) in Sutters, ed. *Archives of the Holocaust*, 82.

16. Ibid, 84.

17. Ibid.

18. Letter from Howard Kershner to Clarence E. Pickett (August 2, 1940) in Sutters, ed. *Archives of the Holocaust*, 63.

19. Joan Beaumont, "Starving for Democracy: Britain's Blockade of and Relief for Occupied Europe, 1939–1945" *War & Society* 8:2 (October 1990), 57–58. On the blockade, see also W. N. Medlicott, *The Economic Blockade* (2 vols.) (London: His Majesty's Stationery Office and Longmans, Green and Co, 1952) and Meredith Hindley, "Blockade Before Bread: Allied Relief for Nazi Europe, 1939–1945." PhD dissertation, American University, 2007.

20. "Feeding of Europe Stirs Sharp Words: Academy of Sciences Hears Plea to Relax Barriers to Succor French." *New York Times* (October 6, 1940), 12.
21. "Quakers Planning to Free Draft Foes." *New York Times* (December 1, 1940). See also "Friends to Ignore British Blockade: Will Continue Endeavors to Feed European Children in Occupied Areas." *New York Times* (December 12, 1940), 12.
22. Beaumont, "Starving for Democracy," 61.
23. Ibid., 62.
24. Navicerts (navigation certifications) were special commercial passports that certified that a ship was not carrying banned items. The debates over the blockade continued throughout the war.
25. In 1940, the AFSC distributed milk to French children in the occupied zone (primarily Paris). The program was suspended in March 1941 following directives from the American government, which limited the distribution of all supplies to the unoccupied zone. See the series of letters between Howard E. Kershner and Robert Garric in USHMM RG 67.007M Box 52 Folder 1.
26. Translation of "Armistice Agreement between the German High Command of the Armed Forces and French Plenitpotentiaries" (June 22, 1940). Available at: https://avalon.law.yale.edu/wwii/frgearm.asp [Accessed December 16, 2019.] Occupation costs are discussed in Article 18. Article 21 charged the French with maintaining "the security of all objects and valuables whose undamaged surrender or holding in readiness for German disposal is demanded in this agreement or whose removal outside the country is forbidden." The French were also responsible for compensating the Germans for any destruction, damage, or unauthorized removal of these items.
27. Polymeris Voglis, "Surviving Hunger: Life in the Cities and Countryside during the Occupation" in *Surviving Hitler and Mussolini: Daily Life in Occupied Europe* edited by Robert Gildea, Olivier Wieviorka, and Anette Warring (Oxford and New York: Berg, 2006), 17, 20.
28. Michel Cépède, *Agriculture et Alimentation en France durant la IIe Guerre Mondiale* (Paris: Editions M-Th. Génin, 1961), 372.
29. "Feeding of Europe Stirs Sharp Words." *The New York Times* (October 6, 1940), 12.
30. Bruno Cabanes, *The Great War and the Origins of Humanitarianism, 1918–1924* (Cambridge: Cambridge University Press, 2014), 219.
31. Cited in Célia Keren, "Autobiographies of Spanish Refugee Children at the Quaker Home in La Rouvière (France, 1940): Humanitarian Communication and Children's Writings," *Les Cahiers de Framespa* Vol. 5 (2010), 7. Available at https://framespa.revues.org/268?lang=es [Accessed May 25, 2020].
32. Ibid., 8. By 1942, the AFSC spent more than $40,000 in publicity. See American Friends Service Committee, "Annual Report—1942," 43.
33. Cabanes, *The Great War*, 250.
34. "Veterans' Plan to Feed French Children Through Quakers Gains Wide Support." *New York Times* (November 28, 1940), 9.
35. "Friends to Ignore British Blockade." *New York Times* (December 12, 1940), 12. Similar statements were made in later articles. See "Friends Face End of Aid

in France: Leaders of Relief Work, Back on Drottningholm, Report Supplies Giving Out." *New York Times* (June 3, 1942), 19; "Plans Aid for Children: Friends Committee Seeks Permit for Work in Europe." *New York Times* (January 23, 1943), 7.

36. "German and British governmental attitudes regarding relief operations in the occupied countries as reported by Quaker representatives" (April 30, 1941). USHMM RG 67.007M Box 34 Folder 10. For an extended study of British policies, see Hindley, "Blockade before Bread."
37. "British Reject Plans for Feeding Europe: Greece Is Only Exception—Foot Justifies Decision." *New York Times* (May 12, 1943), 4.
38. Howard E. Kershner, "Greek Children Need Food: Nazis May Be Feeding Forced Workers but Not Youngsters and Mothers." *New York Times* (May 21, 1943), 18. In addition to the delegations that Kershner mentioned, Theodor Dannecker, the head of the German agency responsible for the long-term planning of anti-Jewish policy in France (the *Judenreferat*), also toured concentration camps in the unoccupied zone on at least two occasions in 1941 and 1942.
39. The Quakers were especially active in providing aid to prison and camp inmates. See, for example, "Activités Accomplies par les Quakers avec l'Approbation des Autorités Allemandes depuis Octobre 1940" (n.d.) USHMM RG 67.007M Box 25 Folder 10.
40. Renée Poznanski, "Rescue of the Jews and the Resistance in France: From History to Historiography," *French Politics, Culture & Society* 30:2 (Summer 2012), 16.
41. "Memorandum to American Friends Service Committee Speakers" (n.d.) USHMM RG 67-007M Box 34 Folder 10. Additional examples in Finn, *A Time to Risk All*, 97–98.
42. American Friends Service Committee, "Activities in France to November, 1942 (Baden-Baden Report)," 46. Available at www.afsc.org/document/activities-france-baden-baden-report-1942.
43. A Quaker representative lived in Gurs after March 1943 (after the AFSC work had been transferred to the Secours Quaker and the Americans had left). Marjorie and Ross McClelland, "Report on Relief Activities of Secours Quaker in France—based on conversations with Helga Holbek." (October 1943). Sutters, ed. *Archives of the Holocaust*, 444.
44. "Memorandum" (July 17, 1941). USHMM RG 67.007M Box 11 Folder 26. An evaluation of the colonies' success and suggestions for future operations were provided in "American Friends Service Committee Activities in France to November, 1942 (Baden-Baden Report), p12–18. Available at www.afsc.org/document/activities-france-baden-baden-report-1942.
45. In 1940 and 1941, any internee with an income of 1,200 francs per month could be released from a camp. See Marrus and Paxton, *Vichy France and the Jews*, 122.
46. On negotiations for deportations for France, see Marrus and Paxton, *Vichy France and the Jews*, 170–176. On the unoccupied zone, see 193–200.

47. Roswell McClelland, "An Unpublished Chapter in the History of the Deportation of Foreign Jews from France in 1942." USHMM 2014.500 McClelland Papers Folder 1 Series 7. Quote from p. 4 of the revised draft.
48. Ibid., 8. The AFSC negotiations with Laval revealed Vichy's own complicity in the deportations.
49. Letter from Marguerite Fischbacher to Mary Elmes (August 24, 1942), 2. USHMM RG 67.007M Box 57 Folder 1.
50. Letter from Mary Elmes to Marguerite Fischbacher (August 27, 1942), 2–3. USHMM RG 67.007M Box 57 Folder 1.
51. Letter from Marguerite Fischbacher to Mary Elmes (August 29, 1942), 1. USHMM RG 67.007M Box 57 Folder 1.
52. Finn, *A Time to Risk All*, 134–138. Elmes was recognized as one of the Righteous Among Nations. There were 174 children and 2,289 Jewish adults deported from Rivesaltes from August to October 1942.
53. Finn, *A Time to Risk All*, 150.
54. Moore, *Survivors*, 141. Moore gives the number as seven. The final report of the AFSC in France from Baden Baden lists nine representatives. See "American Friends Service Committee Activities in France to November, 1942 (Baden-Baden Report)" available online at www.afsc.org/document/activities-from-france-baden-baden-report-1942.
55. USHMM RG 67.0007M Box 25 Folder 14.
56. Shannon L. Fogg, "The American Friends Service Committee and Wartime Aid to Families" in *Vichy France and Everyday Life: Confronting the Challenges of Wartime, 1939–1945* edited by Lindsey Dodd and David Lees (London: Bloomsbury Academic, 2018), 107–122.
57. M. Xavier Vallat, commissioner general for Jewish affairs, Paris to Delegates of the Religious Society of Friends (Quakers), Paris. [n.d. probably July 1941] in Sutters, ed. *Archives of the Holocaust*, 198.

CHAPTER 3

A Women's Occupation?

Female Wehrmacht Auxiliaries in France and Europe, 1940–1944

Julia S. Torrie

The German forces in occupied France, and across Europe, are almost always perceived as male. The majority of occupying troops—foot soldiers, sailors, and aviators—were men, but as the war went on, increasing numbers of women were assigned to desk jobs in occupied areas. In January 1943, for example, as many as 485 women were among 1,482 staff members serving in the administrative offices of the *Militärbefehlshaber Frankreich*. In 1943–1944, there were 8,000 communications auxiliaries (*Nachrichtenhelferinnen*) and 12,500 clerical auxiliaries (*Stabshelferinnen*) in areas controlled by Wehrmacht field units and in occupied territories Europe-wide.[1] By the end of the war, historian Karen Hagemann has estimated, there was one woman for every twenty men in the German army overall.[2]

From the start of the Occupation of France, women served as telephonists and performed clerical work in the offices of the military administration. Their role was formalized into a communications corps (the *Nachrichtenhelferinnenschaft*) in March 1941, and a year later into a clerical auxiliary corps (the *Stabshelferinnenschaft*). These structures grouped auxiliaries and established basic rules for their deployment, conduct, and supervision. At a time when setbacks on the Eastern Front suggested a long war to come, the German army reluctantly decided to recognize what was already evident—female auxiliaries were an essential component of occupation administrations, especially in "safer" occupied areas such as France.

The Third Reich's leaders were torn between their desire to exploit female labor and their unwillingness to challenge traditional gender roles. They worried about young, single women's morals in a masculine environment and the long-term effects of employment on women's capacity to bear children. Military leaders wanted neither to "masculinize" women, nor to "feminize" the German army, and they were concerned about the potential effects of mobilizing women on the morale of their soldier relatives.

Women's presence was especially problematic in occupied areas, where combat soldiers already perceived troops as "soft." Female employment highlighted manpower shortages, and auxiliaries made occupying armies more vulnerable. Guidelines stated that women were not supposed to bear arms.[3] In a volatile situation, they might become a burden on their male colleagues and they were supposed to be evacuated at the first sign of enemy incursions.[4] Beyond any "real" vulnerability, contemporaries attributed characteristics to women, such as a tendency to gossip, that made their presence in occupied areas seem problematic.[5]

Employing women outside the Reich in wartime was particularly difficult to reconcile with a National Socialist emphasis on motherhood. This chapter shows that the regime attempted to resolve this conundrum by trying to maintain auxiliaries' capacity to bear children, and praising it in the abstract, while situating actual motherhood and accompanying virtues, such as nurturing, primarily in the future. Only by turning motherhood into an ideal for the postwar could the regime elaborate a model of femininity that allowed for the large-scale mobilization of young women for a war of conquest in the present.

Female Auxiliaries and Motherhood

Learning more about how National Socialists envisioned femininity in the Wehrmacht, especially among auxiliaries abroad, informs debates in three historiographical areas. First, it intervenes in discussions about female employment in the first half of the twentieth century and debates about women's complicity in the Third Reich. Second, it shows how Nazi-era notions of femininity abroad intersected with, and were shaped by, ideas about women's role in colonial projects since the late nineteenth century. Finally, looking at female auxiliaries suggests how gender interacted with contemporary notions about military occupations. In France, after late 1941, the arrival of growing numbers of female auxiliaries coincided with a shift from an early, relatively calm occupation phase to one of growing oppression, terror, and deportations. As indicated above, the Nazis struggled to reconcile the nurturing functions they associated with women and the "hard" masculinity required of a more brutal occupation.

Auxiliaries' deployment outside the 1939 borders of the Reich was complicated by the way that women's putative "nurturing" or "motherly" characteristics had interacted with their public roles since the late nineteenth century. As Seth Koven and Sonya Michel have explained, the doctrine of maternalism, elaborated at that time, extolled the private virtues of domesticity and used them to legitimate women's public roles. Maternalists argued that as real or potential mothers, they possessed attributes that might, through greater female action in the public sphere, be extended to society.[6] In the context of overseas colonialism, maternalism served to define and justify specifically female contributions to colonial projects.[7] For example, in the interwar period, historian Susan Pedersen has shown, women's supposedly strong nurturing abilities undergirded a growing emphasis on "benevolent" forms of colonial rule in the management of the League of Nations mandates system.[8]

Maternalism and concerns about preserving young women's potential as mothers while also drawing on their labor shaped debates about nursing in the First World War and the so-called "new woman" in the interwar period. Nursing required practical skills, "male" attributes such as bravery and resourcefulness, yet also drew on "female" traits such as empathy and nurturing.[9] Wartime debates spilled over into interwar controversies about the new woman, a young, emancipated, employed female figure who wore both her hemlines and her hair short. While some scholars have argued that the new woman was more a media construct than a reality, others emphasize that especially for young women, this was a time of real opportunity.[10] Historian Rüdiger Graf, for his part, contends that the new woman became a vehicle for expressing competing visions of the future.[11] German observers on the Left saw the new woman as a harbinger of a more equal future along

Soviet lines, while others associated her with a rising America, here too suggesting that "she belonged to a future stage of historical development."[12] Meanwhile, conservatives in Germany rejected both models and feared the potential "masculinization" of women as they took on new styles and roles. For them, women's connection to the future lay not in employment but in bearing children.[13] Specifically National Socialist visions took this perspective to extremes, for a Nazi future had "no space" for women except in their capacity as mothers.[14]

The story of how this tension played itself out after 1933 is well known, as the Nazis first encouraged women to leave their jobs in order to foster full male employment, and then began bringing them back to work as men were mobilized. Unwilling to push especially married women and young mothers into the workforce, they preferred to use forced labor to boost production.[15] Although forced laborers could be exploited in industrial settings, they were ill-suited to sensitive work in a military context, and here, women were preferred. Moreover, many women, especially young, unmarried ones, had never ceased working during the Third Reich. A considerable number had even been employed in German military offices throughout the interwar period, in part to circumvent the Treaty of Versailles that reduced the German army to one hundred thousand men.[16] In view of these circumstances, women's employment as auxiliaries after 1939 constituted a continuity as much as a rupture with previous trends.

Existing studies of Wehrmacht auxiliaries focus on the formation and makeup of women's units, their training, and tasks. Franka Maubach and Rosemarie Killius have illuminated auxiliaries' experiences through interviews, while Wendy Lower and Gudrun Schwarz address the specific question of their complicity in genocide.[17] These accounts acknowledge that women worked outside the Reich but do not problematize auxiliaries' position as representatives of the German forces in foreign lands, nor consider similarities and possible connections between wartime occupations and earlier overseas colonialism.[18] Yet, as this chapter shows, colonial contexts partly shaped contemporaries' ideas about working women abroad.

In recent years, Jürgen Zimmerer and others have argued that military occupations and colonialism are not as different from one another as generations of Eurocentric scholarship have suggested.[19] Applying this perspective to research on Nazi-dominated Eastern Europe and drawing on the literature about European women in overseas colonies, Elizabeth Harvey has shown that, as in colonial settings, German women's role in the Nazi East was to "help maintain the 'superior' culture, promote the cohesion of colonial society, and enforce the boundaries between the colonizing and the colonized 'race' inside and outside the home."[20] Both Harvey and Zimmerer focus on connections between German colonialism and expansion into Eastern Europe, raising the question of whether their observations also apply to the West. Zimmerer argues that his conclusions do not necessarily apply to the West, for "its practices differed greatly from those in the East [and determining] whether colonial structures might also be seen to be at work in the German Occupation of Western Europe would need a separate investigation."[21] Harvey, for her part, downplays East-West distinctions somewhat, noting that women "embarked on programs of 'womanly work' in the conquered territories" both in the West—she points to Alsace—and in Poland, but that these were "pursued with particular ideological fervor in the 'new East.'"[22]

Certainly, National Socialist projects were taken to extremes in Eastern Europe; however, patterns of behavior and thinking that were strongly apparent in occupied Eastern Europe were also present in the West. This included attitudes associated with colonialism, and it is no accident that Frenchman Pierre Audiat, who published a memoir of the war years in 1946, titled a section dealing with the establishment of the German Occupation, "La colonization manquée."[23] The Third Reich's central authorities saw the lands they conquered as one closely connected European zone. Personnel moved back and forth across the continent throughout the war, and a typical female auxiliary might alternate stations in France or Norway with the Balkans, Ukraine, or northern Italy. For this reason, scholarship dealing with colonial attitudes and women in occupied Eastern Europe is relevant to the West. The East-West divide that marks the historiography does not reflect conditions on the ground that, while they were distinct in each occupied area, bore strong similarities Europe-wide.[24]

Notwithstanding Harvey's research and the scholarship on women's roles as auxiliaries and perpetrators cited above, we still know little about women in German-occupied Europe, and broader research about wartime occupations typically overlooks the presence of women among German personnel.[25] Yet it is worth asking not just what women did, but what impact female auxiliaries had on the character of occupations. How did contemporaries reconcile their understanding of women as emotive, nurturing, and empathetic, and the widespread influence of maternalist discourses that legitimated women's public roles by propounding these supposed virtues, with the employment of large numbers of female auxiliaries in a military context abroad?

When the Occupation of France began, Germans gave it continuity by linking it to occupations past. At the same time, they framed it consciously in opposition to specific facets of the way those occupations were remembered. In fact, National Socialist authorities sought to transform the notion of military occupation itself, claiming a moral high ground and espousing notions of partnership and benevolence rather than domination and humiliation. Especially early on, Germans drew on gendered metaphors to style themselves not as dominators, but as chivalrous, "fatherly protector[s]" of a feminized and infantilized French nation.[26] Such rhetoric resonated in a foreign policy context in which, since World War I, conflicts were seen in terms of the victimization of women and children, rather than in more traditional terms, such as treaty violation.[27] Instead of grinding France into submission, Germans argued that they were subjecting the country to a subtler form of discipline and tutelage.[28] In such a context, women's presence made sense—indeed, Pedersen's research into the League of Nations' interwar mandates system suggests that women's involvement in colonies, and by extension, occupations, might be positively desirable because it implied a softer, more benevolent form of rule.[29] However, from late 1941, the German regime in France became more violent and brutal. From this point, even as the number of auxiliaries in France grew because of manpower draining to the Eastern Front, it became more challenging to decide how women fit in.

Female Auxiliaries in Occupied Europe

Soon after the armistice with France was signed, the German army called for female staff to help administer the Occupation. Initially, women from military offices in the Reich were sent out to cover the demand.[30] Deployment to France was viewed as relatively safe—an opportunity to gain positive foreign experience in a place that was sufficiently exotic to be exciting without being uncomfortably or dangerously so. The regime capitalized on these sentiments, promoting army work as a culturally enriching complement to one's education.[31] Once the Reich's invasion of the Soviet Union had stalled and Germany faced an overall labor shortage, women's skills were increasingly valued. By the end of the war, many different subgroups of auxiliaries were working for the army, navy, and air force, and there were others linked to the SS.[32]

In France, along with the communications auxiliaries who worked telephone and telegraph systems, the most important group was the Stabshelferinnen. The designation "Stabshelferin" dated from January 5, 1942, when the high command formalized the status of female clerical employees to unify and standardize their treatment, discipline, and deployment. In occupied areas, women might take over "all tasks that women can also fulfill that have hitherto been undertaken by soldiers capable of field service... in order to make soldiers broadly available for active service."[33] At this time, Stabshelferinnen could be deployed to France, Belgium, and northern France, the Generalgouvernement in Poland, occupied areas of southeastern Europe, the Netherlands, and Norway.[34] Job descriptions notwithstanding, especially in the central offices of the military administration, Stabshelferinnen often did work that went well beyond the secretarial. Of the 176 female staff members working under the military administration in Paris in early 1943, for instance, eighty had been sent out specifically by Reich ministries to perform tasks requiring expert knowledge.[35] A male superior indicated that these women undertook "in many cases no pure clerical work, but rather ought to be viewed as highly-skilled specialists."[36] As demand for frontline soldiers grew, more women moved from strictly secretarial to mid-level administrative work, increasing at the same time their level of complicity in the racist and exploitative projects of the regime.

Auxiliaries were nineteen through thirty-five years old, though in special cases, women up to forty years old might be admitted.[37] Above all, the army sought women who were "of impeccable character, perform well in their work, and are physically healthy."[38] They must also be willing to bend to the highly regimented environment of the military, for the army required, "the fulfillment of duty without taking into account work time and office hours."[39] For the time being, Stabshelferinnen received no uniforms and they were identified using a dark green armband with "Stabshelferinnen des Heeres" (armed forces auxiliary) written in silver, or gold for leaders.[40] Communications auxiliaries were uniformed from the outset.

Auxiliaries were remunerated according to a standard salary grid, and received room, board, and pay supplements while employed in occupied areas. Before deployment, they were required to attend several days of training and to be vaccinated against smallpox, typhus, and cholera.[41] A woman's education and previous work experience were to be considered in her deployment, and the authorities emphasized that "the service of a Stabshelferin is a national service of honour that makes high demands on her strength of character."[42] Explicitly compared to soldiers, Stabshelferinnen were expected to demonstrate "strict breeding, order and comradeship" and to uphold "the worthiness and the reputation of the German woman in occupied areas."[43] Not only during their work hours, but also after work, auxiliaries continued to be under the authority of a (male) military superior, and they were required to abide by "special restrictions" regarding their behavior.[44]

The emphasis on "worthiness" and "reputation," like the many rules regarding women's behavior, reflects the German army's thinking that auxiliaries were both weak and vulnerable. In part to ensure their physical safety, and in part to monitor their morals, while men were often billeted on the population, women were accommodated together in hotels and dormitories, for example, at the Cité universitaire in Paris.[45] Work in military offices during the day and collective accommodation at night made socializing with men, let alone fraternizing with French civilians, difficult or impossible.[46]

Conceptualizing Military Femininity

Even if, given the presence of female staff in German military offices in the interwar period, employing Wehrmacht auxiliaries was not exactly new, recruiting large numbers of young women into full-time employment, often abroad, for the duration of the conflict stood in direct opposition to professed National Socialist doctrine. As a result, young women's employment had to be couched in terms that aligned it with the regime's ideas on femininity and motherhood. Some authors expressed this alignment in terms of women's particular aptitude for routine tasks, including "serving" machines such as typewriters and switchboards.[47] Others emphasized that maintaining connections between far-flung occupied areas and the Reich heartland was ideal for women, given their putative nurturing skills.[48]

At the same time, some contemporaries thought that character traits construed as feminine might make women difficult to manage. Women's attributes included "willingness to help, empathy, patience," while men possessed "toughness, resolve, and drive."[49] Women were viewed as moody and changeable, and a 1944 text by medical officer Dr. Driest warned Luftwaffe officers not to be perturbed by a female tendency to burst into tears. Since Driest believed that women were more sensitive than men, he recommended a calm and gentle approach. Especially when criticizing auxiliaries, officers should aim to gain their trust. Good results could be achieved by appealing to women's pride, ambition (*Ehrgeiz*) and sense of responsibility. Auxiliaries tended to have difficulty following orders, Driest claimed, especially if these orders did not suit them. They might respond by claiming they were ill, weeping, becoming stubborn, "or, when they find no other way out ... even reacting in hysterical fashion."[50] Driest underlined the importance of keeping a professional distance from auxiliaries, who might attempt to gain favors through flirtation. He highlighted the dangers of workplace romance, which would only lead to jealousy and confusion.[51]

Contemporaries were particularly concerned that service as an auxiliary might "militarize" women. "Militarization" was used as a shorthand for "masculinization," and both implied that women might lose the traits of normative Nazi femininity. To address such fears, in June 1942, the army high command issued additional guidelines for the employment of women in military zones, particularly outside the German heartland.[52] Citing the Führer's desire that these women receive the care and protection required to enable them to carry out their duties, the guidelines now emphasized that such attention must "conform to feminine nature and must never lead to a militarization of women, something that is a particular danger in the military sphere."[53] Seeking to contrast German women's participation in war from that of Soviet women, the guidelines went on to insist that, "the 'female soldier' does not at all align with our National Socialist understanding of womanhood."[54] To underscore women's distinctiveness, National Socialist Party Chancellery head, Martin Bormann put Reich Women's Leader (Reichsfrauenführerin) Gertrud Scholtz-Klink in charge of the care and supervision of women working for the German forces. Her deputy in France, Frau von Hoffmann, had an office at the Majestic Hotel alongside other high officials of the military administration.[55]

Guidelines established for the "Betreuung" (care) of Stabshelferinnen maintained that loneliness was the greatest challenge facing women in occupied territories.[56] This was cited as one reason they shared residences. Although these residences were not hotels where one might come and go as one pleased, they should not have the spartan character of military barracks either. Each residence was to have a full-time or part-time "residence leader" (*Heimleiterin*) who was responsible for ensuring respect of the "residence order." Women were to engage in relaxing sporting and cultural activities in their free time, and the regulations now also stated that, "in this regard, too, restraint should be exercised, so that recreational activities are not perceived as [military] service."[57] Auxiliaries were not to be uniformed beyond what was already the practice, though the guidelines admitted that this was also because cloth was required for soldiers' use. Overall, the guidelines revealed a tension between trying to limit women's freedom to avoid behavior that might damage the appearance and reputation of the Wehrmacht, and providing care and supervision "following a feminine point of view" so as not to risk "militarizing," or masculinizing, women by managing them in a military way.[58]

Women in Colonial Spaces

Even as Wehrmacht leaders puzzled over these matters, another model of femininity that might reconcile such concerns had already emerged, in a context quite similar to that of the occupied territories. The so-called "Kolomädel," a young woman in training for future colonial service, offered this alternate model of femininity. Scholar Willeke Sandler has examined the work of two German colonial schools, the Witzenhausen Colonial School for men and, for women, the Koloniale Frauenschule in Rendsburg (Schleswig-Holstein). Despite the loss of Germany's colonies, both institutions continued to function after 1918. The Koloniale Frauenschule prepared women for colonial work from 1926 through the Third Reich, even as Germans' hopes that they might regain their empire slipped away, and attention shifted under Hitler from overseas colonization to imperialism in the European East.

While the Witzenhausen school became a technical college in the first two years of war, and then shut down as potential students were drafted, enrollments at the Koloniale Frauenschule grew, and a 1943 prospectus claimed that many graduates had found work in the "Ostgebieten."[59] The school provided elective classes in Russian and "established a second campus in Potok Zloty [then in Poland]."[60] In 1944, a new prospectus reported that former students were employed as "'settlement advisors' to relocated ethnic Germans, 'as leaders or coworkers in the National Socialist People's Welfare Organization [Nationalsozialistische Volkswohlfahrt program "mother and child" [Mutter und Kind] ... [and] as "German land women" [Landfrauen] on the land administered by the SS.'"[61] Harvey has shown that women became "assiduous empire-builders," in particular as teachers of assimilable ethnic Germans in Nazi-controlled Eastern Europe.[62] The Koloniale Frauenschule readied women to develop and support German communities in Eastern Europe that were, as Sandler points out, "imagined as hermetically sealed off from the local population."[63]

To prepare for this type of work, students at the Koloniale Frauenschule were trained in everything from first aid to housekeeping in the bush. Equally, contemporaries were conscious of a potential conflict between acquiring practical skills such as butchery, blacksmithing, or carpentry, and normative notions of femininity. A 1940 prospectus from the school indicated that the objective was not to make female students into expert craftsmen, but to ensure that they had skills enough to understand various types of work in general terms. Young women should "... overcome, on their own, the traditional prejudice that girls are not fit for such things and ... gain the confidence to help themselves in case of emergencies."[64] The model of the so-called Kolomädel both reinforced and stretched traditional models of femininity. Since training at the Koloniale Frauenschule was focused on home, family, and the care of children, it offered scope for women to support National Socialist goals while acting in accordance with expectations that they would be wives and mothers. At the same time, it was largely practical in nature, took place in the context of overtly colonial projects in Eastern Europe, and involved a wider range of activities than women normally did at home.[65] A Kolomädel was young and fit, "capable and independent, equipped with will and determination as much as skill, and able to handle any situation resourcefully."[66] Were there similarities between the Kolomädel and the military auxiliaries who were employed as typists, stenographers, receptionists, and telephone operators in occupied areas across Europe?

As noted earlier, comparing National Socialist expansionism and overseas colonialism can yield valuable insights.[67] The continued existence of the Koloniale Frauenschule "even well after the battle of Stalingrad when direct colonial engagement was no longer official Nazi policy" underscores the value of such an approach.[68] As we have seen, the school's existence was justified by the fact that it transmitted "the kind of practical knowledge that was also desirable in the East."[69] Further consideration of military occupations in the wider context of colonial projects and colonial discourse is helpful in trying to pin down shifting National Socialist models of femininity among German women outside the Reich, not only in Eastern Europe, but in the West as well.[70]

Contemporaries' understanding of female Wehrmacht auxiliaries and their role in German-occupied Europe was forged in the same context as the Kolomädel. Auxiliaries were also young, typically single women who worked outside the 1939 Reich borders. Like the young women sent to Poland to teach and make homes, auxiliaries in France and elsewhere were supposed to represent a separate and "superior"

German group, whose identity they upheld through their deportment at work and leisure. Whether the authorities admitted it or not, resourcefulness and a certain amount of daring were required in auxiliaries' daily lives, too, just like the Kolomädel.

Yet in the case of the Wehrmacht auxiliaries, the National Socialists' emphasis on women's maternal attributes had the potential to complicate things. Clearly, alongside practical knowledge, women's putative "maternal" skills were valued for German projects in Eastern Europe, as they had been for overseas colonial projects. Harvey emphasized that the settlement advisors, teachers, and kindergarten staff she examined were constructed as "embodying 'cleanliness, purity and maternal fecundity,'" encouraged to combine "motherhood and mastery" as they went about their work.[71] However, while auxiliaries otherwise shared many of the same traits as these women, their role was not to nurture, nor to educate—rather, it was to execute repetitive, routine work with skill, precision, secrecy, and speed. How could this professional work be reconciled with a National Socialist understanding of femininity that emphasized maternal attributes? In his 1944 instructions for Luftwaffe officers, medical officer Dr. Driest addressed this issue head-on when he reminded soldiers that "in the auxiliaries they have before them the bearers of the next generation." "The natural realm of woman," he emphasized, "is and remains the child, the home, the husband and the family."[72]

Auxiliaries were "the bearers of the next generation," but clearly, the time for them to have children was not now, for their labor was needed to run the wartime Reich. To resolve the apparent contradiction between auxiliaries' professional work and their "natural realm" of motherhood, men such as Driest referred to homemaking and motherhood as "future tasks."[73] Occasionally, mothers whose children were being cared for elsewhere were chosen for auxiliary service abroad, but no children were allowed to join their mothers, and any woman who became pregnant was sent home. The lack of accommodation for actual motherhood and positioning it as desirable, but far in the future, underscores how poorly the large-scale deployment of young women as auxiliaries in France and elsewhere aligned with National Socialist notions about femininity.

This is not surprising, given the historical context, but defining women fundamentally as mothers, and then employing thousands of them as military auxiliaries in occupied territories was not simply contradictory. The broad resonance and implications of maternalist discourse in the period meant that it also had the potential to be problematic. If women, perceived as nurturing, empathetic, and emotive, had become essential components of Germany's expansionist apparatus, what did that imply about the core nature of this apparatus? Was it a masculine, powerful engine of European domination, or some kind of softer, female-identified tool for guidance and administrative oversight? A brief detour into the scholarship on maternalism and overseas colonialism explores the potentially pressing nature of these questions.

Maternalism: A Softer Approach?

As noted above, when especially middle-class women became engaged in various public initiatives in the later nineteenth century, many justified their actions through the doctrine of "maternalism." Contemporaries believed that women's special abilities to care and nurture gave them a "natural" affinity for specific types of work, such as nursing, social work, and teaching. More generally, women's presence implied a "softer" approach to public affairs. The broader implications of maternalism, and its relevance for understanding contemporary unease about women's involvement in military occupations, are suggested by Pedersen's research on women's role in the mandates system established at the end of the First World War. Rather than annexing German colonies outright, the victorious powers agreed to divide them up and hold them "in trust" under the oversight of the newly formed League of Nations. The governing powers ruled their mandates more or less as colonies, reporting once a year to the Permanent Mandates Commission [PMC] of the League of Nations.

Pedersen explains that women played a small, but important role in "administering and contesting the mandates."[74] At the PMC's formation, in 1920, international women's organizations lobbied to ensure that one of its nine members was a woman. Throughout its existence, women's organizations petitioned the PMC or its commissioners to bring specific concerns to its attention.[75] Despite their efforts, and women's own hope that their involvement would result in better social programs and a stronger emphasis on development in the mandates, this activity did not amount to very much. No significant changes in governance resulted from female engagement in the process, and the mandates were governed essentially the same way as colonies.

Still, Pedersen argues that women's involvement mattered. She contends that focusing on governance, where women made little or no impact, is beside the point, for "the presence of women on the Mandates Commission ... was politically and ideologically significant in that it helped to legitimate a particular understanding of European imperialism between the wars. Imperial rule, women's presence implied, would henceforth be based on tutelage and not force; social progress guided by women's hands could justify the perpetuation of non consensual alien rule."[76] Women might turn their attention to improving local people's condition, yet also support their (male) colleagues' efforts to suppress any attempts at self-determination. Female involvement updated European imperialism for the interwar era and legitimated it through a new emphasis on social progress, while still ensuring that it was shaped by a "productive symbiosis of benevolence and autocracy."[77] In short, Pedersen shows that because of the underlying concept of maternalism, women's presence stood for a kinder, gentler style of "non consensual alien rule" in the interwar period—one that, while autocratic, now also included benevolence.

Following from these conclusions about the interwar mandates system, women's inclusion as part of an occupying army, regardless of the activities they actually performed, might also be taken to imply benevolence, or at least to raise questions about the nature of the occupations whose work they ensured. Especially in 1940, a connection between women's presence and benevolent rule might not have been a problem. The German authorities were keen to present the Occupation as the beginning of a new style of military domination, far removed from the vindictive occupations of the past. They sent the *Nationalsozialistische Volkswohlfahrt* (National Socialist People's Welfare Organization) to assist French civilian war victims, and bent over backward to demonstrate that their soldiers' behavior was "correct."[78] Despite evidence that German soldiers committed atrocities during the French campaign, and notably murdered 1,500–3,000 French African soldiers, they emphasized repeatedly that they were not barbarians.[79] Now that the fighting was over, they were in France to assist and protect the population, breaking decisively with the brutal occupations of the past.

After 1941, however, the veneer of benevolence faded. Attacks by the Resistance increased, hostage-killings and large-scale deportations began, and the Occupation grew increasingly harsh. If women were organized into formal corps of Nachrichtenhelferinnen and Stabshelferinnen from this point on, it was not only for the practical reason that, as their numbers increased, it was easier to manage them this way. An insistence on proper dress and deportment, clear prohibitions against fraternization, not to mention a preference for housing women together in all-female residences, served to underline the military character of the Occupation. These measures also worked to distance young female auxiliaries from anything potentially "maternal," thus avoiding the suggestion that these women's presence represented either "softness" in the German military forces, or a more benevolent occupation style.

Conclusion

Even as their lives grew more regimented, however, the regime continued to insist that women not become like soldiers. Not wanting to give up on the idea that women were, above all, destined to be mothers, it used the device of locating motherhood, care, and nurturing well into the future to reconcile this notion with its immediate need for dynamic, resourceful, and often ruthless female staff. Indeed, the regime never resolved the tension between a traditional model of femininity and its need to mobilize female labor for occupation work. Rejecting the interwar model of a "new woman," it embraced such characteristics as resolve and resourcefulness only in limited ways, for instance when combined with "motherly" attributes in the Kolomädel.

Perhaps we should not be surprised, however, at the Wehrmacht's struggles to define an appropriate model of military femininity. Barring their work as nurses and nursing assistants, women had never previously been part of military occupations, and even today, it remains difficult to combine motherhood and military work, both at home and abroad. The German authorities tread a fine line. Seeking to avoid the militarization or masculinization of women, they also tried to manage any "softness" or benevolence that women's presence in occupied areas implied. They highlighted putative feminine characteristics when these might support auxiliaries' employment at routine tasks, and lauded motherhood while situating it firmly in the future. Models like the Kolomädel went some way toward reconciling feminine attributes with work outside the home and even the homeland, but in the end, even in wartime—and in some ways perhaps especially in wartime—Germans, like other contemporaries, were unable to close the gap between their understanding of women as mothers and women's potential as competent, professional staff.

Bibliography

Audiat, Pierre. *Paris pendant la guerre*. Paris: Hachette, 1946.

Baranowski, Shelley. *Nazi Empire: German Colonialism and Imperialism from Bismarck to Hitler*. Cambridge: Cambridge University Press, 2010.

Bock, Gisela. "Nazi Gender Policies and Women's History." In *Toward a Cultural Identity in the Twentieth Century*, edited by Françoise Thébaud, 149–76. A History of Women in the West 5. Cambridge, MA: Harvard University Press, 1994.

Bridenthal, Renate. "Beyond Kinder, Küche, Kirche: Weimar Women at Work." *Central European History* 6, no. 2 (June 1973): 148–66.

Darrow, Margaret H. "French Volunteer Nursing and the Myth of War Experience in World War I." *American Historical Review* 101, no. 1 (February 1996): 80.

Gersdorff, Ursula von. *Frauen im Kriegsdienst 1914–1945*. Beiträge zur Militär- und Kriegsgeschichte 11. Stuttgart: Deutsche Verlags-Anstalt, 1969.

Gold, Helmut. "'Hier ist alles Kontakt und Relais:' Zur Wiederentdeckung des 'Fräuleins vom Amt' im Deutschen Postmuseum." *Kultur & Technik: Zeitschrift des Deutschen Museums München* 17, no. 3 (1993): 50–55.

Graf, Rüdiger. "Anticipating the Future in the Present: 'New Women' and Other Beings of the Future in Weimar Germany." *Central European History* 42, no. 4 (December 2009): 647–73.

Grayzel, Susan R. *Women's Identities at War: Gender, Motherhood and Politics in Britain and France during the First World War*. Chapel Hill, N.C.: University of North Carolina Press, 1999.

Hagemann, Karen. "Mobilizing Women for War: The History, Historiography, and Memory of German Women's War Service in the Two World Wars." *Journal of Military History* 75, no. 4 (October 2011): 1055–94.

Harris, Ruth. "The Child of the Barbarian: Rape, Race and Nationalism in France during the First World War." *Past & Present*, no. 141 (November 1993): 170.

Harvey, Elizabeth. *Women and the Nazi East: Agents and Witnesses of Germanization*. New Haven, CT: Yale University Press, 2003.

Killius, Rosemarie. *Frauen für die Front: Gespräche mit Wehrmachtshelferinnen*. Leipzig: Militzke, 2003.

Koonz, Claudia. *Mothers in the Fatherland: Women, the Family and Nazi Politics.* New York: St. Martin's Press, 1987.

Koven, Seth, and Sonya Michel. "Womanly Duties: Maternalist Politics and the Origins of Welfare States in France, Germany, Great Britain, and the United States, 1880–1920." *American Historical Review* 95, no. 4 (1990): 1076–1108.

Lehnstaedt, Stephan. *Occupation in the East: The Daily Lives of German Occupiers in Warsaw and Minsk, 1939–1944.* Translated by Martin Dean. New York: Berghahn, 2016.

Lower, Wendy. *Hitler's Furies: German Women in the Nazi Killing Fields.* Boston: Houghton Mifflin Harcourt, 2013.

Maubach, Franka. *Die Stellung halten: Kriegserfahrungen und Lebensgeschichten von Wehrmachthelferinnen.* Göttingen: Vandenhoeck & Ruprecht, 2009.

———. "Expansionen weiblicher Hilfe: zur Erfahrungsgeschichte von Frauen im Kriegsdienst." In *Volksgenossinnen: Frauen in der NS-Volksgemeinschaft*, edited by Sybille Steinbacher, 9–26. Göttingen: Wallstein Verlag, 2007.

Mazower, Mark. *Hitler's Empire: How the Nazis Ruled Europe.* New York: Penguin Books, 2009.

McClintock, Anne. *Imperial Leather: Race, Gender, and Sexuality in the Colonial Contest.* New York: Routledge, 1995.

Meyer, Ahlrich. "Grossraumpolitik und Kollaboration im Westen: Werner Best, die Zeitschrift 'Reich—Volksordnung—Lebensraum' und die deutsche Militärverwaltung in Frankreich 1940–42." In *Modelle für ein deutsches Europa: Ökonomie und Herrschaft im Grosswirtschaftsraum*, edited by Horst Kahrs et al., 29–76. Beiträge zur nationalsozialistischen Gesundheits- und Sozialpolitik 10. Berlin: Rotbuch, 1992.

Mühlenberg, Jutta. *Das SS-Helferinnenkorps: Ausbildung, Einsatz und Entnazifizierung der weiblichen Angehörigen der Waffen-SS 1942–1949.* Hamburg: Hamburger Edition, HIS Verlag, 2012.

Pedersen, Susan. "Metaphors of the Schoolroom: Women Working the Mandates System of the League of Nations." *History Workshop Journal*, no. 66 (October 2008): 188–207.

———. "The Maternalist Moment in British Colonial Policy: The Controversy over 'Child Slavery' in Hong Kong 1917–1941." *Past & Present*, no. 171 (2001): 161–202.

Reagin, Nancy. "The Imagined Hausfrau: National Identity, Domesticity, and Colonialism in Imperial Germany." *Journal of Modern History* 73, no. 1 (2001).

Reagin, Nancy R. *Sweeping the German Nation: Domesticity and National Identity in Germany, 1870–1945.* Cambridge, UK: Cambridge University Press, 2006.

Rhoades, Michelle K. "Renegotiating French Masculinity: Medicine and Venereal Disease during the Great War." *French Historical Studies* 29, no. 2 (Spring 2006): 293–327.

Roos, Julia. "Racist Hysteria to Pragmatic Rapprochement? The German Debate about Rhenish 'Occupation Children,' 1920–30." *Contemporary European History* 22, no. 02 (May 2013): 155–180.

Sandler, Willeke. "Colonial Education in the Third Reich: The Witzenhausen

Colonial School and the Rendsburg Colonial School for Women." *Central European History* 49, no. 2 (June 2016): 181–207.

Scheck, Raffael. *Hitler's African Victims: The German Army Massacres of Black French Soldiers in 1940*. Cambridge, UK: Cambridge University Press, 2006.

Scheck, Raffael, Fabien Théofilakis, and Julia Torrie, eds. *German-Occupied Europe in the Second World War*. New York: Routledge, 2019.

Schulte, Regina. "The Sick Warrior's Sister: Nursing during the First World War." In *Gender Relations in German History: Power, Agency, and Experience from the Sixteenth to the Twentieth Century*, edited by Lynn. Abrams and Elizabeth Harvey, 121–41. Durham, NC: Duke University Press, 1997.

Schwarz, Gudrun. "'During Total War, We Girls Want to Be Where We Can Really Accomplish Something:' What Women Do in Wartime." In *Crimes of War: Guilt and Denial in the Twentieth Century*, edited by Omer Bartov, Atina Grossmann, and Mary Nolan, 121–37. New York: New Press, 2002.

———. *Eine Frau an seiner Seite: Ehefrauen in der "SS-Sippengemeinschaft."* Hamburg: Hamburger Edition, 1997.

Seidel, Ina, and Hanns Grosser. *Dienende Herzen: Kriegsbriefe von Nachrichtenhelferinnen des Heeres*. Berlin: Limpert, 1942.

Seidler, Franz W., ed. *Blitzmädchen: die Geschichte der Helferinnen der deutschen Wehrmacht im Zweiten Weltkrieg*. Bonn: Bernard & Graefe, 1998.

Steinbacher, Sybille. *Volksgenossinnen: Frauen in der NS-Volksgemeinschaft*. Göttingen: Wallstein Verlag, 2007.

Stephenson, Jill. *Women in Nazi Germany*. New York: Longman, 2001.

Thalmann, Rita. *Frausein im Dritten Reich*. München: C. Hanser, 1984.

Torrie, Julia S. *German Soldiers and the Occupation of France, 1940–1944*. Cambridge, UK: Cambridge University Press, 2018.

———. "The Many Aims of Assistance: The Nationalsozialistische Volkswohlfahrt and Aid to French Civilians in 1940." *War & Society* 26, no. 1 (May 2007): 27–38.

Virgili, Fabrice. "Enfants de Boches: The War Children of France." In *Children of World War II: The Hidden Enemy Legacy*, edited by Kjersti Ericsson and Eva Simonsen, 138–50. Oxford: Berg, 2005.

Westermann, Edward B. *Flak: German Anti-Aircraft Defenses, 1914–1945*. Lawrence: University Press of Kansas, 2001.

Zimmerer, Jürgen. "The Birth of the Ostland out of the Spirit of Colonialism: A Postcolonial Perspective on the Nazi Policy of Conquest and Extermination." *Patterns of Prejudice* 39, no. 2 (2005): 197–219.

Notes

1. In the same period, 300 000 were employed in the area of the reserve army (Ersatzheer), 130,000 in the air force and 20,000 in the navy. Ursula von Gersdorff, *Frauen im Kriegsdienst 1914–1945*, Beiträge zur Militär- und Kriegsgeschichte 11 (Stuttgart: Deutsche Verlags–Anstalt, 1969), 74.

2. Karen Hagemann, "Mobilizing Women for War: The History, Historiography,

and Memory of German Women's War Service in the Two World Wars," *Journal of Military History* 75, no. 4 (October 2011): 1057.
3. Information sheet, Verhalten der Helferinnen des Heeres im Falle der Gefangennahme, n.d. [October 1944] (Bundesarchiv [BArch] RW 60/176). Late February 1945 regulations allowed women to volunteer for aerial defense tasks involving weapons, but they were otherwise not permitted to use them. Radiogram, OKW, "Einsatz von weiblichen Hilfskräften in der Wehrmacht," February 28, 1945, reprinted in Gersdorff, *Frauen*, 504. Cf. Edward B Westermann, *Flak: German Anti-Aircraft Defenses, 1914–1945* (Lawrence: University Press of Kansas, 2001).
4. Armee-Oberkommando 2 O.Qu., Betr. "Einsatz von Stabshelferinnen, October 10, 1944 (BArch: RW 60/176).
5. Militärbefehlshaber Frankreich (MBH), Betr. Belehrung der Stabshelferinnen, 23 November 1943 (Archives nationales [AN]: 40 AJ/451).
6. Seth Koven and Sonya Michel, "Womanly Duties: Maternalist Politics and the Origins of Welfare States in France, Germany, Great Britain, and the United States, 1880–1920," *American Historical Review* 95, no. 4 (1990): 1079.
7. See, e.g., Susan Pedersen, "The Maternalist Moment in British Colonial Policy: The Controversy over 'Child Slavery' in Hong Kong 1917–1941," *Past & Present*, no. 171 (2001): 161–202; Nancy Reagin, "The Imagined Hausfrau: National Identity, Domesticity, and Colonialism in Imperial Germany," *Journal of Modern History* 73, no. 1 (2001); Nancy R. Reagin, *Sweeping the German Nation: Domesticity and National Identity in Germany, 1870–1945* (Cambridge, UK: Cambridge University Press, 2006).
8. Susan Pedersen, "Metaphors of the Schoolroom: Women Working the Mandates System of the League of Nations," *History Workshop Journal*, no. 66 (October 2008): 188–207.
9. Regina Schulte, "The Sick Warrior's Sister: Nursing during the First World War," in *Gender Relations in German History: Power, Agency, and Experience from the Sixteenth to the Twentieth Century*, ed. Lynn Abrams and Elizabeth Harvey (Durham, NC: Duke University Press, 1997), 121–41; Margaret H. Darrow, "French Volunteer Nursing and the Myth of War Experience in World War I," *American Historical Review* 101, no. 1 (February 1996): 80; Michelle K. Rhoades, "Renegotiating French Masculinity: Medicine and Venereal Disease during the Great War," *French Historical Studies* 29, no. 2 (Spring 2006): 293–327.
10. Compare, e.g., Renate Bridenthal, "Beyond Kinder, Küche, Kirche: Weimar Women at Work," *Central European History* 6, no. 2 (June 1973): 148–66. and Helmut Gold, "'Hier ist alles Kontakt und Relais:' Zur Wiederentdeckung des 'Fräuleins vom Amt' im Deutschen Postmuseum," *Kultur & Technik: Zeitschrift des Deutschen Museums München* 17, no. 3 (1993): 50–55.
11. Rüdiger Graf, "Anticipating the Future in the Present: 'New Women' and Other Beings of the Future in Weimar Germany," *Central European History* 42, no. 4 (December 2009): 647–73.

12. Ibid., 664.
13. Ibid., 670.
14. Ibid., 671.
15. See, e.g., Gisela Bock, "Nazi Gender Policies and Women's History," in *Toward a Cultural Identity in the Twentieth Century*, ed. Françoise Thébaud, A History of Women in the West 5 (Cambridge, MA: Harvard University Press, 1994), 149–76; Claudia Koonz, *Mothers in the Fatherland: Women, the Family and Nazi Politics* (New York: St. Martin's Press, 1987); Jill Stephenson, *Women in Nazi Germany* (New York: Longman, 2001); Rita Thalmann, *Frausein im Dritten Reich* (München: C. Hanser, 1984), Ch. 4.
16. Franka Maubach, *Die Stellung halten: Kriegserfahrungen und Lebensgeschichten von Wehrmachthelferinnen* (Göttingen: Vandenhoeck & Ruprecht, 2009), 12.
17. Rosemarie Killius, *Frauen für die Front: Gespräche mit Wehrmachtshelferinnen* (Leipzig: Militzke, 2003). Wendy Lower, *Hitler's Furies: German Women in the Nazi Killing Fields* (Boston: Houghton Mifflin Harcourt, 2013); Gudrun Schwarz, *Eine Frau an seiner Seite: Ehefrauen in der "SS-Sippengemeinschaft"* (Hamburg: Hamburger Edition, 1997). Franka Maubach, "Expansionen weiblicher Hilfe: zur Erfahrungsgeschichte von Frauen im Kriegsdienst," in *Volksgenossinnen: Frauen in der NS-Volksgemeinschaft*, ed. Sybille Steinbacher (Göttingen: Wallstein Verlag, 2007), 9–26; Maubach, *Stellung*. See also Sybille Steinbacher, *Volksgenossinnen: Frauen in der NS-Volksgemeinschaft* (Göttingen: Wallstein Verlag, 2007); Gersdorff, *Frauen*; Jutta Mühlenberg, *Das SS-Helferinnenkorps: Ausbildung, Einsatz und Entnazifizierung der weiblichen Angehörigen der Waffen-SS 1942–1949* (Hamburg: Hamburger Edition, HIS Verlag, 2012); Franz W. Seidler, ed., *Blitzmädchen: die Geschichte der Helferinnen der deutschen Wehrmacht im Zweiten Weltkrieg* (Bonn: Bernard & Graefe, 1998).
18. A partial exception is the work of Gudrun Schwarz, which emphasizes auxiliaries' complicity in National Socialist oppression in Eastern Europe in "'During Total War, We Girls Want to Be Where We Can Really Accomplish Something:' What Women Do in Wartime," in *Crimes of War: Guilt and Denial in the Twentieth Century*, ed. Omer Bartov, Atina Grossmann, and Mary Nolan (New York: New Press, 2002), 121–37. Wendy Lower notes the colonialist attitudes of Germans in Eastern Europe in *Hitler's Furies*, 49–50.
19. Jürgen Zimmerer, "The Birth of the Ostland out of the Spirit of Colonialism: A Postcolonial Perspective on the Nazi Policy of Conquest and Extermination," *Patterns of Prejudice* 39, no. 2 (2005): 199.
20. Elizabeth Harvey, *Women and the Nazi East: Agents and Witnesses of Germanization* (New Haven, CT: Yale University Press, 2003), 7.
21. Zimmerer, "Ostland," 200.
22. Harvey, *Women*, 11.
23. Pierre Audiat, *Paris pendant la guerre* (Paris: Hachette, 1946).
24. See Raffael Scheck, Fabien Théofilakis, and Julia Torrie, eds., *German-Occupied Europe in the Second World War* (New York: Routledge, 2019).

25. See, e.g., Shelley Baranowski, *Nazi Empire: German Colonialism and Imperialism from Bismarck to Hitler* (Cambridge: Cambridge University Press, 2010); Mark Mazower, *Hitler's Empire: How the Nazis Ruled Europe* (New York: Penguin Books, 2009). A partial exception is *Occupation in the East: The Daily Lives of German Occupiers in Warsaw and Minsk, 1939–1944*, trans. Martin Dean (New York: Berghahn, 2016), 43–45; 183–87.
26. Fabrice Virgili, "Enfants de Boches: The War Children of France," in *Children of World War II the Hidden Enemy Legacy*, ed. Kjersti Ericsson and Eva Simonsen (Oxford: Berg, 2005), 139.
27. See, notably, Susan R. Grayzel, *Women's Identities at War: Gender, Motherhood and Politics in Britain and France during the First World War* (Chapel Hill, NC: University of North Carolina Press, 1999); Ruth Harris, "The Child of the Barbarian: Rape, Race and Nationalism in France during the First World War," *Past & Present*, no. 141 (November 1993): 170; Julia Roos, "Racist Hysteria to Pragmatic Rapprochement? The German Debate about Rhenish 'Occupation Children', 1920–30," *Contemporary European History* 22, no. 02 (May 2013): 177.
28. Ahlrich Meyer, "Grossraumpolitik und Kollaboration im Westen: Werner Best, die Zeitschrift 'Reich-Volksordnung-Lebensraum' und die deutsche Militärverwaltung in Frankreich 1940–42," in *Modelle für ein deutsches Europa: Ökonomie und Herrschaft im Grosswirtschaftsraum*, ed. Horst Kahrs et al., Beiträge zur nationalsozialistischen Gesundheits- und Sozialpolitik 10 (Berlin: Rotbuch, 1992), 29–76.
29. Pedersen, "Metaphors."
30. Seidler, *Blitzmädchen*, 11. In September 1940, female staff members were forbidden from riding in military vehicles, which suggests that a sizable contingent was already in Paris. Militärbefehlshaber in Frankreich (MBH) "Benutzung von Wehrmachtfahrzeugen durch weibliche Angestellte," September 13, 1940 (AN: 40 AJ/451).
31. Ina Seidel and Hanns Grosser, *Dienende Herzen: Kriegsbriefe von Nachrichtenhelferinnen des Heeres* (Berlin: Limpert, 1942), 18.
32. On SS auxiliaries, see Mühlenberg, *SS-Helferinnenkorps*.
33. OKH order, January 5, 1942, cited in OKH, "Bildung einer Stabshelferinnenschaft für die Heeresdienststellen in den besetzten Gebieten," February 27, 1942 (AN: 40 AJ/456).
34. OKH, "Bildung," February 27, 1942 (AN: 40 AJ/456). Areas closest to the front lines were excluded until 1944. See AOK 2 O. Qu. "Einsatz von Stabshelferinnen," 10 October 1944 (BArch: RW 60/176).
35. As mentioned, 486 Stabhelferinnen were under the MBH at this time. MBH, Verwaltungsstab, "Die Zusammenlegung der Personalbetreuung," n.d. [ca. 10.1.43] (AN: 40 AJ/450).
36. MBH, Verwaltungsstab, "Zusammenlegung," n.d. [ca. 10.1.43] (AN: 40 AJ/450).
37. Racial criteria were not specifically expressed, perhaps because they were self-evident to contemporaries, or because the women initially sent abroad were

already employed in military offices in the Reich. OKH, "Bildung einer Stabshelferinnenschaft—Ausführungsbestimmungen zu III des Bezugserlasses [OKH 27.2.42], February. 28, 1942, 2 (AN: 40 AJ/456).

38. OKH, "Bildung" February 28, 1942, 2 (AN: 40 AJ/456).
39. OKH, "Bildung" February 27, 1942 (AN: 40 AJ/456).
40. "Ärmelstreifen für Stabshelferinnen des Heeres," from Allgemeinen Anordnungen des Militärbefehlshabers in Frankreich, Nr. 28, July 30, 1942 (AN: 40 AJ/456).
41. OKH, "Dienstordnung für Stabshelferinnen des Heeres," February 28, 1942, 2, 4–5 (AN: AJ 40/456); OKH, "Bildung einer Stabshelferinnenschaft, Ausführungsbestimmungen zu III des Bezugserlasses [OKH 27.2.42]," February 28, 1942, 3 (AN: 40 AJ/456).
42. OKH, "Dienstordnung," February 28, 1942, 1 (AN: AJ 40/456).
43. Ibid.
44. After work hours, supervisory power was delegated to a female leader (Stabshelferinnen-Führerin) who liaised with the local military authorities about all "feminine matters" ("fraulichen Angelegenheiten"). OKH, "Dienstordnung," February 28, 1942, 2–4 (AN: AJ 40/456); OKH, "Bildung einer Stabshelferinnenschaft für die Heeresdienststellen in den besetzten Gebieten," February 27, 1942 (AN: 40 AJ/456).
45. Audiat, *Paris*, 29.
46. In contrast to soldiers' well-documented fraternization with French women, and German women's relationships with French prisoners of war in Germany, auxiliaries do not often seem to have fraternized with French men. Maubach notes that she learned of "no case" of fraternization between an auxiliary and a local man. Maubach, *Stellung*, 119. Cf. Raffael Scheck, *Love between Enemies: Western Prisoners of War and German Women in World War II* (Cambridge, United Kingdom; New York: Cambridge University Press, 2021); Fabrice Virgili, *Naître ennemi: Les enfants de couples franco-allemands nés pendant la Seconde Guerre mondiale* (Paris: Payot, 2009).
47. "Richtlinien über Menschenführung in der Truppe," Oberstabsartzt Dr. Driest, 1944, 1 (BArch: Msg 2/177).
48. Seidel and Grosser, *Herzen*, 13. Before the war, too, women's supposed gentleness, patience and empathy had been thought to make them ideal switchboard operators. Gold, "Kontakt und Relais," 52.
49. The pairs were rendered in the original as, "Hilfsbereitschaft, Mitgefühl, Geduld" and "Härte, Entschlossenheit und Tatkraft." Oberstabsartzt Dr. Driest, "Richtlinien über Menschenführung in der Truppe," 1944, 1–2, 11 (BArch: Msg 2/177).
50. Driest, "Richtlinien," 1944, 4 (BArch: Msg 2/177).
51. Romances were discouraged unless they were serious and neither partner was already married, in which case the relationship was to be encouraged to ensure the future of the "race." Driest, "Richtlinien," 1944, 15 (BArch: Msg 2/177).
52. OKW, signed Keitel, Richtlinien für den Fraueneinsatz im Bereich der

Wehrmacht, insbesondere in den Gebieten ausserhalb der Reichsgrenze, June 22, 1942 (AN: 40 AJ/456).
53. OKW, signed Keitel, Richtlinien, June 22, 1942 (AN: 40 AJ/456).
54. Ibid.
55. Leitender Intendant beim MBH, Betreuung der Stabshelferinnen, hier: Einsetzung von Beauftragten der Reichsfrauenführerin, September 14, 1942 (AN: 40 AJ/456).
56. OKW, signed Keitel, Richtlinien, June 22, 1942 (AN: 40 AJ/456).
57. Ibid.
58. Ibid.
59. Willeke Sandler, "Colonial Education in the Third Reich: The Witzenhausen Colonial School and the Rendsburg Colonial School for Women," *Central European History* 49, no. 2 (June 2016): 202.
60. Zimmerer, "Ostland," 214.
61. Sandler, "Colonial," 202–3.
62. Harvey, *Women*, 11.
63. Sandler, "Colonial," 202.
64. Ibid., 191–92.
65. Ibid., 197.
66. Ibid., 192.
67. Zimmerer, "Ostland," 199.
68. Ibid., 214.
69. Ibid., 214.
70. Cf. Harvey, *Women*.
71. Anne McClintock, *Imperial Leather: Race, Gender, and Sexuality in the Colonial Contest* (New York: Routledge, 1995), 378; Harvey, *Women*, 7, Ch. 6.
72. Driest, "Richtlinien," 1944, 1–2, 11 (BArch: Msg 2/177)
73. See, for instance, Driest, "Richtlinien," 1944, 11 (BArch: Msg 2/177)
74. Pedersen, "Metaphors," 191.
75. Ibid., 191.
76. Ibid., 192.
77. Ibid., 192.
78. Julia S. Torrie, "The Many Aims of Assistance: The Nationalsozialistische Volkswohlfahrt and Aid to French Civilians in 1940," *War & Society* 26, no. 1 (May 2007): 27–38.
79. Raffael Scheck, *Hitler's African Victims: The German Army Massacres of Black French Soldiers in 1940* (Cambridge, UK: Cambridge University Press, 2006). On Germans' desire not to be seen as barbarians, see Julia S. Torrie, *German Soldiers and the Occupation of France, 1940–1944* (Cambridge, UK: Cambridge University Press, 2018), Ch. 1.

CHAPTER 4

The "Wild East" and the "Soft West"

Alcohol, Masculinity, and Geographies of Sexual Violence

EDWARD B. WESTERMANN

Under National Socialism, intoxication in both a literal and metaphorical sense became part of a "hypermasculine" ideal and part of "constellations of violence" in which manhood and male group solidarity were established and reaffirmed by the perpetrators in rituals of celebration, physical and sexual abuse, and mass murder.[1] While the German home front experienced euphoria in mass public spectacles and military victories, the term "*Ostrausch*" (intoxication of the East) emerged as a description of the "imperial high" that characterized the behavior and actions of those participating in the National Socialist conquest of Eastern Europe; a campaign in which "hedonism and genocide went hand in hand."[2] For the army of Nazi Party bureaucrats, the men of the SS (*Schutzstaffel*) and police, and for female auxiliaries who set about the task of conquering and "civilizing" the occupied territories, *Ostrausch* constituted both a feeling and a justification for German rule. These feelings of colonial entitlement reflected elements of a militarized and hypermasculine ethos among the conquerors who "became addicted to the intoxication of the East and became drunk with power (*machttrunken*)."[3] While the expression "drunk with power" served a symbolic purpose, the use of alcohol among the perpetrators was a very real and prevalent fact of life and constituted an important ritual in the preparation, implementation, and celebration of acts of mass killing in the East.

While the occupied East may have been the space in which the apotheosis of the intoxication of conquest occurred, a corresponding if undeclared "*Westrausch*" was involved in the subjugation of France,

Belgium, and the Netherlands. Friedrich Kellner, a German bureaucrat and critic of the Nazi regime in the small town of Laubach, recorded his thoughts in a diary entry on June 14, 1940, concerning the impending fall of France. He observed: "the National Socialists' intoxication with victory will be of an unrestrained nature ... [for] those who plan the premeditated murder of mankind."[4] As Kellner's words reveal, feelings of intoxication and acts of atrocity became inextricably intertwined under the Third Reich. For one German infantryman, the defeat of France was the opportunity for the communal sampling of the heady high of triumph and alcohol as recorded in his diary on June 17, 1940: "[W]e fall into the unprecedented feeling of victory. The wine flows in torrents, the accommodation better than ever before ... The delight of victory was simply too great."[5]

Creating Geographies of Violence

In much the same manner that ideals and standards of masculinity and femininity exist only in relation to one another, such was also the case for Nazi perceptions of the East and the West. Both were imagined areas, but they existed in a very real sense primarily in relation to one another, a point made explicit in the orders of Adolf Hitler and his senior generals concerning each. In preparing for the invasion of the Soviet Union, the Führer told his generals: "This war will be very different from the war in the West. In the East, harshness today means lenience in the future."[6] Three months after the invasion, in a directive of September 16, 1941, Hitler saw no paradox in describing the French as "decent people" and counseling good treatment of the population while at the same time demanding the complete obliteration of Leningrad as a center of "Asiatic poison."[7] In a similar manner, General Hermann Hoth, commander of the Seventeenth Army in Ukraine, issued an order to his own troops on November 17, 1941, in which he referred to "the conception that has been repeatedly expressed by the Führer [that] ... the Eastern Campaign must be led differently to its conclusion than, for example, the war against the French."[8] For their part, senior members of the Nazi SS also emphasized this distinction with one SS leader characterizing the Occupation of France and the Low Countries as "supervisory" while describing that of the occupied East as "colonial."[9]

Recent Holocaust scholarship has focused on the geographic and spatial elements of mass murder. Historian Timothy Snyder described Eastern Europe less as a "political geography" and more as a "human geography of victims." He argued, "The bloodlands were no political territory, real or imagined; they are simply where Europe's most murderous regimes did their most murderous work."[10] Another historian described the occupied territories under German control in the East as "zones of exception" in which "laws simply did not apply as they did at home [i.e., within Germany proper]." In this sense, the occupied East became a colonial space of "unbridled, unaccountable power ... where human beings could be abused in the extreme."[11] Within these areas, the local populations, and especially Jews, became "free game" subject to acts of humiliation, physical and sexual abuse, and murder in which the proscriptions of the center could often be ignored or manipulated by the perpetrators on the periphery.

In one respect, the East also was a gendered geography in which the "masculine battlefront" and the actions of hardened soldiers and SS and policemen distinguished it from the "feminine home front." In the former, acts of violence, atrocity, and mass killing could be justified as a preventative measure to protect one's women in the latter from the sexual danger posed by Russian "hordes."[12] In another respect, the "wild East" was a geography freed of traditional moral and ethical boundaries in which the occupiers and their auxiliaries could even transgress against rules and prohibitions enforced within Germany proper.

The excessive use of alcohol exemplified one of these expanded norms, and high alcohol consumption became an acceptable and, in some locations, a daily practice among the German occupiers.[13] Writing home from the East in August 1944, one soldier remarked, "The way it's whored and guzzled here is incredible."[14] SS and police daily orders in the East make numerous references to prohibitions on drinking during duty hours, including one order requiring that this prohibition be repeated to *all* policemen "*every week*."[15] These repeated prohibitions also can be found in the daily orders issued to SS personnel at Auschwitz; however, it is exactly the ubiquity of such prohibitions that exposes the widespread practice of alcohol consumption and its horrific consequences for the conquered peoples.[16]

The dynamic between sexual aggression and power was prevalent in the occupied East among the German occupiers. Under National Socialism, "sexual gratification" was equated "with masculine power to a degree unprecedented in Germany," historian Annette Timm contends. She also notes, "Masculine vitality was thus viewed as highly dependent on sexual gratification . . . [with] the purpose of achieving the racial state."[17] While Timm focuses on prostitution and the soldiers' use of brothels, the power dynamic she describes related to sexual domination reflects a generalizable mentality among members of the SS and police complex in the Third Reich, especially in the occupied territories. Upon their arrival in Nantes, soldiers "headed straight for the brothels, shooting down the doors," a performative act of masculine bravado in which one's use of a firearm served as an extension of the virility one would display inside the premises.[18] Likewise, SS men on duty in the East routinely employed sexual violence as a means for the "total exploitation of power and the demand for total subjugation [of the victims]" in which the act of rape was followed by the shooting of the victim.[19]

The prevalence of the practice proves as shocking as the number of men who avoided punishment for such acts. One SS judicial investigation of cases of rape and gang rape by SS men estimated that "at least 50 percent of all members of the SS and the police violated the 'ban on undesirable intercourse with ethnically alien women.'"[20] When SS authorities chose to prosecute cases of sexual assault in the East, judicial officers received instructions to consider the "lack of opportunity for sexual intercourse as well as excessive alcohol consumption" as extenuating factors in sentencing; a view that propagated the Nazi concept of masculinity and legitimized sexual violence "especially if it was committed against women from an 'inferior race.'"[21] In comparison, in cases of consensual or nonconsensual homosexual behavior among SS men, excessive alcohol consumption was raised as a mitigating factor, but Reich Leader of the SS and Chief of the German Police Heinrich Himmler and the SS and police courts did not view drunkenness as exonerating this behavior, and punishment could and did include the death sentence.[22] In this sense, the SS and police maintained a gendered distinction in which rape and acts of sexual violence against women were simply one aspect "of a continuum of violence that resulted from genocide" and a natural expression of the perpetrator's "power and dominance through the humiliation and degradation of the other."²³ In contrast, the power and possibility of sexual domination did not exist for German women in the East: these laws were enforced much more severely, and German women who violated them with Slavic men faced fines or jail time compared to German men who "normally g[o]t away scot-free" in their relations with Polish women.²⁴

To a certain degree, the distinction made by Hitler and senior Wehrmacht leaders between the nature of the war in the East versus the West was reflected in the actions and the attitudes of the troops. Historian Felix Römer asserts, "The war in the east possessed a special character even in the eyes of contemporaries ... the fighting in the east was against a different type of opponent, the fighting was conducted under different rules and with no holds barred, to the death."²⁵ However, if visions of the human geography of these areas differed, the masculine ethos of the conquerors effeminized the defeated adversary with clear implications for women in both the East and the West.

The "Soft West" versus the "Hard East"

In her study of Wehrmacht soldiers during the German Occupation of France, Julia S. Torrie exposes the gender-based stereotypes used by the military occupiers in depicting the "hard" East versus the "soft" West.²⁶ In this sense, the feminization and masculinization of geography itself offer a valuable lens for thinking about National Socialist perceptions of masculinity as well as the manner in which the coding of these spaces as feminine or masculine influenced the behaviors of the men in these areas. To be sure, the perspective of distinct female and male spaces, roles, and activities played an integral part in the construction of gender norms from the origins of the Nazi Party.²⁷ However, the outbreak of the war provided an extension of these concepts into the realm of geography, an area in great part represented by the putative racial characteristics of its inhabitants. Furthermore, it was the war that allowed for a reimagining of German space itself with the creation of the "manly battlefront" and the "womanly home front."²⁸

Importantly, the conquest of physical space involved military subjugation and became manifested in the attitudes and actions of German men as well as the methods they employed for ruling the occupied territories. For example, the Wehrmacht's military campaigns throughout Europe offered the ultimate arena for displaying "masculine virtues like will, determination, and action" as part of an "active and aggressive concept of masculinity."[29] Likewise, the glorification of martial virtues and violence as "the highest manifestation of manhood" emerged as defining characteristics of the National Socialist ideal of hypermasculinity, especially within the SS and the police complex.[30] For these men, *The Black Corps*, a newspaper for the SS and police, emphasized to its readers, "war was the father of all things . . . and from it come all manly virtues."[31]

The semantic linkage between procreation, power, war, and masculinity was critical in two respects. First, it promoted a concept of martial masculinity or an exaggerated belief in the necessity for merciless brutality against one's enemies.[32] By extension, it also encompassed a belief among the conquerors that the failure or inability of one's adversary to protect "his" women reflected a failure of their masculinity, but also entitled the winner to claim these women as the right of the victors. However, while the ideal standard of masculinity remained more or less fixed within the SS, the police, and the army, the acceptable means for dealing with conquered female populations demonstrates that geography clearly played a role in establishing limits and boundaries related to their treatment in sexual terms.

Without doubt, geography and space played an important role in the incidents of sexual violence during the Second World War.[33] In his study of Wehrmacht operations in the East, historian Waitman Beorn makes a key point: "At the local level, sexuality in the East seems to have operated under a moral code different from that observed in Western Europe." He continues, "German civil authorities (as well as military men) frequently abused alcohol to excess and participated in depraved sexual acts outside the pale of acceptability in the West."[34] In fact, senior SS, police, and Wehrmacht leaders were clearly aware of the crimes committed by German forces in the East. SS general Kurt Daluege, the chief of the Order Police, sent an order on December 13, 1939, to all Higher SS and Police Leaders (HSSPF) in Germany directing them to remind returning police units that they were "no longer in enemy territory" and were expected to observe the "laws of the homeland."³⁵ In October 1939, the commander in chief of the German army, General Walther von Brauchitsch, lamented the "lack of a firm inner bearing" among army officers after Poland's defeat, based partly on widespread reports of indiscipline, including "drunkenness, insubordination, and rape."³⁶ In fact, the demonstrated misbehavior of troops in Poland led military leaders to "tighten their control over the troops' conduct" during the May 1940 invasion of France "particularly as regards alcohol."³⁷

This existence of a double standard concerning acceptable behavior for troops in the East and the West was primarily a manifestation of Nazi racial ideology and reached into the highest ranks of the German army.³⁸ Such ideas also filtered down to the unit level where bonds of male camaraderie took precedence over official prohibitions on having sex with local women. As one former policeman admitted, "It is true that in the circle of one's comrades such incidents were not relayed [up the chain of command]."³⁹ In the East, physical conquest of territory, racial and gender-based concepts of superiority, and perceptions of male camaraderie combined with excessive alcohol consumption to create a mindset among the perpetrators in which the prohibition of acts of sexual aggression existed as "reality only on paper."⁴⁰

In contrast, the experience of German military Occupation in France indicates that heavy alcohol consumption combined with song and celebratory ritual threatened to, and often did, cross over into acts of violence between soldiers and local civilians. In her study of Wehrmacht sex crimes, Birgit Beck not only identified the consumption of alcohol as a prelude to acts of sexual aggression by soldiers, but also noted the differences in the way military authorities prosecuted such crimes in the occupied territories of Western and Northern Europe and those committed in the East.⁴¹ Drinking not only resulted in acts of sexual aggression, but also in acts of general aggression between males. In one example, a senior German officer ordered a Paris bar closed "when drunken members of the military administration sang Nazi songs ... and physical violence threatened to break out."⁴² The experience of this Parisian bar proved common in drinking establishments throughout the Loire region as "drunken brawls were widespread," a pattern attributed by one French policeman to "the mingling of males and females and above all because of the abuse of alcohol."[43] While intoxication and aggression, including incidents of sexual violence, occurred in France, military authorities "ruthlessly punished" public drunkenness and frequently executed soldiers for rape as the German occupiers "drew on gendered metaphors to style themselves not as dominators, but as chivalrous, "'fatherly protector[s]' of a feminised and infantilised French nation."[44]

One study of French women's reactions to the German invasion in 1940 found two dominant attitudes toward the German army. The first was that the "German army appeared more organized and disciplined than the French," and the second was that "the Germans seemed polite or, as the French say, 'correct.'"[5] A seventeen-year-old French Jewish girl, Jackie De Col, remembered the soldiers offering candy to children and remarked, "they obeyed orders. Plenty of them were not Nazis. There were plenty who were not zealots."[46] To be sure, German forces, especially SS and police units, stationed in France could and did participate in acts of reprisal and atrocity during anti-partisan and anti-resistance operations; however, the choice of means and methods revealed a "large difference between the East and Southeast Europe."[47] Similarly, the general treatment of French civilians in regard to policies of hostage taking and reprisal shootings never approached the extremes experienced in the East, a position expressed by Reinhard Heydrich, the chief of the Security Police and the Security Service, in a visit to Paris in May 1942, where he remarked, "In France, one must pursue a different policy as in the East."[48]

Nevertheless, De Col's perceptions, like the overall positivist narrative of German "correctness" by 1943, increasingly became "a joke in poor taste" as German policies tightened in the face of increasing resistance activities.[49] With respect to sexual violence, historian Fabrice Virgili detailed eighty-six cases of rape or attempted rape in Brittany during the Occupation and highlighted "the 'systematic' deployment of sexual violence as a method of torture" in dealing with the French Resistance after 1943.[50] The use of torture, sexual or otherwise, against women involved in the Resistance was itself an expression of a deeply seated, almost pathological German male paranoia of the so-called "*Flintenweiber*" or "Shotgun wenches" who transgressed gender norms by carrying a weapon and fighting against men. The willingness of soldiers, SS, and policemen to engage in the torture and mass killing of such women crossed spatial geography whether in the Soviet Union, Italy, or France.[51]

In truth, the nature of occupation obliterated the line between consent, instrumental sex, sexual coercion, and sexual assault throughout the *Militärbefehlshaber in Frankreich* (MBF) (the German Military Command in France).[52] In several respects, sexual coercion or acts of sexual violence in the West should not be surprising. First, violent behaviors aimed at both the male and female population in France were almost exclusively tied to the literal intoxication of the perpetrator, a situation in which drunkenness allowed for the free rein of aggression and expressed the victor's masculinity and power over the conquered.[53] The diaries and letters of German soldiers in France are replete with discussions of heavy drinking brought about by the confiscation and consumption of all types of intoxicants including cognac, Benedictine, Cointreau, champagne, and of course wine.[54] Second, the French army's swift and humiliating loss threatened "national virility" and transformed the defeated into "puny," "skinny," and weak old men.[55] In this view, French men "forfeited" their rights to French women through their inability to protect them, a point made by one German military official who exclaimed, "We are the victors! You have been beaten! The women, even the children of your country, are no longer yours!" He continued, "Our soldiers have the right to fun." In the case of the last, however, Robert Gildea asserts, "It was not that the conquerors assumed the right to rape the women of the defeated nation, but the power to seduce was one of the fruits of victory."[56] In contrast, the dictates of masculine hardness and toughness involving mass killing in fact could and did find expression when directed at Communists and Jews, a condition that bound together the spatial geographies of the East and the West.[57]

In contrast to Western Europe, where German soldiers assumed the role of "sexual and gastronomic tourists,"[58] a survey of Nazi Occupation policies in the East emphasized that "Violence against women and girls was part and parcel of the system of persecution established by the occupiers and their helpers."[59] In fact, one Security Police report in

May 1943 for the Polish district of Galicia emphasized that "it is not a minority [of Germans] who stand outside of the written as well as the unwritten laws" as exemplified by an "addiction to pleasure, plans for enrichment, and undignified conduct."[60] The report discussed an array of misbehavior including a district official who "almost only celebrated parties and went hunting" and another police official who "normally in a drunken state regularly had Jewesses in his apartment" and who had tried to force his Polish secretary to spend the night with him ostensibly to read "bible verses" to her.[61] The colonial attitudes of such men and their proclivity for dissolute behaviors not surprisingly promoted numerous acts of sexual coercion and sexual violence.

By December 1941, supplying the *Ostheer* (Eastern Army) with its "fascist feast" became increasingly difficult as evidenced by *wagonloads* of French red wine shipped to the front that had frozen, bursting the bottles and leaving only "chunks of red ice and glass splinters."[62] The shipment of massive quantities of French wines, cognac, schnapps, and even champagne to the East reflected in one sense the regime's attempt to keep the combat front supplied with luxury items such as alcohol and tobacco. The consumption of alcohol itself, however, became an important rite for creating the closed martial and masculine communities of the combat soldier.

As might be expected, acts of indiscipline, especially sexual assaults, were often associated with heavy consumption of alcohol, a trend that existed in both the occupied territories of the East and the West.[63] The Wehrmacht High Command (OKW) was clearly aware of the relationship between heavy drinking and violence among the troops. In a report from a conference of German military doctors in Berlin in 1942, alcohol abuse figured as one of four main reasons for "criminal acts" by soldiers. The report noted that "higher attraction to alcohol through the influence of comrades or increased alcohol availability, especially in the occupied territories, lead a considerable proportion of soldiers of high quality and good character to come into conflict with the law."[64] As this report infers, the consumption of alcohol played a significant role in causing or facilitating "criminal" acts in the occupied territories; an unsurprising revelation based on the historical connection between alcohol and armies and resulting acts of indiscipline, abuse, or atrocity. However, this does not explain the role of alcohol in cases in which atrocious behavior itself had been normalized, including the killing of Jews, Communists, Sinti and Roma, or Slavs. In fact, Nazi racial ideology, criminal orders issued to the Wehrmacht, and the imperial and colonial framework of occupation combined with alcohol consumption to facilitate atrocious behavior far beyond the boundaries of traditional warfare.

Subjugation and the Intoxication of Sexual Violence

While alcohol was neither a necessary nor sufficient cause of sexual violence, it was linked to the intoxication of male power over the victims and played an important role in individual and, more significantly, group acts of sexual assault. The reports of sexual violence involving alcohol consumption by soldiers, policemen, and SS are striking both for their scale and frequency. During the opening weeks of the campaign into Russia, "drunken" German soldiers carried away and raped all of the women between the ages of sixteen and thirty in the village of Beresowka in the district of Smolensk. In Lemberg, intoxicated SS men forced women into a city park where they were brutalized and raped. In this case, a local priest attempted to intervene, but was beaten, had his beard set on fire, and then stabbed to death. In a final example, German soldiers, after capturing seventy-five women near the Belarussian town of Borrisow, raped and murdered thirty-six.[65] In each of these cases, the conquest of territory was accompanied by the sexual subjugation of the women as an expression of racial domination, a practice largely absent from the German invasion and control of areas in the West such as France.[66]

Sexual violence by German troops also included mass rapes of Jewish girls and women in *shtetls* as in the case of Yedintsy in Moldava and Telshyay in Lithuania.[67] One historian estimated that fully one-third of all sexual assaults in the East involved gang rapes, the ultimate expression of male communal bonding.[68] In these cases, the "sexual gratification" of the perpetrators was "secondary to the celebration of fraternity bonding and group pride."[69] These abuses extended into the ghettos and labor camps under German control. Raisa Dudnik fled the Rakovka ghetto in Uman in the fall of 1941, but she could not forget how "[e]very night, drunken bandits [i.e., Germans] burst into our little homes. They raped girls. They beat up old women and took their last belongings."[70] Similarly, SS personnel at the Skarżysko labor camp routinely engaged in drunken orgies in which they victimized Jewish prisoners. During a roll call in October 1942, SS guards selected six recently arrived Jewish female prisoners who "were ordered to serve diners in the nude, and at the end of the meal were raped" before being executed the following day.[71]

The significance of the widespread nature of these transgressions and the fact that they began from the earliest days of the invasion cannot be overstated. Indeed, the accompaniment of the physical conquest of the East with acts of sexual humiliation and subjugation established a precedent and a regular practice that would last throughout the German Occupation. In comparison, acts of sexual violence certainly occurred in the occupied western territories under German military control, but they did not approach the scale and frequency of such behavior in the East.[72] In a secretly recorded conversation of a group of senior German prisoners of war, SS general Kurt Meyer mentioned that he had a German noncommissioned officer executed for raping a French girl in Caen. He stated that the soldier, who was drunk at the time of the assault, was shot the day following the attack with the village mayor and other city officials present as witnesses. During this discussion, Wehrmacht general Heinrich Eberbach remarked, "But I believe that the FÜHRER [sic] issued an order for the East that the raping of women and girls should not be [considered] . . . as a criminal offence, but only as a disciplinary [offense]—as terror was part of the rules of war." Eberbach then commented, "That order wasn't issued for the West, merely for the East."[73]

Eberbach's contention is interesting in several respects. First, although no specific Hitler order allowed German forces to sexually assault women in the East, the *Oberkommando der Wehrmacht* (Wehrmacht High Command) at Hitler's instruction had issued a decree in May 1941, before the invasion of the Soviet Union, that limited the jurisdiction of the courts over "enemy civilians" and established "no obligation to prosecute a member of the Wehrmacht for crimes committed against civilians, even if such crimes constituted offenses against military law."[74] In other words, individual commanders had the discretion to punish troops for criminal offenses committed against civilians, including sexual assaults and murder. Second, this decree along with a series of other "criminal orders" established an environment in which German forces "literally became judge, jury, and executioner."[75] Third, such decrees provide another manifestation of the way in which the geography of the East became a zone of exception in which acts of brutality and atrocity became normalized by statute and in practice. Finally, it demonstrates the way in which the Nazi concept of hypermasculinity, with its emphasis on conceptions of extreme militarized masculinity and a rigid racial hierarchy, exerted its most profound influence in a colonial space populated by "inferior" men and women.

Decline in the West?

After the Allied landings at Normandy in June 1944, France became the frontline for repelling the Allied onslaught. Under these circumstances, German soldiers in France increasingly reached for the bottle to deal with the stress of combat, including the infantryman Helmut Hörner, who started his day on July 2, 1944, in a bunker by filling his canteen with Calvados (brandy). Facing American lines, Hörner wrote in his diary, "I don't want anything to do with food. My friend the good French Calvados tastes much better and I still have two canisters in the bunker ... When the mail arrives I am no longer in any condition to read the letters from far-away Germany."[76] The following day, July 3, he again began his day by sharing his brandy while under attack and reflected, "I believe we will all become drunkards who will have to be treated in hospitals after the war."[77]

Ultimately, the soldiers, SS, and policemen, whether "living like gods in France" or doing "hard duty" in the "Wild East," entered both areas with a martial masculine mentality that explicitly justified the colonization of space and the bodies of the conquered. However, the intrinsic nature of Nazi ideology and its glorification of a hypermasculine ideal, combined with the differing racial perceptions of the French versus the Slavic populations, did influence the degree and the scale of physical and sexual abuse experienced by each area's female populations. In the East, physical conquest of territory, racial and gender-based concepts of superiority, and perceptions of male dominance combined with excessive alcohol consumption to create a mindset among the perpetrators in which sexual aggression was either ignored or even encouraged as the right of the victor. However, these areas did share one characteristic: the "failure" of French and Soviet men in their masculine duties. As a result, German men buoyed by metaphorical and literal intoxication laid claim to these female bodies at times by "seduction" or more often by force, a process characterized by an "active and aggressive concept of masculinity" that prized "hardness" above all and left little room for "softness" for the victims, especially when the strength and potency of Nazi rule began to fail.[78]

Bibliography

Archival Collections
United States Holocaust Memorial Museum Archive (USHMMA)
    LM0343   *Das Schwarze Korps*
    RG 18.002M   *Selected Records from the Latvian Central State Historical Archives, 1941–1945*
Records of the International Tracing Service (ITS)
    Subcollection 1.2.7.8: Persecution Action in the "General Government"/District of Galicia (part of former Poland), ITS Digital Archive. Accessed at the USHMM March–June 2019.
Central Office for the Investigation of National Socialist Crimes (ZStl)
    204 AR-Z 1251/65
National Archives and Records Administration (NARA)
    T 312   *Records of German Field Commands: Armies*

Books and Articles
Bartov, Omer. *Hitler's Army: Soldiers, Nazis, and War in the Third Reich*. Oxford: Oxford University Press, 1992.
Beck, Birgit. "The Military Trials of Sexual Crimes Committed by Soldiers in the Wehrmacht, by Karen Hagemann and Stefanie Schüler-Springorum, 255–73. Oxford: Berg, 2002.
———. *Wehrmacht und sexuelle Gewalt: Sexualverbrechen vor deutschen Militärgerichten, 1939–1945*. Paderborn: Ferdinand Schöningh, 2004.
Benz, Angelika. *Handlanger der SS: Die Rolle der Trawniki-Männer im Holocaust*. Berlin: Metropol, 2015.

Beorn, Waitman. *Marching into Darkness: The Wehrmacht and the Holocaust in Belarus*. Cambridge, MA: Harvard University Press, 2014.

Bloxham, Donald. *The Final Solution: A Genocide*. Oxford: Oxford University Press, 2009.

Burdick, Charles, and Hans-Adolf Jacobsen, eds. *The Halder War Diary, 1939–1942*. Novato, CA: Presidio, 1988.

Burds, Jeffrey. "Sexual Violence in Europe in World War II, 1939–1945." *Politics and Society* 37, no. 1 (2009): 35–73.

Burrin, Philippe. *France Under the Germans: Collaboration and Compromise*. Translated by Janet Lloyd. New York: The New Press, 1996.

Dombrowski, Nicole Ann. "Surviving the German Invasion of France: Women's Stories of the Exodus of 1940." In *Women and War in the Twentieth Century: Enlisted with or without Consent*, edited by Nicole Ann Dombrowski, 85–102. New York: Garland Publishing, 1999.

Frei, Norbert, Thomas Grotum, Jan Parcer, Sybille Steinacher, and Bernd Wagner, eds. *Standort-und Kommandanturbefehle des Konzentrationslagers Auschwitz, 1940–1945*. Munich: K.G. Saur, 2000.

Germany. Auswärtiges Amt. *Documents on German Foreign Policy, 1918–1945*, Series D, Vol. 13 (1937–1945) the War Years, June 23–December 11, 1941. London: Her Majesty's Stationery Office, 1964.

Gildea, Robert. *Marianne in Chains: Everyday Life in the French Heartland Under the German Occupation*. New York, Metropolitan Books, 2002.

Giles, Geoffrey. "The Denial of Homosexuality: Same-Sex Incidents in Himmler's SS and Police." *Journal of the History of Sexuality* 11, nos. 1–2 (2002): 256–90.

Grabowski, Jan, and Zbigniew R. Grabowski. "Germans in the Eyes of the Gestapo: The Ciechanów District, 1939–1945." *Contemporary European History* 13, no. 1 (2004): 21–43.

Halbmayr, Brigitte. "Sexualized Violence against Women during Nazi "Racial" Persecution." In *Sexual Violence against Women during the Holocaust*. Edited by Sonja Hedgepeth and Rochelle Saidel, 29–44. Waltham, MA: Brandeis University Press, 2010.

Herbert, Ulrich. *Best: Biographische Studien über Radikalismus, Weltanschauung und Vernunft*. Bonn: J. H. W. Dietz, 1996.

Hörner, Helmut. *A German Odyssey: The Journal of a German Prisoner of War*. Translated by Allan Kent Powell. Golden, CO: Fulcrum Publishing, 1991.

Kaiser, Wolf, Thomas Köhler, and Elke Gryglewski. *"Nicht durch formale Schranken gehemmt": Die deutsche Polizei im Nationalsozialismus*. Bonn: Bundeszentrale für politische Bildung, 2012.

Karay, Felicja. *Death Comes in Yellow: Skarżysko-Kamienna Slave Labor Camp*. Translated by Sara Kitai. Amsterdam: Harwood Academic Publishers, 1996.

Kellner, Friedrich. *My Opposition: The Diary of Friedrich Kellner-A German against the Third Reich*. Translated and edited by Robert Scott Kellner. Cambridge: Cambridge University Press, 2018.

Kladstrup, Don and Petie. *Wine and War: The French, the Nazis, and the Battle for France's Greatest Treasure*. New York: Broadway Books, 2001.

Koonz, Claudia. *Mothers in the Fatherland: Women, the Family, and Nazi Politics.* New York: St. Martin's Press, 1987.
Krondorfer, Björn, and Edward Westermann. "Soldiering: Men," In *Gender: War.* Edited by Andrea Petö, 19–35. New York: Macmillan, 2017.
Latzel, Klaus. *Deutsche Soldaten-nationalsozialistischer Krieg? Kriegserlebnis-Kriegserfahrung 1939–1945*, 2nd ed., Paderborn: F. Schöningh, 1998.
Lehnstaedt, Stephan. "The Minsk Experience: German Occupiers and Everyday Life in the Capital of Belarus." In *Nazi Policy on the Eastern Front, 1941: Total War, Genocide, and Radicalization.* Edited by Alex J. Kay, Jeff Rutherford, and David Stahel, 240–66. Rochester, NY: University of Rochester Press, 2012.
Lieb, Peter. *Konventioneller Krieg oder NS-Weltanschauungskrieg? Kriegführung und Partisanenbekämpfung in Frankreich 1943/44.* Munich: Oldenbourg Wissenschaftsverlag 2007.
Lower, Wendy. *Hitler's Furies: German Women in the Nazi Killing Fields.* Boston: Houghton, Mifflin, Harcourt, 2013.
Mailänder, Elissa. "Making Sense of a Rape Photograph: Sexual Violence as Social Performance on the Eastern Front, 1939–1944." *Journal of the History of Sexuality* 26, no. 3 (2017): 489–520.
Matthäus, Jürgen, Jochen Böhler, and Klaus-Michael Mallmann, *War, Pacification, and Mass Murder, 1939: The Einsatzgruppen in Poland.* Lanham, MD: Rowman and Littlefield, 2014.
Maubach, Franka. *Die Stellung halten: Kriegserfahrungen und Lebensgeschichten von Wehrmachtshelferinnen.* Göttingen: Vandenhoeck und Ruprecht, 2009.
Mazower, Mark. *Hitler's Empire: How the Nazis Ruled Europe.* New York: Penguin, 2008.
Megargee, Geoffrey, *War of Annihilation: Combat and Genocide on the Eastern Front, 1941.* Lanham, MD: Rowman and Littlefield, 2006.
Mühlhäuser, Regina. "Between 'Racial Awareness' and Fantasies of Potency: Nazi Sexual Politics in the Occupied Territories of the Soviet Union, 1942–1945." In *Brutality and Desire: War and Sexuality in Europe's Twentieth Century.* Edited by Dagmar Herzog, 197–220. New York: Palgrave Macmillan, 2009.
———. *Eroberungen: Sexuelle Gewalttaten und intime Beziehungen deutscher Soldaten in der Sowjetunion, 1941–1945.* Hamburg: Hamburger Edition, 2010.
———. "Sexual Violence and the Holocaust." In *Gender: War.* Edited by Andrea Petö, 101–16. New York: Macmillan, 2017.
Müller, Sven Oliver. *Deutsche Soldaten und ihre Feinde: Nationalismus an Front und Heimatfront im Zweiten Weltkrieg.* Frankfurt/Main: S. Fischer, 2007.
Neitzel, Sönke, ed. *Tapping Hitler's Generals: Transcripts of Secret Conversations, 1942–1945.* Translated by Geoffrey Brooks. London: Frontline Books, 2007.
Neumaier, Christopher. "The Escalation of German Reprisal Policy in Occupied France, 1941–1942." *Journal of Contemporary History* 41, no. 1 (2006): 113–31.
Pezzino, Paolo. "The German Military Occupation of Italy and the War against Civilians." *Modern Italy* 12, no. 2 (2007): 173–188.

Römer, Felix. *Comrades: The Wehrmacht from Within*. Translated by Alex J. Kay. Oxford: Oxford University Press, 2019.

Rubenstein, Joshua, and Ilya Altman. *The Unknown Black Book: The Holocaust in the German-Occupied Soviet Territories*. Translated by Christopher Morris and Joshua Rubenstein. Bloomington: Indiana University Press, 2008.

Sanday, Peggy. "Rape Free versus Rape Prone: How Culture Makes a Difference." In *Evolution, Gender, and Rape*. Edited by Cheryl Brown Travis, 337–62. Cambridge, MA: MIT Press, 2003.

Shepherd, Ben H. *Hitler's Soldiers: The German Army in the Third Reich*. New Haven, CT: Yale University Press, 2016.

Shirer, William L. *Berlin Diary: The Journal of a Foreign Correspondent, 1934–1941*. New York: Alfred A. Knopf, 1941.

Snyder, Timothy. *Bloodlands: Europe between Hitler and Stalin*. New York: Basic Books, 2010.

Stahel, David. *The Battle for Moscow*. Cambridge: Cambridge University Press, 2015.

Stargardt, Nicholas. *The German War: A Nation Under Arms, 1939–1945*. New York: Basic Books, 2015.

Steinkamp, Peter. "Zur Devianz-Problematik in der Wehrmacht: Alkohol- und Rauschmittelmissbrauch bei der Truppe." PhD. diss., Albert-Ludwigs-Universität, Freiburg im Breisgau, 2008.

Tewes, Ludger. *Frankreich in der Besatzungszeit 1940–1943: Die Sicht deutscher Augenzeugen*. Bonn: Bouvier Verlag, 1998.

Timm, Annette. "Sex with a Purpose: Prostitution, Venereal Disease, and Militarized Masculinity in the Third Reich." *Journal of the History of Sexuality* 11, nos. 1–2 (2002): 223–55.

Torrie, Julia S. *German Soldiers and the Occupation of France, 1940–1944*. Cambridge: Cambridge University Press, 2018.

Von Luck, Hans. *Panzer Commander: The Memoirs of Colonel Hans von Luck*. New York: Dell Publishing, 1991.

Westermann, Edward B. *Hitler's Police Battalions: Enforcing Racial Policy in the East*. Lawrence: University Press of Kansas, 2005.

———."Stone-Cold Killers or Drunk with Murder? Alcohol and Atrocity in the Holocaust." *Holocaust and Genocide Studies* 30, no. 1 (2016): 1–19.

Werner, Frank. "'Hart müssen wir hier draussen sein': Soldatische Männlichkeit im Vernichtungskrieg, 1941–1944." *Geschichte und Gesellschaft* 34, no. 1 (2008): 5–40.

Wieland, Christina. *The Fascist State of Mind and the Manufacturing of Masculinity: A Psychoanalytic Approach*. London: Routledge, 2015.

Notes

1. Elissa Mailänder, "Making Sense of a Rape Photograph: Sexual Violence as Social Performance on the Eastern Front, 1939–1944," *Journal of the History of Sexuality* 26, no. 3 (2017): 500–01, 503.

2. Wendy Lower, *Hitler's Furies: German Women in the Nazi Killing Fields* (Boston: Houghton, Mifflin, Harcourt, 2013), 165.
3. Franka Maubach, *Die Stellung halten: Kriegserfahrungen und Lebensgeschichten von Wehrmachtshelferinnen* (Göttingen: Vandenhoek und Ruprecht, 2009), 130.
4. Friedrich Kellner, *My Opposition: The Diary of Friedrich Kellner—A German Against the Third Reich*, trans. and ed. Robert Scott Kellner (Cambridge: Cambridge University Press, 2018), 33, 76.
5. Ben Shepherd, *Hitler's Soldiers: The German Army in the Third Reich* (New Haven, CN: Yale University Press, 2016), 85–86.
6. Charles Burdick and Hans-Adolf Jacobsen, eds., *The Halder War Diary, 1939–1942* (Novato, CA: Presidio Press, 1988), 346.
7. Auswärtiges Amt, *Documents on German Foreign Policy, 1918–1945*, Series D, Vol. 13 (London: Her Majesty's Stationery Office, 1964), 518–20.
8. "Verhalten der deutschen Soldaten im Ostraum," November 11, 1941, T312, reel 771, Frame 516, NARA. Interestingly, both of these orders were issued at the same time that Hitler and the SS sharply criticized the military government in France and its commander, General Otto von Stülpnagel, for their perceived lenience responding to a series of attacks against Wehrmacht personnel.
9. Mark Mazower, *Hitler's Empire: How the Nazis Ruled Europe* (New York: Penguin Press, 2008), 236–37.
10. Timothy Snyder, *Bloodlands: Europe between Hitler and Stalin* (New York: Basic Books, 2010), xviii.
11. Donald Bloxham, *The Final Solution: A Genocide* (Oxford: Oxford University Press, 2009), 282.
12. Frank Werner, "'Hart müssen wir hier draussen sein': Soldatische Männlichkeit im Vernichtungskrieg, 1941–1944," *Geschichte und Gesellschaft* 34, no. 1 (2008): 16, 20.
13. Stephan Lehnstaedt, "The Minsk Experience: German Occupiers and Everyday Life in the Capital of Belarus," in *Nazi Policy on the Eastern Front, 1941: Total War, Genocide, and Radicalization*, eds. Alex J. Kay, Jeff Rutherford, and David Stahel (Rochester, NY: University of Rochester Press, 2012), 255.
14. Sven Oliver Müller, *Deutsche Soldaten und ihre Feinde: Nationalismus an Front und Heimatfront im Zweiten Weltkrieg* (Frankfurt/Main: S. Fischer, 2007), 154.
15. "Der SS- und Polizeiführer Lettland, Kommandeur der Ordnungspolizei, Tagesbefehl 1 [January 21, 1943]," RG 18.002M, reel 9, fond R-82, opis 1, folder 21, USHMMA and "Der SS- und Polizeistandortführer Libau, Standortbefehl [February 4, 1943]," RG 18.002M, reel 30, fond R-83, opis 1, folder 6, USHMMA. Emphasis added.
16. Norbert Frei, Thomas Grotum, Jan Parcer, Sybille Steinacher, and Bernd Wagner, eds., *Standort- und Kommandanturbefehle des Konzentrationslagers Auschwitz, 1940–1945* (Munich: K.G. Saur, 2000), 18, 198, 399–400 and Daily Order Number 4E, item 7 "Drunken Offenses," March 24, 1943, RG 18.002M, reel 9, fond R82, Opis 1, folder 2, USHMMA.

17. Annette Timm, "Sex with a Purpose: Prostitution, Venereal Disease, and Militarized Masculinity in the Third Reich," *Journal of the History of Sexuality* 11, nos. 1–2 (2002): 227.
18. Nicholas Stargardt, *The German War: A Nation Under Arms, 1939–1945* (New York: Basic Books, 2015), 127.
19. Angelika Benz, *Handlanger der SS: Die Rolle der Trawniki-Männer im Holocaust* (Berlin: Metropol, 2015), 213, and Edward B. Westermann, "Stone-Cold Killers or Drunk with Murder? Alcohol and Atrocity in the Holocaust," *Holocaust and Genocide Studies* 30, no. 1 (2016): 11–13.
20. Regina Mühlhäuser, "Between 'Racial Awareness' and Fantasies of Potency: Nazi Sexual Politics in the Occupied Territories of the Soviet Union, 1942–1945," in *Brutality and Desire: War and Sexuality in Europe's Twentieth Century*, ed. Dagmar Herzog (New York: Palgrave Macmillan, 2009), 203.
21. Birgit Beck, "The Military Trials of Sexual Crimes Committed by Soldiers in the Wehrmacht, 1939–1944," in *Home/Front: The Military, War and Gender in Twentieth-Century Germany*, eds. Karen Hagemann and Stefanie Schüler-Springorum (Oxford: Berg, 2002), 266.
22. Geoffrey Giles, "The Denial of Homosexuality: Same-Sex Incidents in Himmler's SS and Police," *Journal of the History of Sexuality* 11, nos. 1–2 (2002): 271, 279, 286.
23. Brigitte Halbmayr, "Sexualized Violence against Women during Nazi "Racial" Persecution," in *Sexual Violence against Women during the Holocaust*, ed. Sonja Hedgepeth and Rochelle Saidel (Waltham, MA: Brandeis University Press, 2010), 30–31.
24. Jan Grabowski and Zbigniew R. Grabowski, "Germans in the Eyes of the Gestapo: The Ciechanów District, 1939–1945," *Contemporary European History* 13:1 (2004): 32. In comparison, Polish men faced execution for involvement with German women while Polish women were arrested and reassigned to a new work place.
25. Felix Römer, *Comrades: The Wehrmacht from Within*, trans., Alex J. Kay (Oxford: Oxford University Press, 2019), 318.
26. Julia S. Torrie, *German Soldiers and the Occupation of France, 1940–1944* (Cambridge: Cambridge University Press, 2018), 6–8, 250–51.
27. Claudia Koonz, *Mothers in the Fatherland: Women, the Family, and Nazi Politics* (New York: St. Martin's Press, 1987), 6, 54–56.
28. Werner, "'Hart müssen wir hier draußen sein,'" 12, 20
29. Werner, "'Hart müssen wir hier draußen sein,'" 12, 20
30. William L. Shirer, *Berlin Diary: The Journal of a Foreign Correspondent, 1934–1941* (New York: Alfred A. Knopf, 1941), 270. Shirer attributes this belief to a quote by Robert Ley, a senior Nazi Party figure. See also Christina Wieland, *The Fascist State of Mind and the Manufacturing of Masculinity: A Psychoanalytic Approach* (London: Routledge, 2015), 26.
31. *Das Schwarze Korps*, June 26, 1941, LM0343, reel 7, USHMMA.
32. For a discussion of militarized masculinity see Björn Krondorfer and Edward B.

Westermann, "Soldiering: Men," in *Gender: War*, ed. Andrea Pető (New York: Macmillan, 2017), 19–35.

33. Regina Mühlhäuser, "Sexual Violence and the Holocaust," in *Gender: War*, ed. Andrea Pető (New York: Macmillan, 2017), 109.
34. Waitman Beorn, *Marching into Darkness: The Wehrmacht and the Holocaust in Belarus* (Cambridge, MA: Harvard University Press, 2014), 172.
35. Wolf Kaiser, Thomas Köhler, and Elke Gryglewski, *"Nicht durch formale Schranken gehemmt": Die deutsche Polizei im Nationalsozialismus* (Bonn: Bundeszentrale für politische Bildung, 2012), 231. This work provides a facsimile of this order.
36. Omer Bartov, *Hitler's Army: Soldiers, Nazis, and War in the Third Reich* (Oxford: Oxford University Press, 1991), 62.
37. Bartov, *Hitler's Army*, 67.
38. Sönke Neitzel, ed., *Tapping Hitler's Generals: Transcripts of Secret Conversations, 1942–1945*, trans. Geoffrey Brooks (London: Frontline Books, 2007), 199.
39. Interrogation protocol of Richard T. on May 24, 1965, 204 AR-Z 1251/65 Band II (René Rosenbauer), 407, ZStL.
40. Jeffrey Burds, "Sexual Violence in Europe in World War II, 1939–1945," *Politics and Society* 37, no. 1 (2009): 38.
41. Beck, *Wehrmacht und sexuelle Gewalt*, 168–69, 182, 327.
42. Hans von Luck, *Panzer Commander: The Memoirs of Colonel Hans von Luck* (New York: Dell Publishing, 1989), 59.
43. Quoted in Shepherd, *Hitler's Soldiers*, 98.
44. Torrie, *German Soldiers*, 50 and Ludger Tewes, *Frankreich in der Besatzungszeit 1940–1943: Die Sicht deutscher Augenzeugen* (Bonn: Bouvier Verlag, 1998), 204, 207–08.
45. Nicole Ann Dombrowski, "Surviving the German Invasion of France: Women's Stories of the Exodus of 1940," in *Women and War in the Twentieth Century: Enlisted with or without Consent*, ed. Nicole Ann Dombrowski (New York: Garland Publishing, 1999), 122; and Philippe Burrin, *France under the Germans: Collaboration and Compromise* (New York: The New Press, 1996), 194–95.
46. Quoted in Dombrowski, "Surviving the German Invasion," 130–31.
47. Peter Lieb, *Konventioneller Krieg oder NS-Weltanschauungskrieg? Kriegführung und Partisanenbekämpfung in Frankreich 1943/44* (Munich: Oldenbourg Wissenschaftsverlag 2007), 506–07. For example, SS and police units committed nine of the ten largest massacres in the anti-partisan campaign in France. Likewise, units who had previous experience in the campaign in the East also tended to be harsher in their treatment of the French population than units who had not seen duty in the East.
48. Ulrich Herbert, *Best: Biographische Studien über Radikalismus, Weltanschauung und Vernunft* (Bonn: J. H. W. Dietz, 1996), 320.
49. Don and Petie Kladstrup, *Wine and War: The French, the Nazis, and the Battle for France's Greatest Treasure* (New York: Broadway Books, 2001), 145.

50. Torrie, *German Soldiers*, 85. For another challenge to the idea of greater German restraint in France versus the East, see Christopher Neumaier, "The Escalation of German Reprisal Policy in Occupied France, 1941–1942," *Journal of Contemporary History* 41, no. 1 (2006): 113–31.
51. Shepherd, *Hitler's Soldiers*, 145, 414 and Paolo Pezzino, "The German Military Occupation of Italy and the War against Civilians," *Modern Italy* 12, no. 2 (2007): 175–79.
52. Tewes, *Frankreich*, 175–88, 205, 209, Torrie, *German Soldiers*, 83–90, and Burrin, *France Under the Germans*, 193–95, 205–07.
53. Tewes, *Frankreich*, 205.
54. Klaus Latzel, *Deutsche Soldaten-nationalsozialistischer Krieg? Kriegserlebnis-Kriegserfahrung 1939–1945*, 2d ed. (Paderborn, Germany: F. Schöningh, 1998), 136–39 and Robert Gildea, *Marianne in Chains: Everyday Life in the French Heartland Under the German Occupation* (New York, Metropolitan Books, 2002), 47.
55. Burrin, *France under the Germans*, 204.
56. Gildea, *Marianne in Chains*, 54, 50.
57. Neumaier, "German Reprisal Policy," 130.
58. Gildea, *Marianne in Chains*, 48.
59. Jürgen Matthäus, Jochen Böhler, and Klaus-Michael Mallmann, *War, Pacification, and Mass Murder, 1939: The Einsatzgruppen in Poland* (Lanham, MD: Rowman and Littlefield, 2014), 77.
60. Report of the Commander of the Security Police and SD for the District of Galicia, May 14, 1943, 1.2.7.8/82187881/ITS Digital Archive. Accessed at USHMMA on March 14, 2019.
61. Report of the Commander of the Security Police and SD for the District of Galicia, May 14, 1943, 1.2.7.8/82187891-92/ITS Digital Archive. Accessed at USHMMA on March 14, 2019.
62. David Stahel, *The Battle for Moscow* (Cambridge: Cambridge University Press, 2015), 255.
63. Beck, *Wehrmacht und sexuelle Gewalt*, 217–18.
64. Quoted in Peter Steinkamp, "Zur Devianz-Problematik in der Wehrmacht: Alkohol- und Rauschmittelmissbrauch bei der Truppe" (PhD diss., Albert-Ludwigs-Universität, Freiburg im Breisgau, 2008), 376–77. The other three factors contributing to criminal offenses included physical overexertion or exhaustion, infectious disease, and psychological pressures related to combat or professional and personal difficulties.
65. Regina Mühlhäuser, *Eroberungen: Sexuelle Gewalttaten und intime Beziehungen deutscher Soldaten in der Sowjetunion, 1941–1945* (Hamburg: Hamburger Edition, 2010), 74–75.
66. Tewes, *Frankreich*, 207–208. In France, for example, soldiers found guilty of rape were shot as a deterrent to their fellow soldiers.

67. Joshua Rubenstein and Ilya Altman, *The Unknown Black Book: The Holocaust in the German Occupied Soviet Territories*, trans. Christopher Morris and Joshua Rubenstein (Bloomington: Indiana University Press, 2008), 157–58, 301–02.
68. Shepherd, *Hitler's Soldiers*, 285.
69. Peggy Sanday, "Rape Free versus Rape Prone: How Culture Makes a Difference, in *Evolution, Gender, and Rape*, ed. Cheryl Brown Travis (Cambridge, MA: MIT Press, 2003), 343.
70. Rubenstein and Altman, *Unknown Black Book*, 198.
71. Felicja Karay, *Death Comes in Yellow: Skarżysko-Kamienna Slave Labor Camp*, trans. Sara Kitai (Amsterdam: Harwood Academic Publishers, 1996), 79.
72. Beorn, *Marching into Darkness*, 173.
73. Neitzel, *Tapping Hitler's Generals*, 198–99.
74. Geoffrey Megargee, *War of Annihilation: Combat and Genocide on the Eastern Front, 1941* (Lanham, MD: Rowman and Littlefield, 2006), 37.
75. Edward B. Westermann, *Hitler's Police Battalions: Enforcing Racial War in the East* (Lawrence: University Press of Kansas, 2005), 166–67.
76. Helmut Hörner, *A German Odyssey: The Journal of a German Prisoner of War*, trans. Allen Kent Powell (Golden, CO: Fulcrum Publishing, 1991), 18, 20.
77. Hörner, *German Odyssey*, 22.
78. Werner, "'Hart müssen wir hier draußen sein,'" 12, 20.

CHAPTER 5

Otto Doberschütz:
A Nazi Officer's Unlikely Relationship with a Basque Double Agent

SANDRA OTT

In a monograph about Franco-German-Basque relations and the trials of suspected collaborators in the French Basque Country and Béarn, I partially reconstructed the experiences of a Basque double agent, Jean Laborde, and a Nazi officer, Otto Doberschütz, in Pau.[1] Laborde worked both as a key agent for a French intelligence network, Alliance, and as an informer for the SS Security Service (the SD, or *Sicherheitsdienst*). Laborde forged an unusual relationship with Doberschütz at a fairly elite level. The Nazi officer headed the SD office in Pau from January 1943 until May 1944.[2] Until now, in various publications about the Doberschütz-Laborde relationship, I have limited my analysis to the Basque and Béarnais side of things with a focus primarily on Laborde and less attention paid to Doberschütz.[3] I also previously underscored the importance of Basque and Béarnais values and social practices, notably in relation to commensality, gift giving, and hospitality as cultural foundations for Franco-German sociability. This chapter explores Franco-German male sociability and bonding by delving more deeply into the "German side" of the Doberschütz-Laborde relationship. I now shift my focus to Nazi German culture and the ways it influenced Doberschütz as he became acquainted and then closely involved with Laborde. I also probe more deeply into the experiences of Doberschütz in Germany during the 1930s and in France during the Occupation.[4] In his fascinating micro-study of an "ordinary" SS officer, Daniel Lee points out that the lives of such low-ranking Nazis are usually "doubly invisible: overlooked by historians, but also forgotten or deliberately suppressed in the memories of living relatives." Understanding the experiences of such men, he argues, "is important for what it communicates about consent and conformity under the swastika."[5] This chapter aims to contribute to our knowledge of "ordinary Nazis" through Doberschütz's experiences.

I also rethink the deeply complicated Doberschütz-Laborde relationship through a gendered lens by injecting the category of comradeship into my analysis to probe further Franco-German male sociability and bonding. Two historians of Nazi Germany—Thomas Kühne and Edward Westermann—offer some insight into "the German side" of the Doberschütz-Laborde relationship. Kühne's recent analysis of the myth and practice of German comradeship, of military masculinity, and male bonding provides a lens through which to explore aspects of Doberschütz's own cultural baggage as a committed Nazi.[6] While some influential historians of Nazi Germany have argued that military masculinity was defined by the repudiation of femininity—such as domesticity, tenderness, and compassion—Kühne argues that "heroic, 'hard' manifestations of manhood" (articulated through aggression, brutality, and control over others) existed alongside German soldiers' routine social interactions that allowed for femininely coded affection: tenderness, empathy, caring, tolerance toward emotional breakdowns, and moments of weakness. Kühne argues that soldiers' comradeship "showed how femininity and masculinity, tenderness and toughness, could be on good terms within one person, one *man*." Manliness entailed the ability to enliven the social dynamic and cohesion of an exclusively male society. This could be accomplished "by heroism on the battlefield, rescuing wounded comrades, or organizing sentimental Christmas parties afterwards."[7] Kühne distinguishes comradeship from friendship, which "caters to the individual self (and is) rooted in the mutual sympathy of individuals and may be abandoned at any time." By contrast, comradeship denotes "the relationship forged by people who work and live together, not by choice but by coercion, by accident and by fate."[8]

I also draw upon Westermann's analysis of Nazi drinking rituals and the National Socialist ideal of hypermasculinity, especially in the SS and the police, to illuminate the nature of the bond forged by Doberschütz and the Basque double agent. During the Third Reich, "alcohol served as both a literal and metaphorical lubricant for acts of violence and atrocity by the men of the SA, SS, and the police." Westermann "explores connections among the perpetrators' consumption of alcohol, their acts of violence, and the use of celebratory ritual as expressions of camaraderie and manifestations of masculinity."[9] Men in the SA, SS, and German police created "exclusive male communities" where men could "demonstrate their masculinity through their knowledge of weapons or their prowess in drinking." "Fellowship evenings" promoted male bonding through alcohol consumption, "male bravado, and song." The ability to drink large amounts of alcohol and to 'hold one's liquor' served as a marker of superior masculinity.[10] As an SD officer, Doberschütz participated in this Nazi subculture before and during his posting to France.

In 2018, Julia S. Torrie provided a much-needed, bottom-up exploration of ordinary German soldiers' daily activities in occupied France in her monograph, *German Soldiers and the Occupation of France, 1940–1944*.[11] Drawing upon letters, photographs, tour guides, and official documents, she revealed that the German authorities encouraged soldiers to sightsee, to photograph, and to "consume" France. Such leisure activities increased Germans' familiarity with the French population, culture, and countryside; they also sustained support for Hitler. Torrie also showed, however, that differences deepened between long-term occupiers who "lived like God in France" and new arrivals from the Eastern Front who embodied the German "fighting spirit" (*Kampfgeist*). The myth "that there was pervasive softness in the West spurred on violence among German soldiers arriving in France from other fronts," especially those in the Waffen-SS and other elite fighting units.[12] As Torrie concluded, "living like gods in France was acceptable only if soldiers did not forget that they were first and foremost Hitler's men."[13]

War and Occupation from a Nazi German Perspective

Unlike most German soldiers in occupied France, Otto Doberschütz was not a short-term German soldier-tourist or an acquisitive shopper-occupier sent to France mainly to recuperate and to enjoy its pleasures.

He had a clear military mission there as a low-ranking Nazi officer who had experienced both the violence and cruelty of the Eastern Front and the subsequent brutal repression of Jews, Communists, and resisters in occupied France. Doberschütz knew the "softness" of the West, as well as the "wild, hard East."

Blond and athletic, Doberschütz was born in Leipzig in 1913, and he graduated from a higher vocational college (*die höhere Handelsschule*) there. On November 1, 1933, he joined the SS (membership number 210,343).[14] From July 1935, Doberschütz worked in the Leipzig regional office of the SD, primarily responsible for analyzing literature, especially in relation to issues of race.[15] The Leipzig Press and Literature Office for which he worked had just been created by the ambitious Nazi intellectual, Franz Six, who extensively rebuilt and expanded the SD's press service into a "well-conceived educational program that reached down through the entire organizational structure."[16]

In 1936, Doberschütz became "a professional in the Special Services of the Third Reich" as a salaried "press principal" (*Referat*) in the central department of the SD Press and Literature Office (SD Main Office, Central Department I-3) in Berlin, still under the direction of Six.[17] Six trusted Berlin-based principals such as Doberschütz to be "intellectually and educationally" suited for a sophisticated evaluation of the press. The central office focused on the most important publications that came to its attention through understaffed regional offices always seeking to expand their networks of unsalaried agents (V-persons).[18] Six boasted that his central department was "the most reliable intelligence source in the entire SD."[19]

In 1936, SS general Heinrich Himmler became chief of all German police and created the Security Police (the Sipo or *Sicherheitspolizei*). He appointed SS general Reinhard Heydrich to head both the Sipo and the SD (*Sicherheitsdienst*).[20] In February 1936, Doberschütz was transferred to an action group of the Sipo in Amt VII in Berlin, which focused on ideological research.[21] On April 1, 1937, he joined the Nazi Party (NSDAP, membership number 4,583, 110).

In early 1938, Doberschütz participated in the German occupation of Austria, in which Heydrich was a driving force in securing police control of the annexed territory, eliminating the opposition,

FIGURE 8. Otto Doberschütz and his wife, Lisa, with their two children in an unknown location, probably taken in 1943–1944. Courtesy of P. J. Snodgrass and Larry Halford.

and orchestrating the terror campaign against Austrian Jews.[22] That same year, twenty-five-year-old Doberschütz filled out an application about his proposed wife, eighteen year-old Lisa Meckelburg, for the consideration of the SS Race and Settlement Main Office (*SS Rasse- und-Siedlungshauptamt*), an SS requirement for marriage.[23] (Himmler wanted to ensure that SS and SD men chose racially pure brides who were able to bear at least four children.[24]) Doberschütz described his fiancée as a "thrifty and industrious" young woman who "dresses simply and tastefully." Meckelburg belonged to the League of German Girls (BdM or *Bund deutscher Mädel*), the female wing of the Hitler Youth in which, from 1936, membership was compulsory.[25] Meckelburg served as an air raid warden and, like Doberschütz, had left the organized church. She worked as a secretary in the SD Main Office, where they likely met. Most secretaries in that notorious office belonged to the Nazi Party and tended to be "serious, self-assured women" attracted by the better pay and not intimidated by the work of the SD.[26] Lisa

Meckelburg and Otto Doberschütz married on November 11, 1938, and lived in the Tempelhof district of Berlin.²⁷

When the war began on September 3, 1939, Heydrich issued state security plans in anticipation of the military onslaught against Poland. On September 27, 1939, he created the Reich Security Main Office (RSHA) by merging the Sipo and the SD.²⁸ Sipo-SD records show that Doberschütz participated in the invasion of Poland (September 9–October 6, 1939). In the district of Warsaw, he had a major posting to work in the office of the Commander of the Security Police and SD, an assignment that indicates Doberschütz was on a fast track in the SD and closely involved in the Nazis' racial and occupation policy in Poland. He remained there until February 1940. An SD officer in Warsaw gave Doberschütz a glowing evaluation, describing him as "clearly Nordic . . . neat and tidy" in appearance, "quiet," "an irreproachable SS-Man."²⁹

In early spring 1940, Doberschütz returned to the RSHA in Berlin.³⁰ He was promoted to the rank of second lieutenant on April 20, 1940.³¹ In terms of his age, educational background, and professional experience in the SD, Doberschütz embodied what German historian Michael Wildt has described as the "generation of the unbound" (*Generation der Unbedingten*), a generational cohort born after 1900, too young to have fought in World War I, but old enough to have been influenced by that heroic, devastating war, and the military values, toughness and ruthlessness of the soldiers who served in it. Doberschütz's "generation of the unbound" came to dominate the RSHA.³²

On March 1, 1940, Lisa Doberschütz gave birth to their first child, a daughter.³³ Soon thereafter, the SD sent her husband to France, though the duration of his stay there seems to have been brief as his duties continued in the RSHA in Berlin. That major posting in the RSHA and his promising career faced a setback, however, when the SD launched an investigation into an alleged theft by Doberschütz that began on June 13, 1941. His personnel file does not indicate the specific charges against him.³⁴

In March 1942, Doberschütz returned to France for a lengthy deployment. His first assignment took him to a hotbed of Nazi and French collaborationist efforts to rid southwestern France of Communists and

FIGURE 9. Otto Doberschütz and his wife, Lisa, with their two children, apparently taken at the same time as figure 8. Courtesy of P. J. Snodgrass and Larry Halford.

Jews, from Bayonne in the Basque Country to Bordeaux in the Gironde. Doberschütz led the anti-Jewish Kommando of the Sipo-SD (KdS, *Kommandeur der Sipo und des SD*) in Bordeaux. The first commander of the Bordeaux KdS was Hans Luther, a "blond, blue-eyed giant, ardent Nazi," and meticulous administrator.[35] In 1942–1943, Luther reported to Helmut Knochen as head of the Security Police and SS Security Service (the BdS, *Befehlshaber der Sicherheitsdienst und des SD*) in Paris. Luther oversaw KdS outposts in Langon, Dax, and the Basque coastal towns of Bayonne and Hendaye.[36] Doberschütz also worked closely with Friedrich Wilhelm Dohse, head of the KdS intelligence service in Bordeaux. A manipulative SS officer, Dohse rapidly recruited a substantial network of agents and informers, aided by his very efficient Swiss deputy, Marcelle Sommer, known as "the Lioness of the Bordeaux Gestapo."[37] Dohse was closely linked to the pro-Nazi police commissioner in Bordeaux, Pierre Poinsot.[38] As we will see, Dohse and Poinsot—an ardent Nazi and an avid French collaborationist—played key roles in introducing Otto Doberschütz to the Basque double agent,

Jean Laborde. Doberschütz's other close connections in Bordeaux included Maurice Papon, the recently appointed secretary general of the Prefecture, and Pierre Garat, appointed by Papon to serve as the head of Vichy's delegation for Jewish Affairs in Bordeaux. Garat was a "privileged interlocutor" of Doberschütz.[39]

In May 1942, Doberschütz sent a cable to the BdS in Paris. Highly rule-oriented, he reported that "around mid-March, [an SS officer named] Ferdinand Hugo aus der Fünten, head of the SD in Amsterdam, travelled to Biarritz to prepare for the passage of several groups of Jews [to Spain], among whom he planned to slip in some of his own agents. At the end of March, one of Fünten's agents, Hochheimer, also showed up in Biarritz, without any mandate whatsoever." In closing, Doberschütz cited Heydrich's general directive to all SD agents operating in France that they must first obtain the permission of the BdS in Paris.[40] Apparently not content with his first cable, Doberschütz sent a second one, with a sharper edge, to "protest that SS Untersturmführer (second lieutenant) aus der Fünten was allowed to be in the southwest of France without informing the BdS in Paris." Doberschütz once again cited Heydrich's directive that "no SD agent should operate in France without the permission of the BdS."[41] The focus of Doberschütz's complaints was the head of the Central Office for Jewish Emigration in Amsterdam from May 1940. Captain Ferdinand aus der Fünten orchestrated the deportation of Dutch Jews to Nazi concentration camps in Poland. Before that appointment, he worked in Office II of the SD Main Office in Berlin under Adolf Eichmann in the section devoted to "Jewry."[42] It is not known whether Doberschütz and Fünten ever met, but Doberschütz clearly knew who he was and resented his meddling in the Bordeaux-KdS domain without permission.

On June 30, 1942, together with other regional KdS leaders, Doberschütz met with Eichmann and Eichmann's representative in Paris, the fanatical anti-Semite, Theodor Dannecker, who played an instrumental role in energizing French anti-Jewish policy.[43] The aim of the Paris meeting was to establish a strategy for the removal of Jews from the occupied zone. On July 2, 1942, following orders by Dannecker, Doberschütz instructed the Vichy head of Jewish Affairs in Bordeaux, Pierre Garat, to arrest two thousand Jewish men and women, between the ages of sixteen and forty-five, by French police in a roundup scheduled to take place July 6–8. The Jews were to be transported to the camp at Mérignac and on "to an unknown destination" with "each French administrator responsible for evacuating every Jew on his list." The order excluded Italian, Spanish, Turkish, Greek, Bulgarian, Hungarian, Finnish, Norwegian, British and American Jews, as well as Jews married to an "Aryan" and their offspring. When Garat asked if mothers (not eligible for exclusion) with very young children should be arrested, Doberschütz ordered that no exceptions would be made and that the children should be sent to the General Union of Israelites in France (UGIF, *Union générale des israélites de France*), whose only representative in the region was Rabbi Joseph Cohen, Chief Rabbi of Bordeaux.[44]

On July 14, Dannecker's former deputy and successor, Heinz Röthke, notified the RSHA that the planned deportation of foreign Jews from Bordeaux on that day had been canceled because of the French national holiday. Röthke at once received an irate telephone call from Eichmann, who roundly admonished him.[45] The roundup took place on the night of July 15–16. Doberschütz played a critical role in organizing the convoys from Mérignac to Drancy; and he frequently intervened in the process of identifying internees who were not in fact Jewish or who had sufficient grounds for claiming "Aryan" status by providing a "family tree" and baptismal records. On July 17, Doberschütz and Garat "examined" 195 Jews at Mérignac on the eve of the first convoy to Drancy. Doberschütz separated the men from the women and ordered them to file in front of him three at a time. On that occasion, he exempted twenty-four internees: ten because of their nationality, another ten because of an "Aryan" spouse, and four more due to illness or infirmity.[46] Doberschütz made the French authorities responsible for accommodating and feeding the Jews in the camp and for providing two twenty-car trains.[47] Doberschütz advised the RSHA that one of the deportees was a Jew from Prague, Liselotte Freund, whom he suspected of espionage.[48] The roundup fell far short of expectations in the RSHA in terms of numbers. In total, 171 Jews left Bordeaux in convoy seventy-eight on July 18, destined for Auschwitz.[49]

The criminal investigation of Doberschütz's involvement in an alleged theft, begun in June 1941, finally ended on August 1, 1942, for reasons unknown. The lengthy case against him explains why further promotion in the SD/SS ranks eluded the Nazi officer for several more years.

On September 22, 1942, in Berlin, Lisa Doberschütz gave birth to their son. Several family photos of Otto, Lisa, and their two children—as infants and young children in Nazi Germany—survive, two of which are included in this chapter. There are no family records about visits Doberschütz made to see his family in Berlin. His daughter scarcely remembers him. She last saw him in 1945, when she was five years old.[50]

During autumn 1942, Doberschütz's primary preoccupation was the arrest and deportation of Jews. He and Luther organized another roundup on the night of October 19–20. They told Garat to "initiate the measures necessary to arrest all foreign Jews" in the area. Garat, in turn, conveyed these instructions to Maurice Papon, whom the SD ordered to provide forty-five inspectors, a police van, a bus, a truck, and a vehicle with two sidecars. The objective was to arrest 250 Jews, based on a list composed of many different nationalities.[51] Although the SD order pertained solely to foreign Jews, Michel Slitinsky later claimed that the Service for Jewish Affairs in Bordeaux contravened German orders by also arresting French Jews that night.[52]

Born in France to Russian Jewish parents, Slitinsky was seventeen years old when two French policemen raided his family's home in Bordeaux during the early hours of October 20, 1942. He escaped, but French police arrested his sister Alice, then twenty-three years old, and interned her at Mérignac. According to Michel Slitinsky, Doberschütz harshly questioned Pierre Garat about the arrest of Alice, who complained vociferously about her treatment as a French Jew. (It is impossible to know what motivated Doberschütz's vigorous defense of her. Was it owing to a measure of compassion, an opportunity for sexual violence, or a determined effort to obey orders?) On October 22, Doberschütz ordered the release of fifteen internees "arbitrarily arrested" in the roundup. The list included Alice, but she gave her place to a younger internee. Contrary to Doberschütz's orders, the camp director detained Alice. "Tired of the laxity" in the Service of Jewish Affairs, Doberschütz ordered her release on December 2, 1942, which became effective on December 5.[53] Two days later, Papon issued his own order to the camp's director. Papon later insisted that he alone had taken this decision.⁵⁴ By the beginning of 1943, Doberschütz had orchestrated the arrest and deportation of eight hundred Jews from the Bordeaux region.⁵⁵

In January 1943, the BdS in Paris sent Doberschütz to Pau to command the border police (*Grenzpolizei*) and to serve as the first regional head of the SD there. He established his headquarters in the elegant Villa St-Albert. Doberschütz took with him an Austrian SD officer, "Tony the Boxer" Enzelberger, known for his extreme brutality during the interrogation of suspected resisters and Communists in Bordeaux.⁵⁶ Enzelberger's nickname derived not only from his role as the former sparring partner of the German heavyweight boxer, Max Schmeling. "The boxer," a masculine trope, was a common nickname for SS men who took great pride in their ability to knock out a prisoner with one punch.⁵⁷ Contemporaneous witnesses often described Doberschütz and Enzelberger as "hard" and "unconditionally tough," terms that Westermann cites as "defining features of masculinity within the Nazi Party's paramilitary organizations" and extended to the entire SS and police complex.⁵⁸ Hitler and Nazi propaganda elevated "hardness" and "toughness" as virtues.⁵⁹ Doberschütz remained in Pau until May 1944, when the SD transferred him to the KdS office in Nancy.⁶⁰

War and Occupation from a French Basque Perspective

How did Otto Doberschütz meet the Basque spy, Jean Laborde? Laborde was a highly decorated air force veteran of the First World War and an elite machine gunner and bomb expert during the Moroccan campaign from 1919 until 1934. These experiences no doubt shaped his perceptions of masculine behavior and a militarized masculine identity. Heavy drinking, sexual exploits, and counting the number of aerial victories became key markers of male prowess among airmen during the First World War; and such manifestations of performative masculinity extended into the Second World War.⁶¹

In 1927, Laborde married a Belgian woman, Stephanie Dumont.⁶² In Morocco, the couple socialized with a network of extreme right-wing, ardently anti-Communist French military men, including Georges Loustaunau-Lacan, Colonel Jean-Baptiste Morraglia, and

Pierre Poinsot. Laborde served under Morraglia, himself a highly decorated bomber pilot, for eight years in Morocco.[63] Poinsot served in the French air force in Casablanca from 1923 until 1930, when he became a police inspector there.[64] The intense anti-Communist sentiments these men shared soon served as a driving force in the relationship Laborde forged with Doberschütz.

From 1934 until 1939, Lieutenant Laborde served in the thirty-third air force squadron in Nancy. His son was born in 1936. When France declared war, Laborde transferred to the thirty-sixth air force squadron in Pau and was promoted to captain because of his "excellent conduct."[65] He, his wife, and son settled in Pau for the war's duration.[66] Laborde had spent his youth in Gelos, a commune adjacent to Pau and was thus now back in familiar territory among some familiar acquaintances, including Georges Loustaunau-Lacau, a native of Pau.

It is also quite possible that Laborde's return to Pau renewed his connection with Marie-Madeleine Fourcade, a longstanding and close confidante of Loustaunau-Lacau. She had spent a few years in Morocco with her first husband (a member of the military elite, Édouard Méric) while Laborde was based there. When France fell in June 1940, Fourcade arranged to meet Loustaunau-Lacau near Pau in the Béarnais town of Oloron, where his family lived. They were now about to launch an ambitious intelligence initiative, Alliance.[67] Loustanau-Lacau appointed his friend, the staunchly anti-Communist and initially anti-Gaullist Fourcade, as second in command. Vichy police arrested him in Pau on July 18, 1941.[68] The Germans called the group "Noah's Ark," because its agents used the names of animals, fish, birds, and insects as code names.[69] At the height of its operations in 1942, Alliance ran three thousand operatives across France.[70] Led by Fourcade, the *réseau* quickly became one of Britain's most valuable sources of intelligence.[71]

With the code name "Bear," Jean Laborde joined Alliance in June 1942. He initially operated just north of the Dordogne and briefly in Limoges.[72] Laborde then shifted his focus to Bordeaux. Laborde gathered gather military intelligence about German submarine bases and minefields along the Atlantic coast.[73] Both French and German intelligence networks appreciated the value of his extensive military experience and high-level contacts in the French air force. Laborde had a powerful connection in Bordeaux, his friend and former junior air force colleague in Morocco, Pierre Poinsot. Driven by professional ambitions and a visceral hatred of Communists and resisters, Poinsot had advanced quickly through the ranks to become a special police commissioner in Bordeaux by 1938.[74]

When the RSHA dispatched Herbert Hagen and his SD agents to Bordeaux in July 1940, Poinsot eagerly exchanged intelligence with them. As Hagen observed after the war, Poinsot had helped to make Bordeaux "a kind of laboratory" for a Nazi-controlled Europe.[75] Poinsot also established close relations with Friedrich Dohse, head of section IV in the Bordeaux KdS. Both men played key roles in the dismantlement of the Resistance movement, OCM, whose controversial, anti-Communist leader, André Grandclément, had forged compromising relations with them. From November 1940 to January 1942, Poinsot orchestrated the arrest of almost five hundred Communists in the Gironde.[76]

Poinsot came to Laborde's rescue when German police arrested and imprisoned the Basque spy in September 1942 during an intelligence mission on the coast. After sixty days of detention in Fort du Hâ, Laborde contacted his former junior colleague, Poinsot, who at once went to see Otto Doberschütz. Poinsot negotiated his Basque friend's release just before Christmas 1942. Laborde then enjoyed three days as Poinsot's houseguest. Soon thereafter, Dohse asked to meet Laborde and invited him to dinner. He also invited Doberschütz, who was about to move to Pau as head of the regional SD office. Over dinner, Doberschütz and Laborde quickly struck up an animated conversation about Pau and Communists, whom they both hated. The Basque agent knew many farmers and shepherds in the region who could supply Doberschütz with ample supplies of food and alcohol. Soon thereafter, the two men set off for the Béarnais countryside where they bought eggs, flour, potatoes, lard, and a few hens. Laborde told the SD officer to pose as "a Spanish consul," an unlikely disguise that apparently amused Doberschütz.[77]

A few days after Laborde returned to Pau, he told his wife that he was "on probation" (*liberté surveillée*) and had "to report quite often to the German police."[78] He got official permission from his handler in Alliance, Édouard Kauffmann, to "play a double game" and to establish close relations with Doberschütz. Kauffmann knew Laborde from their days together in Morocco.[79] Kauffmann instructed Laborde to "gain (the Germans') trust by providing them with food and entertainment" and to give them the impression that he was "a pleasure-seeker."[80] According to Mme. (Stephanie) Laborde, her husband invited Doberschütz and his interpreter to dinner at the Laborde's home "to thank them for his freedom." A short time later, Laborde invited them to dine again in their home to put himself "on a good footing with the Germans. I always cooked these meals myself," Mme. Laborde observed, "and never heard anything suspect in their conversations."[81]

French, Basque, and German Sociability: Boozing and Bonding

Kauffmann's instructions suited the Basque agent and his new "frenemy." Both he and Doberschütz enjoyed the Armagnac, fine wines, and good food that Laborde sourced through his Basque and Béarnais connections. The two men regularly drove into the countryside to buy black-market goods. Once in Pau, Doberschütz transitioned into a "softer" occupier whose leisure activities centered on commensality, alcohol consumption, parties, and sex.[82] Laborde shared his propensities for excessive drinking and sexual conquests. At one point, the Basque agent had three mistresses simultaneously in Pau. Doberschütz's German mistress regularly accompanied him when he and Laborde enjoyed lavish meals in the SD villa and in the home of Laborde's brother, who was a chef and restaurateur. Stephanie Laborde usually accompanied her husband. (Doberschütz's wife, Lisa, and two young children lived in Germany. It is not known whether he visited them.)

Stephanie Laborde, her sister-in-law Alice Laborde, and Doberschütz's French cook provide a tantalizing glimpse into Franco-German sociability and bonding that was not confined to men with similar, militarized masculine identities. These women participated avidly in the dinner parties. As Stephanie Laborde observed, the Germans ate at her brother-in-law's restaurant on many occasions. The guest list always included Doberschütz, his German mistress, his cook (a thirty-four year-old widow from the Landes), her lover (an SD chauffeur), Karrika (a notorious carouser and Basque friend of

Laborde whom he had recruited into Alliance) and Karrika's Basque wife. Stephanie Laborde offers insight into these evenings: "In late 1942, early 1943, I went to dine at the Villa St-Albert. The dinner took place in the dining room, where there was also a piano. Jean's brother, his wife Alice, Doberschütz, Bauer, Schmidt (both SD officers), the interpreter, my husband and I were there.... After this meal a lot of empty bottles were smashed, and my sister-in-law fell down in the living room. I had to help her get up. Just to clarify, my brother-in-law, who was also very drunk, said some insulting things in Basque about the Germans. I was afraid of what the Gestapo might do. This was the only time I ate in the Villa St-Albert."[83]

Contrary to her statement, the same Franco-German couples dined together at the Villa St-Albert on several other occasions. One night in February 1943, the group enjoyed a particularly excellent dinner that started at nine o'clock in the evening and ended at three o'clock in the morning. The French cook described the gathering in detail: "Doberschütz provided a guinea fowl, a duck, and a chicken. Laborde's brother had bought two pigs for the occasion and his wife contributed a ham, *confit de canard, saucisson* (sausage), and pastries to the feast. Laborde's brother and sister-in-law prepared the meal. Gaiety reigned. Doberschütz was especially drunk," she observed, "as was (Jean) Laborde, to the extent that, by the time morning came, when (Doberschütz and I) tried to drive the Labordes home, we drove past their place for about a kilometer without realizing our mistake."[84] According to Alice Laborde, "many bottles were emptied that night. The Germans smashed lots of them on the parquet floor and waved their revolvers in the air."[85] She also admitted that she had danced exuberantly on a tabletop and had (again) fallen onto the floor.[86] Drunken Germans waving their pistols in the air offer an additional perspective for considering the manner in which SD men flaunted their weapons in both public and private spaces as a manifestation of their virility.[87]

Alice Laborde may well have been one of Doberschütz's sexual conquests. According to his Swiss interpreter, she was "always with Doberschütz on the many occasions when her husband was absent and I called in to see him. The two of them spoke in familiar terms. She called him by his first name, Otto. She once told him: 'When we see each other again, I will remember the nice meals that we had together in the Villa St-Albert.'"[88]

These accounts of Franco-German commensality in Pau are reminiscent of the "fellowship evenings" and celebratory drinking rituals through which SS men and other Nazis bonded as comrades and expressed their masculinity—except, of course, that these evenings in Pau included women. Unlike German women who visited male-dominated Nazi taverns in Germany, female companions at Doberschütz's parties were not prohibited from drinking alcohol, and some drank to excess.[89]

In normal circumstances, women in traditional Basque and Béarnais society did not consume alcohol, and if they did so, it was only in small amounts. People regarded alcohol consumption as a social activity to be enjoyed in moderation with a meal. Drinking was associated with masculinity, but men were expected to control their consumption of alcohol. Men who drank excessively, whether or not they could "hold their liquor," risked social alienation for being out of control and "in disorder." In rural communities, heavy drinkers were also often judged incapable of controlling their sexual "power"/procreative "force" (*indarra*, in Basque) and were thus deemed to be sexually dangerous. Such men often had difficulty finding a marriage partner.[90] Although Jean Laborde had rural roots, he moved in cosmopolitan circles during his air force and intelligence careers in Morocco and France. For Laborde, excessive alcohol consumption and sexual "conquests" served as male bonding mechanisms aimed at social inclusion in Pau's SD community.

In the summer of 1943, the regional head of Alliance, General Morraglia, dined with Laborde and his wife and gave them some quite tardy advice: "Now you have to move to the second stage in your relations with the Germans. You must now invite them to dine with you from time to time. . . . And you, Madame, I know that you detest the Boches at least as much as I do. You must forget your hatred and smile at them. Offer them drinks until the early hours of the morning, if necessary. Be gracious and likeable in their presence. That is the price we will pay for your husband to succeed in his mission."[91] His emphasis upon her role as hostess gives her agency in the forging of male camaraderie among men who increasingly blurred the lines between occupier and occupier, friend and enemy.

Doberschütz and Laborde also enjoyed gambling at the horse races in Pau. They socialized with a member of the Pau nobility, Baron d'Ariste, who raised racehorses and organized hunting parties at his chateau in Lescar. Baron d'Ariste was the nephew of Jean Ybarnegaray, the notoriously anti-Communist French Basque politician who represented the Basses-Pyrénées in the Chamber of Deputies from 1914 until 1939.[92] Laborde had grown up around horses; his father worked for the national stud in Gelos just outside Pau. It is likely that Laborde participated in the baron's hunting parties. Hunting "is heavily invested with concepts of masculinity and incorporates a competitive element of performative masculinity associated with marksmanship" and a man's "prowess in bringing down prey."[93] A favorite hobby of Basque men, hunting occupied (and still does) a central place in rural Basque culture. Basque hunters sometimes found the "deep psychic gratification involved in killing the prey, which results in 'internal heat,' heart pounding, (the) discharge of adrenaline... comparable (to) lovemaking."[94] If Doberschütz also participated in the hunting parties, he and Laborde would have competed and bonded not only in heavy drinking and profligate sexual activity, but also in "killing the prey."

In late May 1943, an SD officer saw Doberschütz's Basque housekeeper pass a note to Laborde while they drank coffee in the villa's kitchen. The officer reported the suspicious activity to Doberschütz. The note contained information about "suspect individuals" she had stolen from Doberschütz's desk. Doberschütz scolded Laborde "quite harshly" and threatened to ban him from the villa. When Laborde responded angrily, Doberschütz sought reconciliation, combining tenderness and toughness. The two men then drank wine together, not as "comrades" in the strictly National Socialist sense, but in keeping with French and Basque expectations of camaraderie.[95]

Soon after the "scolding" incident, Doberschütz caught Laborde and the housekeeper, walking together one evening and later "charmingly" told the Basque spy that she was not his "type." The remark (recalled by Laborde after the war) could be interpreted as a form of teasing between two men who, after all, knew quite a bit about each other's sexual exploits. Laborde, however, argued that the exchange revealed Doberschütz's suspicions about his undercover activities, which was why he had banned the spy from the villa's kitchen. The kitchen was the center of Basque and Béarnais sociability to which only the most trusted individuals gained access. Exclusion from the domestic domain was a deep insult.[96] In both Basque and German cultures, the kitchen is a female domain, the essence of domesticity. Laborde's exclusion had both a symbolic value and a practical one—limiting his access to the Germans' female domestic staff.

In July 1943, Laborde's superiors in Alliance urged him to relocate. The Germans had arrested several Alliance agents and had found Laborde's radio. Yet he refused to leave Pau, claiming that he feared German reprisals against his family. During the course of 1943, Laborde did provide Doberschütz with some intelligence about local resisters, one particularly prominent Communist resister, and a few other "enemies of the Reich." In November, Doberschütz summoned Laborde to his bedroom, apparently seeking comfort during an illness he suffered. Doberschütz noted the recent infrequency of the Basque's visits. According to Laborde: "He needed alcohol and seemed rather annoyed with me. He said that I wasn't my usual self. I said it was dangerous for me to visit him, because the Resistance tracked my movements ... Soon thereafter Doberschütz was hospitalized." Laborde visited him on several occasions.[97]

In March 1944, Doberschütz confronted Laborde a few times about his suspected resistance activity but chose to do nothing. In April, Doberschütz told him that the SD in Toulouse had ordered his arrest "because he worked for a resistance group." Twenty days passed before Doberschütz "reluctantly" arrested the Basque and held him in the basement of the Villa St-Albert.[98] When Doberschütz asked if his code name was "Bear," Laborde admitted that it was. Doberschütz then shook his hand and promised he would petition the KdS in Toulouse for Laborde's release. He kept his promise but failed to persuade his superiors.

As Stephanie Laborde noted in a post-liberation testimony, "I visited the Villa St-Albert two times following my husband's arrest in April 1944. On each occasion Doberschütz looked very embarrassed in my presence and never once looked me in the eye. He told me he would do everything possible to sort out my husband's situation."[99] Embarrassed because the Nazi officer had failed to protect his Basque "friend"? Or was it because of Franco-German male complicity in extramarital affairs?

While in prison, Laborde heard that Doberschütz thought highly of him. "He is a charming man," Laborde allegedly replied. On August 17, 1944, a German military court condemned Laborde to death. They had irrefutable evidence of his espionage for Alliance. The FFI liberated him on August 19. Laborde disappeared and likely never saw Doberschütz again.

By November 1944, Laborde lived in an apartment on the Champs Élysées owned by Marie-Madeleine Fourcade. The police arrested him on charges of treason. During discovery before Laborde's trial, Laborde reflected on the choices Doberschütz had made. He suggested that Doberschütz "perhaps had no interest in arresting" him, because he knew too much about Doberschütz's private life, claiming that Doberschütz had begun to neglect his duties because of his involvement with women.[100]

Postwar Trajectories

Laborde faced the court of justice in Pau May 18–21, 1946. The court found him guilty of intelligence with the enemy and endangering the lives of French citizens, with extenuating circumstances. He received twenty years in prison with hard labor and national degradation for life. By May 1948, the chief prosecutor in Pau had received two petitions for a reprieve. In July 1957, the French air force informed him that Laborde had been "reinstated in the reserve corps of air force officers by a decree dated June 11, 1957." He had also been promoted, backdated to August 1953. The court of appeal granted Laborde full amnesty in October 1957.

What happened to Otto Doberschütz? In October 1944, the German authorities transferred the entire KdS office in Nancy (including him) to Vienna. In November, Doberschütz and most of his unit were reassigned to a recently formed SS paramilitary death squad of the Sipo-SD, *Einsatzgruppe H/Sonderkommando 29*. This special task force had been sent to Slovakia in August 1944 to murder any remaining Jews. Doberschütz became one of a hundred senior SS officers in the unit and headed its base camp in Trnava.[101] In January 1945, he was finally promoted to senior SS storm leader and first lieutenant.[102] As the end of the war rapidly approached, Doberschütz led a "people's militia" (*Volkssturm*) under Himmler's control. These militias included boys and men from sixteen to sixty years old, called up to replace the losses sustained that summer as Allied forces advanced into Germany.[103] Doberschütz, who was thirty-two year old, died in combat involving the "people's militia" in Berlin-Spandau, just a day before or during the city's capitulation on the night of May 1–2, 1945.[104] By then, the Red Army controlled Slovakia.

In 1948, the restored Slovakian People's Courts "punished war criminals who had evaded justice in the preceding years," including Eichmann's deputy, Dieter Wisliceny, in May 1948. He "had played a central role in the Holocaust of Slovak and Hungarian" Jews.[105] The Slovakian People's Court in Bratislava also tried Otto Doberschütz (mistakenly under the surname Oberschütz and *in absentia*), along with nine other members of the *Einsatzgruppe H/Sonderkommando* on December 3, 1948.[106]

In 2018, the step-grandson of Otto Doberschütz, Larry Halford, contacted me. He wanted to know what I knew about his grandmother's first husband. Larry sent me a copy of Doberschütz's death certificate, a few photos of his grandmother with Otto and their two children, as well as several lengthy emails about what Larry, his aunt, and uncle had found out about the mysterious "Otto." Otto's wife, Lisa, had never spoken to her American family about her experiences in Nazi Germany. Soon after Otto's death in 1945, Lisa began to date an American GI, Johnny Snodgrass, who had already served in Germany before returning home, only to find his wife pregnant with another man's child. Snodgrass rejoined the US Army and returned to Germany with the intention of settling there. He and Lisa married and had a child, P. J. Snodgrass. Somehow, in the chaos of postwar Berlin, the army lost track of Johnny Snodgrass, who ran a lucrative black-market coffee network. The army eventually found out and forced him to return to Tennessee alone. Lisa and her baby emigrated there a few months later, but she left her two children fathered by Doberschütz in Germany with her parents. Lisa kept in touch with the children, unbeknownst to her American family.

In 1996, during a trip to Germany, the daughter of Lisa and Johnny Snodgrass, P. J. or "Peachie," discovered that she had two stepsiblings (Otto's children) and went to see them. On her return to Tennessee, she confronted her parents, who responded furiously. As one family member recalled, Johnny Snodgrass "was a good man but his temper was akin to a dump-truck full of dynamite." He and, unsurprisingly, Lisa refused to answer any family members' questions about their past, or about Otto.[107]

Peachie Snodgrass claims that during his trial in 1998, Maurice Papon insisted that Otto Doberschütz—not Papon—was "the real criminal" behind the deportation of Jews from Bordeaux.[108] In a retranscription of his pleading at Papon's trial on March 9, 1998, one of the prosecutors complained about "the unjustified attacks against the magistrate" made by Papon and his defense attorneys; they criticized the court "for not having pursued SS Doberschütz . . . someone who had died in 1945."[109]

Conclusions

The Doberschütz-Laborde relationship invites us to think about the German Occupation of southwestern France not as something fleeting that might soon disappear, but rather as something more layered and, above all, more permanent.[110] The two men relied upon each other to improve their day-to-day lives at a time of constant shortages and threats from above. Both men brought their experiences of the prewar years to bear on their own evolving relationship as they variously moved in the elite wartime circles of notorious French collaborationists, ardent resisters, and committed Nazis. Some of the men with whom they worked were key protagonists in the Vichy regime, the Third Reich, and the Resistance. Laborde's relationship with Doberschütz muddies the two categories (resistance and collaboration) that once dominated historians' understanding of French behavior during the Occupation and challenges the boundaries of Burrin's concept of accommodation and Gildea's notion of Franco-German cohabitation. Nor does the relationship fit neatly into the framework of occupied and occupier.

Exploring their unusual relationship through a German lens reveals the "hard" side of Nazi manliness alongside some curious interactions between the two men that allowed for femininely coded affection, tenderness, empathy, caring, and moments of weakness. They did not treat each other as the "enemy" and both took immense risks to forge a social bond that fell somewhere in between comradeship and friendship. Even as the ideals and expectations of the SD shaped Doberschütz's masculine identity, Laborde's experiences as a highly decorated soldier, airman, elite machine gunner, and double agent reflected a similar manifestation of militarized masculine identity, performed through excessive drinking and sexual conquests. Jean Laborde and Otto Doberschütz also brought their own cultural baggage into their extraordinary relationship. If we had letters, diaries, and other personal primary sources relating to these men, we would be better able to see more clearly and more deeply the Basque, the French, and the Nazi German "side of things."

Bibliography

Archival Collections
Archives départmentales, Pyréneées-Atlantiques, 30W42, dossier of S.P.
Archives Nationales, Pierrefitte-sur-Seine
    AJ38/5815
    F/7/15389, Professionels des Services Speciaux de III Reich
Centre des archives contemporains de Fontainebleau (CAC)
    850 671, carton 64, dossier of police commissioner Pierre Poinsot
Deutsche Dienstelle, Berlin. Ref. VIBII.

Books and Articles
Boulanger, Gérard. *Plaidoyer pour quelques Juifs obscurs victims de M. Papon*. Paris: Calmann Lévy, 2005.
Browder, George C. *Hitler's Enforcers: The Gestapo and the SS Security Service in the Nazi Revolution*. New York: Oxford University Press, 1996.
Cointet, Michèle. *Marie-Madeleine Fourcade: un chef de la Résistance*. St-Armand-Montrond, France: Perrin, 2006.
Conan, Éric. *Le procès Papon*. Paris: Gallimard, 1998.
Deacon, Valerie. "Fitting into the French Resistance: Marie-Madeleine Fourcade and Georges Loustaunau-Lacan at the Intersection of Politics and Gender," *Journal of Contemporary History* 50, no. 2 (April 2015): 259–273.
Fourcade, Marie-Madeleine. *L'Arche de Noé, réseau Alliance, 1940–1945*. Paris: Plon, 2007.
Frommer, Benjamin. *National Cleansing: Retribution Against Nazi Collaborators in Postwar Czechoslovakia*. Cambridge: Cambridge University Press, 2005.

Gerwarth, Robert. *Hitler's Hangman: The Life of Heydrich*. New Haven, CN: Yale University Press, 2012 edition.

Gibas, Monika, ed. *"Ariserung" in Leipzig*. Berlin: Leipzig University Press, 2007.

Haynes, Stephen R. "Ordinary Masculinity: Gender Analysis and Holocaust Scholarship," in *Genocide and Gender in the Twentieth Century: A Comparative Survey*, edited by Amy E. Randall. London: Bloomsbury Academic, 2015.

Imlay, Talbot. "The German Side of Things: Recent Scholarship on the German Occupation of France." *French Historical Studies* 39, no. 1 (February 2016): 183–215.

Koscielniak, Jean-Pierre and Philippe Souleau, eds. *Vichy en Aquitaine*. Paris: Les Éditions de l'Atelier, 2011.

Kühne, Thomas. *The Rise and Fall of Comradeship: Hitler's Soldiers, Male Bonding and Mass Violence in the Twentieth Century*. Cambridge: Cambridge University Press, 2017.

Lee, Daniel. *The SS Officer's Armchair: Uncovering the Hidden Life of a Nazi*. New York: Hachette Books, 2020.

Leruste, Florent. *Juifs internes à Bordeaux (1940–1944): Le camp de Mérignac-Beaudésert*. Suresnes: Éditions du Net, 2014.

Lower, Wendy. *Hitler's Furies: German Women in the Nazi Killing Fields*. London: Vintage Books, 2014 edition.

Marrus, Michael R. and Robert O. Paxton. *Vichy France and the Jews*. Stanford: Stanford University Press. 1995 edition.

Moore, Bob. *Survivors: Jewish Self-Help and Rescue in Nazi-Occupied Europe*. Oxford: Oxford University Press, 2010.

Ott, Sandra. *Living with the Enemy: German Occupation, Collaboration and Justice in the Western Pyrenees, 1940–1948*. Cambridge: Cambridge University Press, 2017.

———. "Indarra": Some Reflections on a Basque Concept." In *Honor and Grace in Anthropology*, J. G. Peristiany and Julian Pitt-Rivers, eds. Cambridge: Cambridge University Press, 1992.

Poullenot, Louis. *Basses-Pyrénées, occupation libération 1940–1945*. Biarritz: Éditions J&D, 1995.

Šindelárová, Lenka. *Finale der Vernichtung: Die Einsatzgruppe H in der Slowakei 1944–1945*. Damstadt: WBG, dissertation, University of Stuttgart, 2013.

Slitinsky, Michel. *Procés Papon: Le devoir de justice*. La Tour d'Aigues: Éditions de l'Aube, 1997.

Souleau, Philippe. "De l'exclusion à la deportation: les politiques répressives et ses acteurs en Gironde occupée," Jean-Pierre Koscielniak and Philippe Souleau, eds. *Vichy en Aquitaine*. Paris: Les Éditions de l'Atelier, 2011.

Stargardt, Nicholas. *The German War: A Nation Under Arms, 1939–1945*. New York: Basic Books, 2015.

Steinberg, Lucien. *Les autorités Allemandes en France Occupée*. Vol II. Paris: Centre de Documentation Juive Contemporaine, 1966.

Terrisse, René. *Bordeaux, 1940–1944*. Paris: Perrin, 1993.

———. *À la botte de l'occupant, itinéraires de cinq collaborateurs*. Bordeaux, France: Aubéron, 1998.

Torrie, Julia S. *German Soldiers and the Occupation of France, 1940–1944*. Cambridge: Cambridge University Press, 2018.

Vaughan, David, ed. *Letters from a War Bird: The World War I Correspondence from Elliott White Springs*. Columbia: University of South Carolina Press, 2012.

West, Nigel. *MI6 British Secret Service Operations 1909–1945*. London: Random House, 1983.

Wildt, Michael. *An Uncompromising Generation: The Nazi Leadership of the Reich Security Main Office*, trans. Tom Lampert. Madison: University of Wisconsin Press, 2010.

Westermann, Edward B. "Drinking Rituals, Masculinity, and Mass Murder in Nazi Germany." *Central European History*, Vol. 51 (2018): 367–389.

Zulaika, Joseba. *Basque Violence: Metaphor and Sacrament*. Reno: University of Nevada Press, 1988.

Notes

1. Sandra Ott, *Living with the Enemy: German Occupation, Collaboration and Justice in the Western Pyrenees, 1940–1948* (Cambridge, UK: Cambridge University Press, 2017).
2. Jean Laborde is a pseudonym. I have, however, used the "real" name of Doberschütz, as he appears briefly, and tantalizingly, in several scholarly books about the Holocaust, the Occupation of France, and the trial of Maurice Papon.
3. Ott, chapter 12, "Duplicitous Accommodation."
4. I presented an earlier version of this paper at the forty-seventh annual meeting of the Western Society for French History in Bozeman, Montana, in October 2019. I am extremely grateful to the commentary provided by Daniel Lee during the panel and address the key issues he raised.
5. Daniel Lee, *The S.S. Officer's Armchair: Uncovering the Hidden Life of a Nazi* (New York: Hachette Books, 2020), 4.
6. Thomas Kühne, *The Rise and Fall of Comradeship: Hitler's Soldiers, Male Bonding and Mass Violence in the Twentieth Century* (Cambridge: Cambridge University Press, 2017).
7. Ibid., 293.
8. Ibid., 291.
9. Edward B. Westermann, "Drinking Rituals, Masculinity, and Mass Murder in Nazi Germany," *Central European History*, Vol. 51, 2018, 367.
10. Ibid., 374.
11. Julia S. Torrie, *German Soldiers and the Occupation of France, 1940–1944* (Cambridge: Cambridge University Press, 2018).
12. Ibid., 251.
13. Ibid., 251.
14. Documents provided by P. J. Snodgrass and Larry Halford show that Doberschütz received both an SA and a Reich Sports Badge (both in bronze), indications of his athleticism.

15. Monika Gibas (ed.), *"Arisierung'in Leipzig* (Berlin: Leipzig University Press, 2007), 121; George C. Browder, *Hitler's Enforcers: The Gestapo and the SS Security Service in the Nazi Revolution* (New York: Oxford University Press, 1996), 179–180. Working in an SD office gave Doberschütz an official affiliation with the SD and membership of it. See Browder, 131.
16. Browder, 180, 220. Germanist intellectual Wilhelm Spengler created the Leipzig Literature Post in 1933 for the evaluation of German literature. His efforts reflect the close interest the SD took in education and culture.
17. Archives Nationales, Paris, file F/7/15389, Professionels des Services Speciaux du III Reich, 191.
18. Browder, 131, 180.
19. Browder, 180.
20. Browder, 3.
21. Archives Nationales, Paris, file F/7/15389, Professionels des Services Speciaux du III Reich, iv, under II., le RSHA.
22. Robert Gerwarth, *Hitler's Hangman: The Life of Heydrich* (New Haven, CN: Yale University Press, 2012 edition), 1, 121–122.
23. Photocopy of the marriage application, no date, kindly provided by Larry Halford, June 20, 2020.
24. Lee, 109. See also Browder on assessing "suitable fiancées" for SD men, 213.
25. Wendy Lower, *Hitler's Furies: German Women in the Nazi Killing Fields* (London: Vintage Books, 2014), 23.
26. Lower, 57.
27. I am extremely grateful to P. J. Snodgrass (daughter of Lisa Meckelburg by her second husband) for access to questionnaires completed by her mother about her mother's suitability to be the bride of Otto Doberschütz, i.e., that she was in good health, of "Aryan stock," etc. I am also grateful to Ed Westermann for having translated much of the German in these documents.
28. Robert Gewarth, *Hitler's Hangman: The Life of Heydrich* (New Haven, CN: Yale University Press, 2012 edition), 163.
29. Recommendation for promotion to the head of the Sipo-SD in Berlin, sent from Warsaw, February 20, 1940, sender's name illegible. I am grateful to the stepgrandson of Otto Doberschütz, Larry Halford, for having sent me this document.
30. Undated "personal report" on Hauptscharführer Otto Doberschütz, SD, Warsaw. I am grateful to P. J. Snodgrass for having provided a copy of this document, June 28, 2020.
31. Monika Gibas (ed.), *"Arisierung'in Leipzig* (Berlin: Leipzig University Press, 2007), 121.
32. I owe this observation to Ed Westermann (commentary on an earlier version of this chapter for the workshop on "Nazi Germany and Occupied France" at the University of Nevada, Reno, March 6–7, 2020) and for reference to the work of Michael Wildt, *An Uncompromising Generation: The Nazi Leadership of the Reich Security Main Office*, trans. Tom Lampert (Madison: University of Wisconsin Press, 2010), 45.

33. Personal communication, P. J. Snodgrass, June 20, 2020. Doberschütz belonged to the infamous SS-initiated association *Lebensborn* (literally "Fount of Life"), founded to increase Germany's declining birthrate by providing pregnant "Aryan" women with financial assistance, adoption services, and private maternity homes.
34. The investigation closed on August 1, 1942. Details of the alleged theft are not known. I thank P. J. Snodgrass and Larry Halford for having provided me with a copy of the report.
35. Lucien Steinberg, *Les autorités Allemandes en France Occupée*, Vol. II (Paris: Centre de Documentation Juive Contemporaine, 1966), 106, entry 327, f. Doberschütz responded to Dannecker's cable of January 19, 1942, on March 12, 1942, reporting that all German Jews in the Bordeaux area had "emigrated." René Terrisse, *Bordeaux, 1940–1944* (Paris: Perrin, 1993), 27, indicates that Doberschütz became head of the anti-Jewish Kommando in June 1942, but German records indicate an earlier arrival.
36. Steinberg, 26.
37. Terrisse, 29, 33n.12.
38. AN, Paris, F/7/15389, iv-v.
39. Michel Slitinsky, *Procès Papon: Le devoir de justice* (La Tour d'Aigues: Éditions de l'Aube, 1997), 76–77.
40. Steinberg, entry 349, May 9, 1942, 111.
41. Steinberg, entry 1293, May 9, 1942, 311.
42. Ferdinand Hugo aus der Fünten was well known for his heavy drinking, a factor that helped Walter Süskind and colleagues rescue Jewish children through the Schouwburg theater and crèche in Amsterdam. See Bob Moore, *Survivors: Jewish Self-Help and Rescue in Nazi Occupied Europe* (Oxford: Oxford University Press, 2010), 311. Fünten achieved notoriety in his postwar trial for war crimes as one of the so-called "Breda Four," the only German war criminals to be imprisoned in the Netherlands. He died soon after his release in 1989.
43. Michael R. Marrus and Robert O. Paxton, *Vichy France and the Jews* (Stanford: Stanford University Press, 1995 edition), 81–82.
44. Slitinsky, 76–77.
45. Sternberg, entry 385, a. (July 14, 1942), c. (July 15, 1942); entry 386 (July 14, 1942), entry 387, a. (July 18, 1942), b. (July 18, 1942), 118.
46. Florent Leruste, *Juifs internés à Bordeaux (1940–1944): Le camp de Mérignac-Beaudésert* (Suresnes: Éditions du Net, 2014), 168, 170, testimony by a young female Russian Jew who witnessed the "selection" process.
47. AN, Pierrefitte-sur-Seine, AJ38/5815, Direction Régionale de Bordeaux, 1941–1944, letter from Garat to Papon, July 2, 1942, also cited in Slitinsky, 76–77. The deadline for these arrests was July 6, 1942. The letter does not indicate the number of Jews to be arrested. In Éric Conan, *Le procès Papon* (Paris: Gallimard, 1998) 91, Conan reports that Doberschütz ordered the prefect to arrest two thousand Jews and quotes portions of the letter from Garat that I cite. Conan's source relates to the thirty-first day of Papon's trial when the court interrogated Papon about the

roundup of July 16, 1942 (when the roundup slated for July 6 actually took place) and the convoy of July 18. *See also* Jean-Pierre Koscielniak and Philippe Souleau (eds.), *Vichy en Aquitaine* (Paris: Les Éditions de l'Atelier, 2011), 241.
48. Steinberg, entry 387, July 18, 1942, 118.
49. Philippe Souleau, "De l'exclusion à la deportation: les politiques répressives et ses acteurs en Gironde occupée," Jean-Pierre Koscielniak and Philippe Souleau (eds.), *Vichy en Aquitaine* (Paris: Les Éditions de l'Atelier, 2011), 241.
50. Personal communication (P. J. Snodgrass, June 28, 2020).
51. Slitinsky, 9.
52. Slitinsky, 30.
53. The files give no indication of any personal motives for her release. Doberschütz was following the rules set by the RSHA regarding foreign and French Jews.
54. In *Procès Papon*, Slitinsky reproduced the letter from Papon (writing on behalf of the prefect of the Gironde) to the director of the Mérignac camp and stamped December 7, 1942, 257.
55. Koscielniak and Souleau, 241–242.
56. René Terrisse, *À la botte de l'occupant, itinéraires de cinq collaborateurs* (Bordeaux: Aubéron, 1998), 214.
57. Personal communication from Ed Westermann, September 22, 2019.
58. Edward B. Westermann, "Drinking Rituals, Masculinity, and Mass Murder in Nazi Germany," *Central European History*, Vol. 51, 2018, 376.
59. Stephen R. Haynes, "Ordinary Masculinity: Gender Analysis and Holocaust Scholarship," *Genocide and Gender in the Twentieth Century: A Comparative Survey*, Amy E. Randall (ed.) (London: Bloomsbury, 2015), 170.
60. Archives Nationales, Paris, file F/7/15389, Professionels des Services Speciaux du III Reich, 191. Lenka Šindelárová, *Finale der Vernichtung: Die Einsatzgruppe H in der Slowakei 1944–1945* (Darmstadt: WBG, dissertation University of Stuttgart, 2013), 58.
61. I owe this observation to Ed Westermann, as well as the reference to David Vaughn (ed.), *Letters from a War Bird: The World War I Correspondence from Elliott White Springs* (Columbia: University of South Caroline Press, 2012).
62. Archives Départementales, Pyrénées-Atlantiques (hereafter AD, P-A), file 30W42, dossier of S. P., testimony by S. P. to a police commissioner in Territorial Surveillance, Pau, November 29, 1944.
63. AD, P-A, file 30W42, dossier of S. P., testimony of General Jean-Baptiste Morraglia to an examining magistrate in Algiers, April 19, 1945.
64. René Terrisse, *Bordeaux, 1940–1944* (Mesnil-sur-l'Estrée: Perrin, 1993), 44.
65. AD, P-A, file 30W42, dossier of S. P., testimony by General Morraglia, air force commander in Algeria, Algiers, April 19, 1945.
66. AD, P-A, file 30W42, Pau, testimony of S. P. to a police commissioner in Territorial Surveillance, Paris, no. 643, November 29, 1944.
67. Michèle Cointet, *Marie-Madeleine Fourcade: un chef de la Résistance* (St-Armand-Montrond: Perrin, 2006), 42.

68. AD, P-A, file 30W42, dossier of S. P., document 32, testimony of Marie-Madeleine Fourcade to a police commissioner in Pari, April 25, 1945. In this testimony, Fourcade claimed that she "directed" Alliance from September 1940. In other primary sources, she claims to have done so as soon as Loustaunau-Lacau was arrested in July 1941.
69. Marie-Madeleine Fourcade, L'Arche de Noé, réseau Alliance, 1940–1945 (Paris: Plon, 2007), 97.
70. Nigel West, MI6 British Secret Service Operations 1909–1945 (London: Random House, 1983), 152.
71. Valerie Deacon, "Fitting into the French Resistance: Marie-Madeleine Fourcade and Georges Loustaunau-Lacau at the Intersection of Politics and Gender," Journal of Contemporary History, Vol. 50, No. 2 (April 2015), 263.
72. AD, P-A, file 30W42, file of S. P., document 32, testimony of Marie-Madeleine Fourcade to a police commissioner in Paris, April 25, 1945.
73. AD, P-A, file 30W42, Pau, testimony of S. P. to a police commissioner in Territorial Surveillance, Paris, no. 643, November 29, 1944.
74. Centre des archives contemporaines de Fontainebleau (CAC), 850 671, carton 64, dossier of commissioner Poinsot.
75. Souleau, 231.
76. René Terrisse, À la botte de l'occupant, itinéraires de cinq collaborateurs (Bordeaux: Aubéron, 1998),]29–30.
77. AD, P-A, 30W42, first testimony of S. P. to a police commissioner in Territorial Surveillance, Pau, November 29, 1944. See Ott, Living with the Enemy, 249.
78. AD, P-A, 30W42, intelligence note marked "secret," no signature, October 26, 1944.
79. AD, P-A, 30W42, testimony of Marie-Madeleine Méric (Fourcade) to the examining magistrate, Pau, February 28, 1946.
80. AD, P-A, 30W42, testimony of Marie-Madeleine Méric (Fourcade) to the examining magistrate, Pau, February 28, 1946.
81. AD, P-A, 30W42, testimony of S. H. to the inspector for Territorial Surveillance, Pau, October 13, 1944.
82. Available sources to date on his time in Bordeaux do not mention any of his leisure habits other than dinner invitations. It may well be that Doberschütz engaged in heavy drinking and extramarital sex there, too.
83. AD, P-A, 30W42, testimony of S. H. to an inspector of Territorial Surveillance, Pau, October 13, 1944.
84. AD, P-A, 30W42, testimony by O.D., Doberschütz's cook, Pau, October 19, 1944.
85. AD, P-A, 30W42, testimony of A. L., Pau, October 16, 1944.
86. AD, P-A, 30W42, testimony of A. L., Pau, October 16, 1944.
87. I am grateful to Ed Westermann for this observation (March 6, 2020).
88. AD, P-A, 30W42, testimony of K. H. to a police inspector, Pau, October 11, 1944.
89. Westermann, 374–375.
90. See Sandra Ott, "Indarra": Some Reflections on a Basque Concept," in Honor and Grace in Anthropology, J. G. Peristiany and Julian Pitt-Rivers (eds.), (Cambridge: CUP, 1992), especially 208–209.

91. AD, P-A, 30W42, letter from General Morraglia to the president of the departmental liberation committee, sent from Algiers to Pau, April 1, 1945.
92. AD, P-A, 30W42, testimony of Baron d'Ariste to police commissioner Lorenzi, no date, file marked "secret."
93. I am again grateful to Ed Westermann for this observation in relation to this chapter (March 6, 2020).
94. Joseba Zulaika, *Basque Violence: Metaphor and Sacrament* (Reno: University of Nevada Press, 1988), 199.
95. AD, P-A, 30W42, testimony of S. P. to a police commissioner in Territorial Surveillance, no. 6314, Pau, November 29, 1944.
96. Ott, *Living with the Enemy*, 252.
97. AD, P-A, 30W42, first testimony of S. P. to a police commissioner, Paris, November 29, 1944.
98. AD, P-A, 30W42, second testimony of Hochstrasser to a police inspector, Pau, October 12, 1944. Doberschütz and Tony "The Boxer" Enzelberger regularly beat and tortured resisters in that basement.
99. AD, P-A, 30W42, testimony of S. H. to an inspector in Territorial Surveillance, Pau, October 13, 1944.
100. AD, P-A, 30W42, first testimony of S. P. to a police commissioner, page 14, Paris, November 29, 1944.
101. Šindelárová, 210.
102. Monika Gibas (ed.), " '*Arisierung'in Leipzig* (Berlin: Leipzig University Press, 2007), 121; Lena Šindelárová, "*Einsatzgruppe H* in Slovakia during the uprising, 1944–1945, and postwar prosecutions," *Soudobé dejiny*, Vol. 20, No. 4, 82–603.
103. I am grateful to Ed Westermann for providing background on the *Volkssturm*. See Nicholas Stargardt, *The German War: A Nation Under Arms, 1939–1945* (New York: Basic Books, 2015), 456–458.
104. Deutsche Dienststelle, Berlin, ref. VIB111, notice sent to P. J. Snodgrass ("Peachie," daughter of Doberschütz's wife by her second marriage) in Tennessee on September 28, 1998, and kindly shared with me in May 2018.
105. Benjamin Frommer, *National Cleansing: Retribution Against Nazi Collaborators in Postwar Czechoslovakia* (Cambridge: Cambridge University Press, 2005), 335.
106. Šindelárová, 247.
107. Personal communications with Larry Halford, on various occasions in the summer of 2018 and in January 2020.
108. Personal communication with Larry Halford via email, 2018.
109. Gérard Boulanger, *Plaidoyer pour quelques Juifs obscurs victimes de M. Papon* (Paris: Calmann Lévy, 2005), 23.
110. I am most grateful to Daniel Lee for this observation.

CHAPTER 6

Dining at the Tour d'Argent

Ernst Jünger, Power and the Othering of Paris

BERTRAM M. GORDON

On July 4, 1942, after enjoying a dinner of sole and the famous duck at the Tour d'Argent restaurant, "that silver tower where Henry IV [reigned 1589–1610] dined on egret pies," Ernst Jünger described a "diabolical" sense of power in looking down on German-occupied Paris during the Second World War "upon the gray sea of roofs at their feet, beneath which the starving eke out their living. In times like this—eating well and much—brings a feeling of power."[1] A well-known and accomplished author who had written about his experiences in the First World War, Jünger was keenly aware of his power as the conquering uniformed military officer during the Occupation. His *War Journals*, in which he repeatedly discussed his fascination with Paris and its culture, however, expressed this power in a variety of ways, including dining, his social and literary contacts, and his strolls through the streets of the French capital. As Patrick Buisson noted in his study of "the erotic years" of 1940–1945 in France, Jünger's comment was a very rare example of "bad conscience . . . on the menu at these feasts."[2]

A Decorated Veteran of the First World War

A study of Jünger (1895–1998) in occupied France during the Second World War, this chapter began as a review of his wartime *Journals*, translated into English in 2019 and published on the digital H-Diplo network.[3] The timing of the English translation may not have been completely fortuitous: charts compiled from counts of references to "Ernst Jünger" in Google digitized books, while spiking in German and French books about the time of his death, have more recently increased to unprecedented heights, though with a slight decline in the second half of the 2010s in the English-language literature. While the German- and French-language publication numbers declined after Jünger's death, the figures increased again in French during the twenty-first century, reflective perhaps of the interest of some on the political Right there, such as Alain de Benoist and the *Identitaire* movement, to be discussed later in this chapter. Whether the seemingly increased interest in the English-language world relates to a heightened presence of the political Right remains to be explored.

A highly decorated German veteran of the First World War, Jünger had been wounded some fourteen times during that conflict. He spent much of the Second World War as an officer stationed in Paris, where his *Journals* are an almost daily record of the views and impressions of a well-read literary figure, entomologist, and cultural critic, although as Julia S. Torrie has noted, they were published only after the war, first appearing in 1949, giving Jünger the opportunity to edit them in the light of the changed political circumstances of the postwar era.[4] The *Journals* became available for the first time in English translation in 2019 in *A German Officer in Occupied Paris*.[5]

A captain in the Wehrmacht who was posted in white-collar positions in Paris with the German military during the 1940–1944 Occupation, Jünger had visited the city before the war, was fluent in French, and now had the contacts and the time to become even more familiar with the French capital. He was given a room in the Hôtel Raphael, then as now, one of the most luxurious lodgings in Paris, on the Avenue Kléber in Paris's sixteenth arrondissement, not far from the Arc de Triomphe, and one of the many hotels in Paris commandeered by the Germans to house their offices and personnel in the occupied city. His office was in the Hotel Majestic, on a side street around the corner, also commandeered for German use.[6] By the time of his arrival in France during the Second World War, Jünger was already widely known as a consequence of the reception of his earlier literary work, notably his *In Stahlgewittern*, an account of the trench warfare of the First World War. A restless young man with a quest for adventure in 1911, he had joined the Wandervogel (Wandering Bird) movement of youth groups who went hiking in the countryside to commune with nature and escape modern industrial society. The Wandervogel also sought to revive a romanticized vision of old Teutonic values and strongly supported German nationalism. At age seventeen in 1913, he traveled to Algeria where he joined the French Foreign Legion, only to flee to Morocco, where he was placed in prison. Released through the efforts of his well-connected father, he returned to school in Germany. With the outbreak of the First World War only a few months later, he joined the German army in Hanover. By the beginning of 1915, he was at the Western Front. Because of his service at the front and many injuries in battle, Jünger was awarded the Pour le Mérite, the highest honor in the Prussian army on September 22, 1918. He was the youngest man ever to receive it.[7] In the words of Alex Colville,

> *In Stahlgewittern* narrates one mass slaughter after another with calm detachment, even coldness—comrades repeatedly blown to bits or shot in the head. The book bristles with militarism, with no room for individual suffering. Men are briefly sketched and swiftly killed, to be replaced by new faces indistinguishable from those before.[8]

In Stahlgewittern was first published privately in German in 1920 where it became a best seller and was translated into English as *The Storm of Steel* (New York: Doubleday) in 1929. In addition to his literary work, Jünger also wrote about entomology, a field that would retain a lifelong attraction for him. Infused with a Nietzschean anti-liberalism and a critic of the Weimar Republic, he was also active politically during the early post-First World War years in the movements of "National Bolshevism" and "Prussian Socialism" that, according to Elliot Neaman, meant "a new state to be run by steely-eyed workers and soldiers in full mobilization to restore Germany to its status as a world power."[9] By the late 1920s, Jünger had become "less focused on strident German nationalism," retaining, however, an anti-populist elitism that kept him aloof from the Nazis and their racialism, despite their attempts to win him over as they took power in 1933.[10] His novel *Auf den Marmorklippen* (*On the Marble Cliffs*), published just before the Second World War (Hamburg: Hanseatische

Verlagsanstalt, 1939), was often seen as a subtle critique of the Nazi dictatorship in Germany, although Jünger later denied that this had been his intent.[11]

The Second World War and the *Journals*

With the outbreak of war again in 1939, Jünger was drafted as a lieutenant, eventually rising to the rank of captain in the Wehrmacht. A member of the advancing German forces in the spring of 1940, he participated in their victory over France. In April 1941, he was posted to the German military headquarters in Paris, where his duties included helping to prepare plans for the invasion of England, censoring the mail of the Occupation soldiers, and the occasional supervision of the execution of deserters.[12] The assignment pleased Jünger who noted in his *Journals* that "I would be in a better position here in Paris than I would be elsewhere."[13] He would remain for much of the war period in Paris, the city that, with no effort of his own, now lay open to him. Having visited Paris during the interwar years, Jünger found it even more brilliant during the Occupation than before. He became very much a part of the salon culture of Paris that continued and flourished during the German Occupation.[14]

Reviewing the English translation of Jünger's *Journals* in H-France, Torrie notes that because Jünger edited his *Journals* after the war and they were published four years later, they are to be read more as memoirs than as a contemporary diary of the events described. His style, she adds, "is dream-like and impressionistic, with an eye for arresting details that the author then uses as a window onto whole landscapes." She cites a reviewer, Peter de Mendelssohn, who emphasized the idiosyncratic nature of Jünger's *Journals*, a "construction," in his words, rather than an "authentic" record of the war.[15] Jünger's memoir should be seen as having been written from a position of power both of the occupying military officer during the war and the veteran who had successfully negotiated his way back into society and literary acceptance afterward. He shared with many, although not all, occupying German soldiers the privileged opportunity of touring Paris as victors, "manifestations of the relationships of power, similar to those seen by Walter Benjamin expressed in the medium of film."[16] Not many Germans in occupied Paris, however, wrote of dining in the Tour d'Argent, and Jünger's account of wartime Paris must be seen as the idiosyncratic document that it is.

Well aware of the misery of so many of the French, Jünger described in his *Journals* the high lifestyle of the German officers, of which the Tour d'Argent account is only one example. People mentioned repeatedly include Florence Gould, the wife of the American railway magnate Frank Jay Gould, both of whom were living in France during the Occupation. When Jünger "left Paris at the very last moment, in August of 1944," wrote Charles L. Robertson, "it was to Florence Gould's apartment that he went to say his last goodbyes."[17] As Neaman notes in his foreword to the *Journals*, Jünger "rubbed shoulders with Braque, Picasso, Sacha Guitry, Julien Gracq, Paul Léautaud, and Jean Paulhan," among other literary and artistic luminaries. He also frequented the Hôtel George V, a luxury spot, where he mingled with "a roundtable of exclusive French and German intellectuals, including the writers Morand, Cocteau, Montherlant as well as the publisher Gaston Gallimard."[18] His *Journals*, meticulously compiled during the war, were first published in German as *Strahlungen* (Tübingen: Heliopolis Verlag) in 1949. Brought out in a French translation (*Journal de Guerre et d'Occupation 1939–1948*, translated by Henri Plard, Paris: René Julliard), in 1965, they appeared, as noted, in 2019 in English for the first time as *A German Officer in Occupied Paris: The War Journals, 1941–1945*. Holding his white-collar position, Jünger had time to wander around Paris, where, as Melanie Gordon Krob writes, "he could be a part of a long, continuous and unbroken thread of history."[19] Together with his walks, Jünger had the opportunity to meet many leading French cultural figures and note his impressions in his journals, which begin en route to Paris in February 1941 and extend through the American conquest of his hometown of Kirchhorst in Saxony in mid-April 1945.

Having been called for military service shortly after the start of the Second World War, Jünger participated in the Blitzkrieg military victory over France, although he was not involved in the fighting. His journal, *Gärten und Strassen* (*Gardens and Streets*), published in 1942, covered the period from early April 1939 through July 1940.[20] With his unit he traveled as far south as Bourges with stops in Paris but quickly returned to Germany, "both frustrated and relieved not to have participated in the Blitzkrieg," in the words of François Dufay, writing at the time of the publication of a French-language translation of the *War Journals* in the prestigious Pléiade book collection in 2008.[21]

Jünger returned to France in the spring of 1941, arriving in Paris in April. There is a break in October 1942 when he was transferred to the Eastern Front where he remained through January 1943, when he was sent back to Paris. Accordingly, the *War Journals* are divided into four parts: the "First Paris Journal," his writings from 1941 through October 1942; "Notes from the Caucasus," continuing his account through February 1943; the "Second Paris Journal," covering the period from his return to Paris through the liberation of France in the late summer of 1944; and lastly, the "Kirchhorst Diaries," his account of having been placed in charge of the local militia *(Volkssturm)* and his reflections on the bombings and imminent defeat of Germany.

The "First Paris Journal" reflects the *flânerie* of a German officer and writer happy to rediscover Paris at a time when it seemed clear that Germany had won the war and would dominate France and perhaps Europe indefinitely. Following the German invasion of the Soviet Union, tensions mounted in occupied France. In December 1941, attacks against German soldiers in France, described as "assassinations" by Jünger, were beginning to change the atmosphere; and he found extended curfews dimming the activity and sparkle of Paris.

> Walked through the deserted streets of the city in the evening. Because of the assassinations, the populace is under curfew in the early evening. Everything lies lifeless in the fog. The sound of radios and chattering children came from the houses, as if I were walking among birdcages.[22]

Closer physically to combat following his transfer to the East in October 1942, Jünger devoted greater attention to the fighting and the raw nature of the German-Soviet struggle in "Notes from the Caucasus." By the time he returned to Paris and began his "Second Paris Journal" in February 1943, the Germans had been defeated at Stalingrad and it had become increasingly evident that a titanic struggle loomed and that the Germans might well lose the war. As the tide of war turned increasingly against Germany, Jünger, as many others in France, became more preoccupied with a potential Allied landing. On May 8, 1944, he wrote: "the landing is on everyone's mind; the German command as well as the French believe that it will happen in the next few days."[23] The German defenses were based on the Atlantic Wall, a mammoth undertaking that employed thousands of workers. In an allusion reminiscent of an earlier description of the Maginot Line, the magazine *L'Illustration* described it in 1943 as comparable in history only to the Great Wall of China.[24] Upon hearing of the June 6, 1944, landings in Normandy, he predicted it would be a "historic day," but expressed surprise at the time and place, about which people would be talking "well into the distant future."[25]

On Gender, Power, and Cultural Sophistication

Jünger's views of gender emerge most clearly in comments about cities and, in particular, Paris, whose beauty and, by implication, "yielding" nature he considered feminine. Writing that "cities are feminine and only smile on the victor," he visited the Sacré Cœur Cathedral terrace in early August 1944, two weeks before the liberation, for a nostalgic final "last glance" at occupied Paris.[26] To Jünger, the streets of Paris offered presents to the *flâneur*, such as views of the locals bending over and kissing one another, conveying sentiments such as might be given by a man's girlfriend, in other words, a feminized view of the city that he shared with other Germans stationed there.[27] Paris, he wrote, in another feminine allusion, "had been founded at the altar of Venus."[28] His view of a feminized Paris was in keeping with other gendered images of France, expressed in French as "la belle France."

Previously, shortly after the defeat of France, he had written that Paris was "the only city with which I have a relationship as to a woman."[29] The nostalgia at the thought of leaving Paris was not unique to Jünger. A German columnist, in the August 8, 1944, issue of the *Pariser Zeitung*, the German-language newspaper published during the Occupation, without mentioning his own forced withdrawal, wrote wistfully of Normandy's having grown on him after several years of service there. Already he had seemed to miss Normandy's calvados, trees, wind, and brooks.[30]

The final section of Jünger's work, the "Kirchhorst Diaries," is set against the backdrop of the Allied invasion of Germany, accompanied by intense bombing and the destruction of German cities and homes including his own, together with the seemingly countless numbers of civilian refugees seeking shelter and food. Through it all, Jünger continues his reading, including that of the Bible, his book collecting and visits to antiquarian booksellers when possible, and his chats with various literary figures in Paris and, at times, in Germany.

Most of the editions of Jünger's *Journals*, including the recent English-language translation, begin with his posting to occupied Paris in February 1941, omitting his participation in the German invasion of France in May 1940, during which time he had watched German soldiers lowering bottles of Burgundy wine, looted from the upper floors of houses in Sedan. "I snatched one in mid-air," he wrote, "like a fish snapping at bait: a Châteauneuf-du-Pape 1937," a comment that Julian Jackson notes had been omitted when *Gärten und Strassen*, his earlier diaries, had been first published in 1942 and was included only after the war.[31]

During his stay in Paris, Jünger met painters including Georges Braque and Pablo Picasso, as well as literary figures such as Louis-Ferdinand Céline and Jean Cocteau, all of whom figure in his *Journals*, which reflect a view of a Paris that had become a tourism mecca during the late nineteenth and early twentieth centuries.[32] For many in Germany, an appreciation of French culture in general and Paris in particular, even if in some ways seen as decadent, reflected a self-image of sophistication in which they could take pride. This perspective was reflected in the picture books edited by Heinrich Hoffmann, Hitler's official photographer, *Mit Hitler im Westen*, an album of the German victory in the West in 1940, and *Mit Hitler in Polen*, a parallel account of their 1939 defeat of Poland. While Hoffmann's book on the West included photos of several tourist sites in France that represented French culture, this was not true of *Mit Hitler in Polen*, with the possible exception of the old city of Gdansk (Danzig), which was considered a German city anyway. German soldiers stationed in occupied France were encouraged to learn French, whereas those on duty in Poland were said to have less need to know the local language.[33] Jünger shared this feeling of sophistication in his appreciation of French culture. As Torrie noted in a comment on an earlier version of this essay, in his view of France as the "other," "he never quite saw it as his equal, for Jünger was always superior." Paris and France were viewed as feminine, whereas he was masculine; they represented the past, he and the Germans the present and the future.[34] In an essay about the *Journals* published in 1993, Richard Griffiths noted that Jünger's interest in French literature was centered on the later nineteenth century, in particular fin-de-siècle poets and novelists.[35] Although Jünger came to Paris in 1941 as a soldier, many of his activities there, not least of which were his solitary strolls through the city, were those of a tourist. His predilection for the writers of the fin-de-siècle years is of interest in placing him, for all his idiosyncrasies, into a broader context of the emergence of Paris as a tourist attraction at that time.

To Jünger, writing in May 1941, Paris was the citadel of a grand style of life and ideas, transmitted through the centuries. Expressing a romanticized nostalgia for a unspecified time in the past, he described Paris as "a capital, symbol and fortress of an ancient tradition of heightened life and unifying ideas, which nations especially lack nowadays."[36] More than a year later, reflecting on an afternoon's walk with a female friend through Paris, from l'Étoile along the rue du Faubourg Saint-Honoré and ending at the Place du Tertre and the Sacré-Cœur Cathedral in the Montmartre section, he wrote: "The city has become my second spiritual home and represents more and more strongly the essence of what I love and cherish about ancient culture."[37]

At the same time, Jünger was aware of the "shafts of glaring looks" with which he was sometimes viewed by locals as he wandered in uniform through the city's streets and byways.[38] Paris, however, remained for Jünger a kind of glorious past, to be assimilated from a position of power. Summarizing the *Journals*, Griffiths wrote:

> Junger's attitudes epitomize those of many of the old Wehrmacht, serving Germany in war, suspicious of the new forces that were ruling their country, disapproving but subservient. Only with the imminent prospect of defeat and chaos did real distress visit Junger; by 1944 his diaries are far from the insouciance of his arrival in Paris in 1941.[39]

Introspection, Virility, and Politics

Much of the material in the *Journals* is introspective, with Jünger addressing his innermost thoughts and dreams. Snakes appear with some frequency, for example, in the entry of July 13, 1943, where during a restless night disturbed by air raid sirens in Paris, he recalls having dreamt of dark black snakes devouring more brightly colored ones. In the *Journal* entry, he linked snakes back to primal forces incarnating life and death, and good and evil. This connection, he maintained, was the reason people fear the sight of a snake, "almost stronger than the sight of sexual organs, with which there is also a connection."[40] Following a conversation with the "Doctoresse," the name that Jünger used for Sophie Ravoux, a pediatrician, with whom he was intimate and had an affair in Paris, he described his own manner of thinking as "atomistically by osmosis and filtration of the smallest particles of thoughts."[41] His thought process, he explained, ran not according to principles of cause and effect but rather at the "level" of the vowels of a sentence, on the molecular level. "This explains [he wrote] why I know people who couldn't help becoming my friends, even through dreams."[42] Addressing Eros and sexual organs, Jünger added that he wished to study the connections between language and physique. Colors also had spiritual values, "Just as green and red are part of white, higher entities are polarized in intellectual couples—as is the universe into blue and red."[43]

Given his own at times tense relations with the Nazi authorities, Jünger often wrote elliptically to avoid potential trouble and frequently used pseudonyms for the people about whom he was writing. Ravoux was the "Doctoresse." His wife, Gretha, appears as "Perpetua," an apt nickname as Neaman points out, in that it alluded to the women who did household chores in Catholic monasteries, and Gretha was sensitive to the fact that she was left maintaining the household, amid increasing Allied bombings in Germany as the war went on, while her husband enjoyed the delights of Paris.[44] Hitler was "Kniébolo," a choice of names not entirely clear, although it has been suggested that it came from "*knebelnder Diabolus*," or "repressive devil."[45]

A quality that Jünger admired in "Charmille," another pseudonym for Ravoux, was her "sense of freedom, which is evident in the shape of her forehead." There were, he maintained, individuals who "know by instinct what freedom is" and who "belong to the race of the falcon or the eagle."[46] He referred nostalgically to the clandestine meeting of "national revolutionaries" at Eichhof in Germany in 1929, adding that the "Munich version—the shallowest of them all," in other words, the Nazi movement, "had now succeeded in the shoddiest possible way."[47] In August 1943, he described his political views as a combination of Guelph (relating to the medieval supporters of the Pope against the Holy Roman Emperor), Prussian, *Gross-Deutscher* (in support of a Greater Germany including Austria), European, and citizen of the world "all at once." As he put it, "My political core is like a clock with cog wheels that work against each other." However, he added: "Yet, when I look at the face of the clock, I could imagine a noon when all these identities coincide."[48]

What is clear is that Jünger was uncomfortable with the liberal, pluralistic, and what he saw as regimented social order that he believed characterized the direction of world history in the late nineteenth and early twentieth centuries. Influenced by his own predilections for the culture of the Wandervogel and his subsequent experiences during the First World War, the picture of Jünger's political views that emerges in his *Journals* is of a highly chivalric and military elitist imagery in which a small number of bold idealists, for lack of a better term, struggle against *demos* and technocracy, democracy and technicians, whom he saw as destroying the soul of an older more virile European society. Writing while back home in Kirchhorst on November 6, 1944, following the expulsion of the Germans from France and walking around viewing the destruction wrought by the Allied bombs in Germany, he observed:

> As I walked, I thought about the cursory style of contemporary thinkers, the way they pronounce judgment on ideas and symbols that people have been working on and creating for millennia. In so doing they are unaware of their own place in the universe, and of that little bit of destructive work allocated to them by the world spirit.[49]

He went on to criticize "the old liberals, Dadaists, and free-thinkers, as they begin to moralize at the end of a life devoted to the destruction of the old guard and the undermining of order." Jünger then referred to Fyodor Dostoevsky's novel *The Demons*, in which the sons of Stepan Trofimovich "are encouraged to scorn anything that had formerly been considered fundamental." Having destroyed their father, these "young conservatives," now sensing "the new elemental power" of "the *demos*," are then dragged to their deaths. In the ensuing chaos, "only the nihilist retains his fearsome power." Jünger mentions Paul von Hindenburg, and the destruction of the conservatives by the Nazis is clearly implied.[50] He leaves the impression of a longing for the old European knighthood embodying heroism, virility, and a militaristic sense of honor. Jünger's view of the Nazis was hostile, if not outright contemptuous, and he was aware that he needed to be careful in his writing, lest his *Journals* fall into the wrong hands. It was as if, in his view, the Nazis, their militarism notwithstanding, had debased the older nobility of knighthood.

A Detached Witness of a Brutal Regime

In his study of Jünger, Allan Mitchell notes (as has Torrie more recently) that the *Journals* are highly idiosyncratic and that the diarist "seems to slouch through the city, imperturbable, protected by a thick emotional carapace that enabled him to maintain his habitual aloofness."[51] There is much that Jünger omits, Mitchell continues, particularly in regard to suffering. Mitchell notes that Jünger's mentions of the Allied bombings in Paris say little about those killed or displaced. He made few comments about the fate of the Jews, though he did write about feeling "embarrassed to be in uniform" when for the first time he saw the yellow star being worn by "three young girls" on the rue Royale in June 1942.[52] As Mitchell notes, however, Jünger wrote little about the extensive deportations.[53] In his recent book about the German soldiers in occupied Paris, Bernd Wegner points out that Jünger wrote frequently about the Allied bombings in the city but with his "stylized habit of commenting laconically on the terrible [events]."[54]

There are also some discrepancies in his account of his own role in the execution of a German charged with desertion in 1941. Torrie cites Felix Krömer's argument that Jünger may have revised his entry of

May 29, 1941, changing his original account in the original unpublished version, where Jünger described himself as having led a firing squad in an execution of the soldier, to a version in the published account of his having been an unwilling participant with the firing squad led by a higher officer.[55] In another sequence of events described by Torrie, Jünger expressed fear that Hitler's ordering of the extensive killing of hostages as reprisals for Resistance attacks could lead to a longstanding, if not permanent, enmity between the French and the Germans. The assassination of Karl Friedrich Hotz, the German field commander of the city of Nantes, in October 1941, led to Hitler's order to kill 100–150 hostages, later reduced to 50–100, as reprisal. In a secret report prepared by Jünger for his commanding officer, General Otto von Stülpnagel, Torrie notes that Jünger expressed fear that such reprisals might enflame relations not only between the Occupation authorities and the local population but also between the French and German people as a whole.[56]

Jünger may well have disapproved of the Nazis and their racial policies, especially as the war turned increasingly against Germany and disaster loomed, but he kept this to himself, possibly seeking some sort of vindication in a postwar and post-Nazi world. In a study of the Germans in occupied France, Ahlrich Meyer noted that the quotidian bureaucratic activities of Germans such as Jünger and Gerhard Heller, the latter in charge of literature for the German *Propagandastaffel* in Paris, combined with the attractions of Paris, enabled them to avert their gazes from the German Occupation policy in France that dictated privations for most of the French and the rounding up of Jews to be sent to the extermination camps, as well as the losses of both soldiers and civilians in the war against the Soviet Union.[57]

Aware of the plight of the Jews in Nazi-occupied Europe, Jünger wrote in April 1943 of the "horror" he felt upon hearing of the shooting of Jews, adding that the shooting was soon to be replaced by gassing.[58] Six months later, he wrote of the gassing and shooting of Jews in the Lodz ghetto. Crematoria were built near the ghetto, and victims were taken there in vehicles designed so their exhaust fumes "were piped into the interior so that they become death chambers."[59] Jünger added: "This is the landscape that reveals Kniébolo's nature, and which not even Dostoyevsky could have predicted."[60] Despite his not always disguised loathing of the Nazis, however, he argued that assassinations "change little and improve nothing," and remained aloof from the plot of July 1944 against Hitler.[61] Although not involved in the conspiracy, he appears to have had advance knowledge of it and he was summarily dismissed from the army.[62] Four months later he learned that his son Ernst Jr. had been killed in action in Italy while on duty with a penal battalion after having been court-martialed for what had been termed "subversive" talk.[63] Aware of the many executions at Mont-Valérien, not far from Paris, of French resisters and German soldiers found guilty of desertion, Jünger again described the bloodshed, in the words of Wegner, as a "distanced observer."[64]

Postwar Successes

As the Allies approached Paris, Jünger checked out of the Hotel Raphael on August 14, 1944.[65] He survived the war and had a successful postwar career as a writer. His eighteen-volume *Sämtliche Werke* (*Complete Works*) were published (Stuttgart: Klett-Cotta) 1978–1983, and he was invited to speak at the Verdun Memorial in 1984 in the presence of French president François Mitterrand and West German chancellor Helmut Kohl. On the occasion of his 100th birthday in March 1995, Kohl and German president Roman Herzog defied snow and windy cold weather to attend a celebration for him in Wilflingen, a village in Upper Swabia, where he was living.[66] Following his death in 1998, his house in Wilflingen was turned into a museum. A society was established to collect and promote Jünger's work, together with those of his younger brother Friedrich, a poet, novelist, and essayist.[67]

Honored and accepted into French and German society in the later twentieth century, Jünger remains, however, a figure of controversy as a consequence of his ideals and his service to Nazi Germany during the Second World War. As Richard Vinen wrote, "Jünger's opposition to Nazism seems mainly to have been confined to the pages of his diary and to private conversations."[68] Writing about French artists and intellectuals under the Nazi Occupation, Frederic Spotts described Jünger:

Renowned for his cold, steely demeanour, he looked at the world with gimlet-eyed detachment. Hitler, for example, he regarded not so much as monstrous as ridiculous and 'a man with no sense of refined cuisine.'[69]

Adding that Jünger had expressed shock at seeing Jews wearing the yellow star and also witnessing a roundup of Jews, Spotts adds: "Shock! Where had he been since Hitler came to power? Otherwise he took no notice of arrests, executions or deportations." Jünger, he concluded, "was typical of the fun-loving Germans in Paris, untypical only in the sophistication of his artistic and gastronomic tastes."[70]

In her study of German soldiers during the Occupation, Torrie writes that in his *Journals*, published after the war (she reminds the reader): "Jünger interpreted the regime's brutality as the work of Hitler and his henchmen, external to himself."[71] As the Resistance grew and German killings of hostages, at Hitler's order, increased in February 1942, General von Stülpnagel, who had commanded the Wehrmacht in occupied France and opposed the killing of hostages, resigned. Jünger, Torrie continues, was part of the hostage-killing machine.

> For Jünger, publishing after the war, von Stülpnagel and his staff had served the role of brakes—they were the only people able to keep German leaders and French collaborators from working the bellows together to fan the flames of hatred. It had been essential that they act in secret, however, for any "appearance of humanity" would have given them away. Even after 1945, Jünger refused, or was unable, to see the extent to which von Stülpnagel, and by extension, he himself, were implicated in the crimes of the Nazi regime.[72]

Jünger's postwar view of von Stülpnagel and his staff, including himself, as brakes mitigating the evils of the Nazi state has parallels with the retrospective "sword and shield" argument in France, which held that Marshal Philippe Pétain and the Vichy government had acted as a shield protecting the French from worse German exactions while General Charles de Gaulle had represented the sword, ready to strike when the time was right.[73]

Addressing the French who collaborated with Germany during the war in his 1972 book on Vichy France, Robert Paxton, who also strongly critiqued the postwar "sword and shield" argument in France, concluded:

> Even Frenchmen of the best intentions, faced with the harsh alternative of doing one's job, whose risks were moral and abstract, or practicing civil disobedience, whose risks were material and immediate, went on doing the job. The same may be said of the German occupiers. Many of them were "good Germans," men of cultivation, confident that their country's success outweighed a few moral blemishes, dutifully fulfilling some minor blameless function in a regime whose cumulative effect was brutish.[74]

Ernst Jünger most evidently was one of the Germans who, whatever his private feelings about Hitler and the Nazis, "went on doing the job." Summing up his review of the *Journals*, Alex Colville writes that Jünger:

> paints himself as the detached botanist-scholar, determined to survive and help the world recover in peacetime. For him, the best way to avoid being sucked into the vortex of violence was to disconnect from emotion and group mentalities: to feel nothing and be on no one's side, only bearing witness.[75]

Jünger, however, as Colville adds, "tweaked reality to create this image of detachment." Whatever his private thoughts, he served Hitler and the Nazi state through his work censoring letters and newspapers in Paris. He wrote little about his extramarital affair in Paris. Neither, however, did he picture himself as a hero, "omitting how he passed on to Jews information of upcoming deportations, buying them time to escape."[76] As Paxton concludes, readers would prefer to identify with the Resistance rather than the types he described above. Jünger may have sought to disconnect from emotion, as Colville wrote, but undoubtedly he had feelings and made choices. Enjoying a sense of "frisson," to use Torrie's term, while dining well at the Tour d'Argent restaurant, and gazing down at the hungry civilians in the buildings below was the choice Jünger made.[77] Would Paxton or his readers have behaved differently in similar circumstances? How would one behave in a similar situation today?

The Limits of Jünger's Uniqueness

Jünger's work is that of a cultured and literary person in service to a brutal regime. Concluding her review of Jünger's *Journals* in H-France, Torrie writes: "If his writing can be taken to represent anyone at all beyond himself, it is only a very small cadre of highly educated officers in Paris."[78] Although unusual because of the erudition with which he wrote, on a broader level, Jünger's experiences in occupied France were shared by many others among the German forces. An average 2,910 German military personnel signed up for group tours of Paris organized by the Wehrmacht from October 9 through December 29, 1940, a figure that would total more than 800,000 for the period from July 1940 through April 1941, as claimed by a German-language tourism guide to Paris in 1941.[79] Sexual tourism involving nightclubs and even casual encounters, as Jünger relates in having met a woman in a movie theater in 1941, were not uncommon in occupied France. It was following this meeting that he commented to the effect that Paris had been founded at the altar of Venus.[80] His affair with Sophie Ravoux has already been mentioned. In a variety of circumstances, 200,000 babies were born to local women in France with German fathers during the Occupation.[81]

None of this detracts from the uniqueness of Jünger's erudition and style except to say that he was hardly alone in enjoying the pleasures of occupied Paris, even if he described them in terms that were exceptional. He may well have best summarized his *Journals* in describing—not joyfully—his sense of power while dining at the Tour d'Argent and gazing down on the suffering Parisians.[82] His fine dining tastes, however, were very much in contrast to the rustic dining motifs promoted by Nazi ideology from Hitler down in Germany.[83] Ironically, perhaps, the sense of power he described was very much in line with the power perspectives promoted by the Nazis, especially when they had the opportunity to defeat and dominate other peoples, as in the case of France in 1940. Jünger's expression, however, of the power he felt as he dined in the top restaurants, while aware of the food privations in occupied Paris and the stated embarrassment he felt as a German officer seeing Parisian Jews wearing the yellow star, made him very much an exception among the German chroniclers of life in occupied France.[84] It would be simple to say that for Jünger, the suffering French civilians upon whom he gazed from his perch at the Tour d'Argent during the Occupation were the "others" but in reality, it appears more likely that for him, the "others" were virtually everyone who did not share his table at the Tour d'Argent.

In a book about the nature of war in general, Margaret MacMillan suggests that while war is essentially fighting and killing, it is "intimately bound up with what it means to be human."[85] Indeed, the tens of thousands of tours of occupied Paris offered by the German military command to their Occupation troops undoubtedly helped humanize the war for many of them, as did Jünger's experiences for him, even if they, unlike Jünger, did not express it as eloquently as did he, nor get to dine in the Tour d'Argent.[86]

Conclusion: A Subject of Continuing Relevance

Jünger remains a subject of interest, perhaps increasingly so in the English-language world (see the Google counts in the appendix), as well as to marginal political groups in France. As a postscript to this chapter, one could speculate that he might well have found an acceptable table-mate at the Tour d'Argent in the person of Alain de Benoist, one of the major theoreticians of France's *Nouvelle Droite*, or New Right, during the 1970s and in the years since. A prominent member of *GRECE* (*Groupement d'études et de recherche pour la civilisation européenne*), de Benoist now edits two journals, *Nouvelle École*, since 1968, and *Krisis*, since 1988. I had a chance to interview him in 1989 when he explained his concept of a Europe of the "*ethnies*" (ethnicities), a continent within which, for example, the Bretons and the Occitans, would have their own states, ending what he called the artificial centralized state of France that had existed since the 1789 Revolution. A new neopagan Europe would form based on these states in what he called an ethno-pluralism, anti-Christian, anti-liberal, and decidedly anti-American world.[87] De Benoist was especially drawn to the National Bolshevism of interwar Germany and more recently to the *gilets jaunes*, or Yellow Vests in France.[88] His ideas have also influenced the *Identitaire* movement in recent France.[89] Not surprisingly, he has been attracted to some of the ideas espoused by Jünger. In 1996, shortly after Jünger's centennial birthday, when he was receiving at least some accolades, de Benoist devoted an entire issue of *Nouvelle École* to him. Looking back in an article titled "Ernst Jünger & the French New Right," in 2010, de Benoist wrote: "The editorial that I signed there began with these words: 'The 20th century is the century when the Nobel Prize was not given to Ernst Jünger. It is as good a way to define it as any other.'"[90] So, Jünger is still alive and relevant for some. The rise of the *Front National*, now the *Rassemblement National*, in France and the *Alternative für Deutschland*, in Germany may be a reminder of William Faulkner's saying: "The past is never dead. It's not even past."[91]

Appendix

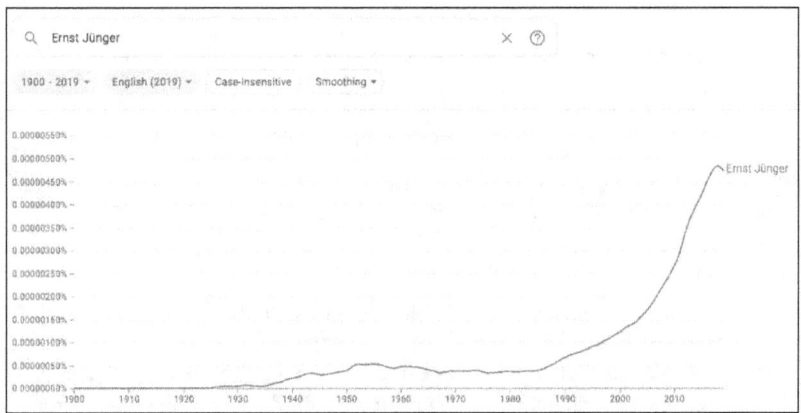

Google Books Ngram Viewer. Frequency of references to "Ernst Jünger" in English-language books, 1900-2019.

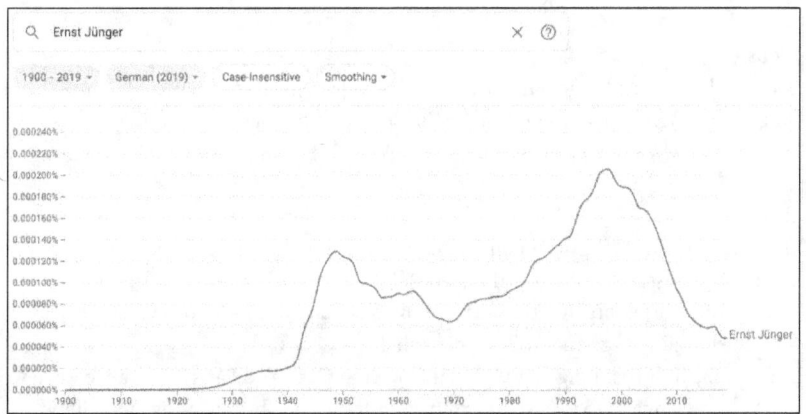

Google Books Ngram Viewer. Frequency of references to "Ernst Jünger" in German-language books, 1900–2019.

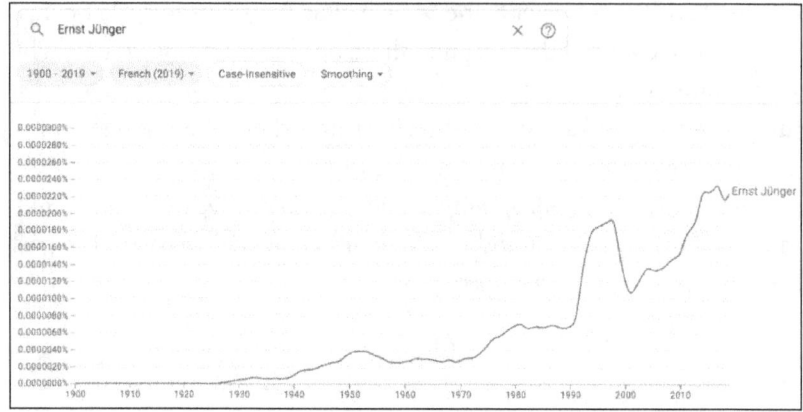

Google Books Ngram Viewer. Frequency of references to "Ernst Jünger" in French-language books, 1900–2019.

Bibliography

Interviews

Author's interview with Alain de Benoist, Paris, December 3, 1989.

Newspapers

Binder, David. "Ernst Junger, Contradictory German Author Who Wrote About War, Is Dead at 102," New York Times (February 18, 1998): D, 22.

Blin, Simon. "Alain de Benoist, faiseur de droits," Libération (November 28, 2019); <https://www.liberation.fr/debats/2019/11/28/alain-de-benoist-faiseur-de-droites_1766127/>, retrieved November 29, 2019.

Dorza, Th. "Im Calvados: Impressionen aus der Normandie," Pariser Zeitung (August 8, 1944): 6.

Websites

Ernst und Friedrich Jünger Gesellschaft e.V., <https://juenger-gesellschaft.com>.

Jünger-Haus Wilflingen. Gedenkstätte für Ernst und Friedrich Georg Jünger; <https://www.juenger-haus.de>.

Reviews

Gordon, Bertram M. "Gordon on Jünger. A German Officer in Occupied Paris," H-Diplo Essay No. 171 (April 19, 2019), URL: http://tiny.cc/E171; also <https://networks.h-net.org/node/28443/discussions/4007640/h-diplo-review-essay-171-gordon-jünger-german-officer-occupied>.

Torrie, Julia S. "Ernst Jünger, A German Officer in Occupied Paris," H-France Review Vol. 20 (January 2020), No. 15; <https://h-france.net/h-france-review-volume-20-2020/>, retrieved February 5, 2020.

Books and Articles

Bieber, Konrad. "Ernst Jünger," in Bertram M. Gordon, ed., Historical Dictionary of World War II France: The Occupation, Vichy, and the Resistance. Westport, CT: Greenwood Press, 1998: 203–204.

Bouron, Samuel. "Un militantisme à deux faces: Stratégie de communication et politique de formation des Jeunesses identitaires," Agone 54, 2 (2014): 45–72.

Buisson, Patrick. 1940–1945 Années érotiques: Vichy ou les infortunes de la vertu. Paris: Albin Michel, 2008.

Colville, Alex. "Ernst Jünger—reluctant captain of the Wehrmacht," The Spectator (January 19, 2019); <https://www.spectator.co.uk/2019/01/ernst-junger-reluctan-captain-of-the-wehrmacht/>, retrieved February 1, 2020.

de Benoist, Alain. "Ernst Jünger & the French New Right," trans. by Greg Johnson. Counter-Currents Publishing (July 21, 2010); <https://www.counter-currents.com/2010/07/ernst-junger-and-the-french-new-right/>, retrieved February 14, 2020.

Desquesnes, Rémy. Normandy 1944: the Invasion, the Battle, Everyday Life, trans. by John Lee. Rennes: Éditions Ouest-France, 1993.

Dufay, François. "Ernst Jünger—Un occupant si korrekt," L'Express (February 14, 2008), 77; <https://www.lexpress.fr/informations/ernst-junger-un-occupant-si-korrekt_721403.html. Retrieved May 25, 2021.

Gordon, Bertram M. "Fascism, the Neo-Right and Gastronomy: A Case in the Theory of the Social Engineering of Taste," *Taste: Proceedings of the Oxford Symposium on Food and Cookery, 1987*. London: Prospect Books, Ltd., 1988, 82–97.

———. "'To Live in France': The Confluence of Tourism, Memory, Migration and War," in Sabine Marschall, ed., *Memory, Migration and Travel*. Abingdon, UK: Routledge, 2018, 104–124.

———. *War Tourism: Second World War France from Defeat and Occupation to the Creation of Heritage*. Ithaca, NY: Cornell University Press, 2018.

Griffiths, Richard. "A certain idea of France: Ernst Jünger's Paris Diaries 1941–44," Journal of European Studies, 23 (1993): 101–120.

Heller, Gerhard. Un Allemand à Paris, 1940–1944. Paris: Éditions du Seuil, 1981.

Jünger, Ernst. A German Officer in Occupied Paris: The War Journals, 1941–1945. Foreword by Elliot Neaman, translated by Thomas H. Hansen and Abby J. Hansen. New York: Columbia University Press, 2019.

———. Gärten und Strassen. Berlin: E. S. Mittler & Sohn, 1942.

Krob, Melanie Gordon. "Paris through enemy eyes: the Wehrmacht in Paris 1940–1944," Journal of European Studies 31:1 (2001): 3–28.

Jackson, Julian. France: The Dark Years 1940–1944. Oxford: Oxford University Press, 2001.

Lehrer, Steven. Wartime Sites in Paris 1939–1945. New York: SF Tafel, 2013.

Marty, Alan T. A Walking Tour of Occupied Paris: The Germans and Their Collaborators. Unpublished manuscript, ©2007, 2013.

Meyer, Ahlrich. L'occupation allemande en France, translated from the German by Pascale Hervieux, Florence Lecanu, and Nicole Taubes. Paris: Privat, 2002.

Mitchell, Allan. The Devil's Captain: Ernst Jünger in Nazi Paris, 1941–1944. New York and Oxford: Berghahn Books, 2011.

Neaman, Elliot Y. A Dubious Past: Ernst Jünger and the Politics of Literature after Nazism. Berkeley, Los Angeles, and London: University of California Press, 1999.

Paxton, Robert O. Vichy France: Old Guard and New Order, 1940–1944. New York: Alfred A. Knopf, 1972.

Riding, Alan. And the Show Went On: Cultural Life in Nazi-Occupied Paris. New York: Alfred A. Knopf, 2010.

Rosbottom, Ronald C. When Paris Went Dark: The City of Light Under German Occupation, 1940–1944. New York, Boston, London: Back Bay Books, Little, Brown and Co., 2014.

Rousso, Henry. La dernière catastrophe: L'histoire, le present, le contemporaine. Paris: Gallimard, 2012.

Rousso, Henry. The Vichy Syndrome: History and Memory in France since 1944, trans. by Arthur Goldhammer. Cambridge, MA: Harvard University Press, 1991.

Spotts, Frederic. The Shameful Peace: How French Artists and Intellectuals Survived the Nazi Occupation. New Haven, CN, and London: Yale University Press, 2008.

Torrie, Julia S. German Soldiers and the Occupation of France 1940–1944. Cambridge: Cambridge University Press, 2018.

Vinen, Richard. The Unfree French: Life under the Occupation. London: Penguin, 2006.

Wegner, Bernd. Das deutsche Paris: Der Blick der Besatzer 1940–1944. Paderborn: Ferdinand Schöningh, 2019.

Notes

1. Ernst Jünger, *A German Officer in Occupied Paris: The War Journals, 1941–1945* (New York: Columbia University Press, 2019), entry of July 4, 1942, 73. Jünger's statement about the feeling of power while dining at the Tour d'Argent is also cited by Julia S. Torrie, *German Soldiers and the Occupation of France 1940–1944* (Cambridge: Cambridge University Press, 2018), 81; especially note 86 which references additional citations related to his comment about dining in the Tour d'Argent. See also Bernd Wegner, *Das deutsche Paris: Der Blick der Besatzer 1940–1944* (Paderborn: Ferdinand Schöningh, 2019), 114.

2. Patrick Buisson, *1940–1945 Années érotiques: Vichy ou les infortunes de la vertu* (Paris: Albin Michel, 2008), 412–413.

3. "H-Diplo Review Essay 171-Gordon on "Jünger, A German Officer in Occupied Paris: The War Journals, 1941–1945." Foreword by Elliot Neaman, translated by Thomas H. Hansen and Abby J. Hansen (New York: Columbia University Press, 2019), H-Diplo Essay No. 171 (April 19, 2019), URL: http://tiny.cc/E171; also <https://networks.h-net.org/node/28443/discussions/4007640/h-diplo-review-essay-171-gordon-jünger-german-officer-occupied>.

4. Julia S. Torrie, H-France Review Vol. 20 (January 2020), No. 15; *Ernst Jünger, A German Officer in Occupied Paris: The War Journals, 1941–1945.* Foreword by Elliot Neaman. Translated by Thomas S. Hansen and Abby J. Hansen. New York:

Columbia University Press, 2019; <https://h-france.net/h-france-review-volume-20-2020/>, retrieved February 5, 2020.
5. Ernst Jünger, *A German Officer in Occupied Paris: The War Journals, 1941–1945*. Foreword by Elliot Neaman, translated by Thomas H. Hansen and Abby J. Hansen (New York: Columbia University Press, 2019).
6. Allan Mitchell, *The Devil's Captain: Ernst Jünger in Nazi Paris, 1941–1944* (New York and Oxford: Berghahn Books, 2011), 22.
7. Ibid., 89. See also Elliot Y. Neaman, Foreword, *Jünger, The War Journals, 1941–1945*, x–xi; and Steven Lehrer, *Wartime Sites in Paris 1939–1945* (New York: SF Tafel Publishers, 2013), 210.
8. Alex Colville, "Ernst Jünger—reluctant captain of the Wehrmacht," *The Spectator* (January 19, 2019); <https://www.spectator.co.uk/2019/01/ernst-junger-reluctant-captain-of-the-wehrmacht/>, retrieved February 1, 2020.
9. Elliot Y. Neaman, Foreword, Jünger, *The War Journals, 1941–1945*, xii.
10. Ibid., xii-xiii.
11. Ibid., xiv.
12. Lehrer, *Wartime Sites in Paris 1939–1945*, 211.
13. Jünger, *The War Journals, 1941–1945*, May 30, 1941, 18.
14. Wegner, *Das deutsche Paris*, 136. On Jünger and the salon culture of Paris, especially that around Florence Gould, see also Alan Riding, *And the Show Went On: Cultural Life in Nazi-Occupied Paris* (New York: Alfred A. Knopf, 2010), 255–268.
15. Torrie, H-France Review Vol. 20, No. 15; Ernst Jünger, *A German Officer in Occupied Paris: The War Journals, 1941–1945*. Foreword by Elliot Neaman. Translated by Thomas S. Hansen and Abby J. Hansen. New York: Columbia University Press, 2019); <https://h-france.net/h-france-review-volume-20-2020/>, retrieved February 5, 2020. See also Elliot Y. Neaman, *A Dubious Past: Ernst Jünger and the Politics of Literature after Nazism* (Berkeley, Los Angeles, and London: University of California Press, 1999), 6.
16. See Vanessa R. Schwartz, "Walter Benjamin for Historians," *American Historical Review*, 106, no. 5 (December 2001): 1736; cited in Bertram M. Gordon, *War Tourism: Second World War France from Defeat and Occupation to the Creation of Heritage* (Ithaca, NY: Cornell University Press, 2018), 99.
17. Charles L. Robertson, *They Stayed: Americans in Paris Under the German Occupation*, VI, 15; manuscript in preparation; cited in Alan T. Marty, "A Walking Tour of Occupied Paris: The Germans and Their Collaborators" (unpublished manuscript, ©2007, 2013), 48.
18. Neaman, foreword, Jünger, *The War Journals, 1941–1945*, xvi.
19. Melanie Gordon Krob, "Paris through enemy eyes: the Wehrmacht in Paris 1940–1944," *Journal of European Studies*, 31:1 (2001), 9.
20. Jünger, *Gärten und Strassen* (Berlin: E. S. Mittler & Sohn, 1942).
21. François Dufay, "Ernst Jünger—Un occupant si korrekt," *L'Express* (February 14, 2008), 77; <https://www.lexpress.fr/informations/ernst-junger-un-occupant-si-korrekt_721403.html. Retrieved May 25, 2021.

22. Jünger, *The War Journals, 1941–1945*, December 8, 1941, 36.
23. Jünger, *The War Journals, 1941–1945*, May 8, 1944, 319.
24. *L'Illustration*, May 23, 1943, cited in Rémy Desquesnes, *Normandy 1944: the Invasion, the Battle, Everyday Life*, trans. by John Lee (Éditions Ouest-France, 1993) 22–23. For German Field Marshal Erwin Rommel's repeated visits to Normandy and his urgent requests for more extensive building of the Atlantic Wall, see Tonie and Valmai Holt, *The Visitor's Guide to Normandy Landing Beaches Memorials and Museums* (Ashbourne, Derbyshire: Moorland, 1994), 33–34.
25. Jünger, *The War Journals*, 1941–1945, May 8, 1944, 319.
26. Jünger, *The War Journals, 1941–1945*, June 6, 1944, 329.
27. Wegner, *Das deutsche Paris*, 154. Wegner cites Jünger's entry of July 14, 1941.
28. Ibid., 86. Wegner cites Jünger's entry of May 1, 1941.
29. Cited in Mitchell, *The Devil's Captain*, 18. The quotation is taken from a letter by Jünger to Carl Schmitt, June 28, 1941, cited by Heimo Schwilk, *Ernst Jünger*, 381. See Mitchell, 96, chapter 2, note 14. It is not clear which of two books by Schwilk and titled *Ernst Jünger* is meant; see Mitchell, p. 111.
30. Th. Dorza, "Im Calvados: Impressionen aus der Normandie," *Pariser Zeitung*, August 8, 1944, 6.
31. Julian Jackson, *France: The Dark Years 1940–1944* (Oxford: Oxford University Press, 2001), 273.
32. Gordon, *War Tourism*, 20–21.
33. Ibid., 132.
34. Julia S. Torrie, "Comment: Bertram Gordon, 'Dining at the Tour d'Argent in Occupied Paris: Ernst Jünger, Power, and the Othering of Paris,'" for the conference on Nazi Germany and Occupied France, Center for Basque Studies, University of Nevada, Reno, March 6, 2020.
35. Richard Griffiths, "A certain idea of France: Ernst Jünger's Paris Diaries 1941–44," *Journal of European Studies*, 23 (1993), 107.
36. Jünger, *The War Journals, 1941–1945*, May 30, 1941, 15.
37. Jünger, *The War Journals, 1941–1945*, September 18, 1942, 98.
38. Jünger, *The War Journals, 1941–1945*, 18 August 18, 1942, 89, and September 29, 1943, 259.
39. Griffiths, "A certain idea of France," 102–103.
40. Jünger, *The War Journals, 1941–1945*, July 13, 1943, 220.
41. Neaman, foreword, Jünger, *The War Journals, 1941–1945*, xviii. A suggestion has been made that through Sophie Ravoux's husband, Jünger may have had contact with the French Resistance; see "Dandy Club," Review of Tobias Wimbauer, ed., *Ernst Jünger in Paris. Ernst Jünger, Sophie Ravoux, die Burgunderszene und eine Hinrichtung* (Hagen-Berchem: Eisenhut Verlag, 2011); <https://www.dandy-club.com/2011/10/ernst-junger-als-pariser-dandy.html>, retrieved February 16, 2020. By coincidence, the Ravoux couple inhabited an apartment at 72 rue du Cherche Midi in Paris (see Mitchell, *Ernst Jünger in Nazi Paris*, 84), a building in which my wife, Suzanne, and I rented an apartment during the 1990s.

42. Jünger, *The War Journals, 1941–1945*, January 22, 1944, 292.
43. Ibid., 293.
44. Neaman, foreword, Jünger, *The War Journals, 1941–1945*, xviii–xix.
45. Jünger, *The War Journals, 1941–1945*, 409, footnote 12. See also Mitchell, *The Devil's Captain*, 41.
46. Jünger, *The War Journals, 1941–1945*, December 3, 1941, 34.
47. Jünger, *The War Journals, 1941–1945*, April 19, 1943, 190. For his use of the term "national revolutionaries," see the entry of January 20, 1942, 43.
48. Jünger, *The War Journals, 1941–1945*, August 1, 1943, 229–230.
49. Jünger, *The War Journals, 1941–1945*, November 6, 1944, 356.
50. Ibid.
51. Mitchell, *The Devil's Captain*, 58.
52. Jünger, *The War Journals, 1941–1945*, June 7, 1942, 356.
53. Mitchell, *The Devil's Captain*, 58.
54. Wegner, *Das deutsche Paris*, 101; see also 224, note 36.
55. Torrie, H-France Review Vol. 20, No. 15; *Ernst Jünger, A German Officer in Occupied Paris: The War Journals, 1941–1945*. Foreword by Elliot Neaman. Translated by Thomas S. Hansen and Abby J. Hansen. New York: Columbia University Press, 2019); <https://h-france.net/h-france-review-volume-20-2020/>, retrieved February 5, 2020. See also Jünger, *The War Journals, 1941–1945*, May 29, 1941, 14.
56. Torrie, *German Soldiers and the Occupation of France 1940–1944*, 177–179.
57. Ahlrich Meyer, *L'occupation allemande en France*, translated from the German by Pascale Hervieux, Florence Lecanu, and Nicole Taubes (Paris: Privat, 2002), 29. For an example of a postwar self-serving apologia for living the good life in occupied Paris while Germany carried out its belligerent policies, see Gerhard Heller, *Un Allemand à Paris, 1940–1944*, (Paris: Éditions du Seuil, 1981), 168.
58. Jünger, *The War Journals, 1941–1945*, April 21,1943, 190–191.
59. Jünger, *The War Journals, 1941–1945*, October 16, 1943, 267.
60. Ibid.
61. Jünger, *The War Journals, 1941–1945*, July 21, 1944, 336.
62. Konrad Bieber, "Ernst Jünger," in Bertram M. Gordon, ed., *Historical Dictionary of World War II France: The Occupation, Vichy, and the Resistance* (Westport, CT: Greenwood Press, 1998), 203.
63. David Binder, "Ernst Junger, Contradictory German Author Who Wrote About War, Is Dead at 102," *New York Times* (February 18, 1998), section D, 22.
64. Wegner, *Das deutsche Paris*, 175.
65. Alan T. Marty, "A Walking Tour of Occupied Paris: The Germans and Their Collaborators" (unpublished manuscript, ©2007, 2013), 42. See also Riding, *And the Show Went On*, 306.
66. Binder, "Ernst Junger, Contradictory German Author Who Wrote About War, Is Dead at 102."
67. See the museum website, Jünger-Haus Wilflingen. Gedenkstätte für Ernst und Friedrich Georg Jünger; <https://www.juenger-haus.de> and for the Ernst and

Friedrich Jünger Society, the Ernst und Friedrich Jünger Gesellschaft e.V., see <https://juenger-gesellschaft.com>, both retrieved May 30, 2021.

68. Richard Vinen, *The Unfree French: Life under the Occupation* (London: Penguin, 2006), 108.
69. Frederic Spotts, *The Shameful Peace: How French Artists and Intellectuals Survived the Nazi Occupation* (New Haven, CN, and London: Yale University Press, 2008), 31.
70. Ibid., 32.
71. Torrie, *German Soldiers and the Occupation of France 1940–1944*, 185.
72. Ibid.,185.
73. Henry Rousso, *The Vichy Syndrome: History and Memory in France since 1944*, trans. by Arthur Goldhammer (Cambridge, MA: Harvard University Press, 1991), 9–10; and Rousso, *La dernière catastrophe: L'histoire, le present, le contemporaine* (Paris: Gallimard, 2012),182–183. See also Gordon, "Preface," in Gordon, ed., *Historical Dictionary of World War II France*, xvii.
74. Robert O. Paxton, *Vichy France: Old Guard and New Order, 1940–1944* (New York: Alfred A. Knopf, 1972), 383.
75. Alex Colville, "Ernst Jünger—reluctant captain of the Wehrmacht," *The Spectator* (January 19, 2019); <https://www.spectator.co.uk/2019/01/ernst-junger-reluctant-captain-of-the-wehrmacht/>, retrieved February 1, 2020.
76. Ibid.
77. For Jünger's sense of "frisson," see Torrie, *German Soldiers and the Occupation of France 1940–1944*, 81.
78. Julia Torrie, H-France Review Vol. 20 (January 2020), No. 15; *Ernst Jünger, A German Officer in Occupied Paris: The War Journals, 1941–1945*. Foreword by Elliot Neaman. Translated by Thomas S. Hansen and Abby J. Hansen. New York: Columbia University Press, 2019); <https://h-france.net/h-france-review-volume-20-2020/>
79. Gordon, *War Tourism*, 120.
80. Jünger, *The War Journals, 1941–1945*, May 1, 1941, 19.
81. Bertram M. Gordon, "'To Live in France': The Confluence of Tourism, Memory, Migration and War," in Sabine Marschall, ed., *Memory, Migration and Travel* (Abingdon, UK: Routledge, 2018), 113.
82. For a listing of references to the fine dining of Jünger, together with others of his German colleagues in occupied Paris, see Wegner, *Das deutsche Paris*, 111 and 225, note 29.
83. See Bertram M. Gordon, "Fascism, the Neo-Right, and Gastronomy: A Case in the Theory of the Social Engineering of Taste," *Oxford Symposium on Food and Cookery 1987, Taste, Proceedings* (London: Prospect Books, Ltd., 1988), 82–97.
84. See Jünger, *The War Journals, 1941–1945*, July 4, 1942, 72–73.
85. Margaret MacMillan, *War: How Conflict Shaped Us* (New York: Random House, 2020), cited in Dexter Filkins, "What Is It Good For? War has affected society in many ways, both positive and negative," *New York Times Book Review* (November 29, 2020), 8.

86. For a discussion of the humanization of war through tourism, see Gordon, *War Tourism*, 6.
87. Author's interview with Alain de Benoist, Paris, December 3, 1989.
88. Simon Blin, "Alain de Benoist, faiseur de droits," *Libération* (November 28, 2019); <https://www.liberation.fr/debats/2019/11/28/alain-de-benoist-faiseur-de-droites_1766127/>, retrieved November 29, 2019.
89. Samuel Bouron, "Un militantisme à deux faces: Stratégie de communication et politique de formation des Jeunesses identitaires," *Agone* (2014/2), vol. 54, 31.
90. Alain de Benoist, "Ernst Jünger & the French New Right," trans. by Greg Johnson, Counter-Currents Publishing (July 21, 2010); <https://www.counter-currents.com/2010/07/ernst-junger-and-the-french-new-right/>, retrieved February 14, 2020.
91. Scott Horton, "The Past Is Not Past. Or Is It?," Browsings, The Harper's Blog, *Harper's Magazine* (March 24, 2008); <https://harpers.org/blog/2008/03/the-past-is-not-past-or-is-it/>, retrieved February 15, 2020.

CHAPTER 7

"Millions of men in Germany and elsewhere have more than one reason to be ashamed"[1]

Franco-German Commemorative Scripts and the Gurs Camp

SCOTT SOO

The inaugural two-day commemoration of the newly renovated cemetery of the Gurs camp in southwest France involved aspects that might, at first sight, appear to be out of kilter with the site's history. During the official lunch that followed the morning's remembrance ceremony on March 23, 1963, the mayors of Navarrenx, France, and Karlsruhe, Germany, compared the merits of the local salmon of the Béarn to trout from the Black Forest. It was followed by mutual displays of admiration for West German chancellor Konrad Adenauer and French president Charles de Gaulle. And finally, the mayor of Freiburg, Germany presented his French counterpart with an authentic Black Forest clock.[2] But the after-meal speeches were not the only incongruity. The morning's ceremony had involved the inspection of French parachutists, and the following day French officials accompanied the German delegation to a visit of the region's petrol refinery.

If some of the events appear at odds with the camp's history, it should be noted that the organizers had no precedent from which to draw. This was the first time a former "concentration camp"/internment center in France had been the subject of an official Franco-German commemoration. The developing relations between the two countries during this period might thus explain the emphasis on Franco-German friendship and mutual national interests. Aside from political considerations, the event also needed to address the human need to mourn the death and suffering of more than a thousand people who had died through incarceration in the Gurs camp. Commemoration was thereby shaped by both political and social influences. The participation of state authorities was evident in the form and content of commemoration, and the event invariably engaged with the politics of remembrance in France and Germany. At the same time, the impetus of both French and German civic and religious organizations was apparent. Consequently, different, but sometimes interwoven, agendas were at work, which raises the question of what issues were privileged or indeed cast aside as part of the two-day event.

Understanding the commemorative script of the 1963 inaugural event at the Gurs camp constitutes the primary aim of this chapter. Given the transnational character of the commemoration and the development of Franco-German relations, the potential for the emergence of a more universal or indeed proto-European narrative existed. One of the key points in the Karlsruhe mayor's speech that's in this chapter's title seemingly provided a tentative step in this direction through the reference to the shame of millions of men in Germany and elsewhere. However, nuances of this kind were not repeated in the French official's speeches or reflected upon in the French press. Indeed, as this chapter will endeavor to demonstrate, while the German and German-Jewish speeches at the 1963 event internationalized the cause of and response to racial discrimination, they simultaneously fed into a French commemorative framework that represented the camp as an exemplar of Nazi brutality. Although the particular fate of the German Jews in the Gurs camp was acknowledged, the diversity of the camp's internees, their voices, and the circumstances of the camp's creation before the start of the Second World War remained largely absent from the commemorative script.

Commonalities and Specificities of the Gurs Camp

Historians in France were the first to research the postwar history of the French camps by exploring the creation of monuments and early examples of commemoration. Annette Wieviorka's impressive study, *Déportation et Génocide: Entre la Mémoire et l'Oubli*, contains a chapter on commemoration that discusses the ceremonies at Drancy that occurred in 1944, 1946 and 1947. The book also contains brief details of the earliest attempt to construct a monument at the Gurs camp.[3] A follow-up study with Serge Barcellini on the myriad monuments and plaques that were created after the end of the Second World War identified monuments at the camps of Pithiviers in 1957 and Beaune-La-Rolande in 1965.[4] More recently, other scholars have analyzed the commemorative trajectories of Drancy and Rivesaltes over a longer period of time; and my recent article on Gurs has charted the closure process and emergence of a French patriotic commemorative narrative.[5]

In many respects, the Gurs camp was not so dissimilar from the other internment centers created in response to the 1939 exodus of half a million refugees from the Spanish Civil War. As at many other sites, the camp continued to be used by the Vichy regime and the provisional government during the liberation of France. The distinctiveness of Gurs, however, dates back to the Vichy administration's decision to incarcerate German Jews who had been deported from their homes in the autumn of 1940. The result was disastrous. Atrocious conditions, a cold winter, and the frailty of many of the Jewish internees rapidly led to more than 900 deaths. By 1945, the Gurs camp cemetery contained 1,077 graves representing at least seventeen different national backgrounds. It was not only the largest burial ground of any internment camp in France; it also contained the highest number of German-Jewish tombs.[6]

The cemetery and preponderance of German Jewish graves largely explain the distinctiveness of the camp's commemorative trajectory. First, a monument was erected in the late 1940s well before the examples of Pithiviers and Beaune-La-Rolande. Regular and sustained commemorative activities then developed from the early 1960s before any comparable form of activity elsewhere in the country.[7] The political and social dynamics also differed. Annual commemoration began at Gurs partly because of the French state's neglect of the camp cemetery. An eventual solution for the restoration, maintenance and subsequent commemorations of the cemetery emanated from a Jewish organization and the municipal authorities of Karlsruhe in the Federal Republic of Germany.

Significantly, the Gurs camp cemetery became a commemorative focus of Jewish suffering during a period that historians initially characterized as involving silence or indeed the repression of the Holocaust in remembrance practices occurring in France, Germany, and further afield.[8] The study of commemoration at Gurs, therefore, contributes to a more nuanced understanding of Jewish suffering in remembrance narratives of postwar France and Germany. Furthermore, it provides insight into an early, if not the first, example of sustained Franco-German commemoration of a site in France associated with the mass repression and genocide of Jews during the Second World War.

The specificity of Gurs raises the question of whether existing concepts are entirely suitable for understanding the development of commemoration at this site. With its emphasis on the national arena, Pierre Nora's influential concept of *"lieu de mémoire"* or "site of memory" is unable to capture the complex nexus of the local, regional, national, and transnational influences that came to bear on the commemorative transformation of the Gurs camp. A similar emphasis on what might or might not resonate at the national level also appears to influence Barcellini and Wieviorka in their wide-ranging study of Second World War monuments and plaques where Drancy and other camps such as Gurs are characterized as representing *"lieux du souvenir"* or "sites of remembrance."[9]

The focus on *"souvenir,"* or remembrance, certainly broadens our understanding of the complexities involved in the proliferation of plaques, monuments, and other signifiers of deaths from the Second World War in France. It also offers a counterpoint to the top-down and national perspective encapsulated by Nora's concept of a site of memory.[10] From a longer term perspective, the breadth of examples contained in Barcellini and Wieviorka's study can also be viewed as further evidence, if not an additional stage, in the democratization of remembrance practices that developed during the twentieth century. Moreover, as the two historians emphasized, in some cases sites of remembrance could develop into sites of memory.[11] All the same, the framework does not quite correspond to the emergence and development of commemoration at Gurs. This involved a more complex process of local, regional, national and pannational negotiation that neither a top-down or bottom-up approach suggests. In many respects, the Gurs commemorative topography lay at the intersection of the aforementioned processes.

Commemoration at Gurs was partly a result of pressure from non-state organizations and the public wishing to create a fitting place of remembrance. The 1963 event, however, would not have occurred without either Franco-German diplomacy or significant state support from both German and French authorities. In turn, the respective officials were mindful of the widespread attention that the commemoration of an internment/concentration camp in France would attract for this and future commemorative events. Nora's definition of a *lieu de mémoire* involving "any significant entity, whether material or nonmaterial in nature, which by dint of human will or the work of time had become a symbolic element of the memorial heritage of any community" is clearly relevant.[12] But while commemorative activity at Gurs involved processes associated with both sites of memory and sites of remembrance, additional pan-national influences were at work. The French authorities' neglect of the Gurs cemetery was the catalyst for German and German Jewish intervention that was shaped by dynamics in the German city of Karlsruhe. This resulted in the renovation of the Gurs cemetery within a German Jewish aesthetic framework and an annual commemorative event that operated within but also across national remembrance narratives. For the purposes of this study, the Gurs camp is therefore analyzed as a site of transnational commemoration.

Given the transnational background to commemoration at Gurs, the question arises as to whether there was any divergence from practices at former camps in East and West Germany. Early examples of commemoration certainly existed. The German Democratic Republic incorporated the concentration camps into its national commemorative framework from 1959 as examples of communist and antifascist resistance. However, the mass scale of Jewish deaths was elided. In the Federal Republic of Germany, commemorative activity also occurred in the decades after the end of the war, but this was frequently through the impetus of survivors' associations. As in East Germany, the fate of Jews in these camps tended to be obscured through an emphasis on all victims of National Socialism.[13]

Bergen-Belsen appears to have been an exception. In April 1946, on the first anniversary of the camp's liberation, Jewish survivors posted a column with an inscription in English and Hebrew that read

"Israel and the world shall remember thirty thousand Jews exterminated in the concentration camp of Bergen-Belsen at the hands of the murderous Nazis. Earth conceal not the blood shed on thee!" In 1952, a larger monument with a wall of inscriptions was dedicated and similarly evoked the fate of the Jews in the camp. It also alluded to the international scale of the killings with fourteen inscriptions in various languages (the deceased originated from forty different countries) that were, in turn, reinforced through the attendance of representatives from nine European countries and the United States of America.[14] However, regular commemorative activity did not ensue. Instead, Bergen-Belsen was subject to lengthy discussions surrounding French attempts to exhume some of the bodies from the nearby cemetery; Franco-German diplomacy, survivors' associations and religious authorities were involved.[15]

Mass Internment at Gurs

The origins of the Gurs camp date back to the last years of the Third Republic and the intensifying political and social malaise in France. Partly because of its geographical location and partly because of the Republic's claim to be a country of asylum, France had received refugees from Russia, Armenia, Italy, Germany, and Austria across its eastern borders and refugees from the Spanish Civil War in the southwest. By the time the Radical Party came to power under Édouard Daladier in April 1938, xenophobia was intensifying alongside anti-Semitism and anticommunism. The Radicals were acutely aware of the growing threat of war against Germany and of the increasing political polarization of French society. Under these circumstances, the Daladier government endeavored to balance national security with refugee welfare but concentrated more heavily on the former. It was this context that explains the steps taken to intern refugees from the Spanish Civil War. Just one month after taking office, the Daladier government had ordered a survey for potential sites where refugees suspected of being a threat to national security could be interned.[16] A decree on November 12, 1938, permitted the incarceration of "undesirable" foreigners in "special camps."[17] It enabled the interment of foreigners in France from the Third Republic through to the end of the Vichy regime.

With the legislation in place, the Gurs camp was created as part of a vast network of internment centers in response to the mass exodus of close to half a million refugees from the Spanish Civil War. Over the last week of January and first week of February 1939, the French authorities interned 275,000 of the refugees in hastily constructed camps on the beaches of the Mediterranean coast. To relieve overcrowding, a temporary internment center was then constructed at Gurs in six weeks and opened its gates in April 1939.

From the start, French administrators referred to Gurs and the other such sites as either centers or camps through a variety of qualifications of which the most frequent were "accommodation," "concentration," "internment," and "reception." For the French minister of the interior, Albert Sarraut, the concentration camps in France were very much different to the camp system in Germany:

> The Spanish will never be submitted to any harmful regime or to forced labor. Let us repeat that: the camp of Argelès-sur-Mer will not be a penitentiary center but a concentration camp. It is not the same thing.[18]

In practice, correspondence by administrators across France suggests that the terminology was not especially consistent. Even so, exclusion remained the essential rationale of the camps even if the factors driving exclusion changed over time. If national security concerns fueled the treatment of the refugees from the Spanish Civil War under the Third Republic, the anti-Semitism of the Vichy administration resulted in the internment of both foreign and French Jews in the country's camps.[19]

The first internees at Gurs originated from the Spanish Civil War and more specifically were composed of refugees from the Basque Country, Galicia, and the International Brigades. By mid-May, the number had increased to 18,985.[20] During the outbreak of war against Germany, the camp held French nationals accused of communist activity alongside Germans and Jews originating from Germany and the European regions annexed by Nazi Germany. The most tragic episode of the camp, however, followed the defeat of France with the "Wagner-Bürckel-Aktion." The name comes from two Nazi administrators who declared the Baden and Saarland regions to be free of Jews after deporting more than 6,500 to France in October 1940. Once in France, it was not the German authorities but rather the Vichy administration that took the decision to intern the German Jews based on the recent legislation of October 4.[21] More than 7,000 Jewish men, women, and children were sent to Gurs from other camps in southern France in the two years that followed. A combination of fragile health, age, and the "medieval conditions" of the Gurs camp resulted in a rapid and exponential increase in deaths.[22] Within the first two months, 470 men and women died and by November 1, 1943, the figure had risen to 1,038.[23] By this time, the French authorities had also organized a series of deportations with 3,907 Jews leaving for Auschwitz from August 6, 1942, to March 3, 1943.[24]

The camp continued to be used during the liberation of France to hold German prisoners of war along with French nationals accused of collaboration and black market activities. Finally, the site was used for newly arriving Spanish refugees fleeing the Francoist regime to join relatives already in exile. The order to close the camp was issued on November 17, 1945.[25] The fate of the camp was similar to the majority of other internment sites. The French government ordered its closure, the camp was dismantled, and the terrain was used for other activities. The area where the main camp once stood was thus turned over to forestry, obscuring the remaining vestiges of internment. The one trace that could never be removed was the camp cemetery. With more than thousand graves, it was the largest camp cemetery of its kind and is a prime reason why commemorative activities began so early compared to other camps.

The Origins of Commemoration at Gurs

In 1946, Joseph Weill published a study of the French camps on behalf of the Centre de Documentation Juive Contemporaine (CDJC) or Center for Contemporary Jewish Documentation, an organization that had been created by French Jews to collect and publish information on the genocide. The book and indeed the work of the CDJC signaled the will of Jews in postliberation France to call public attention to the concentration camp network that existed in France and to the specificity of Jewish persecution. It also acknowledged the origins of the camp system in the opening sentence of the first chapter: "It is the Spanish republicans who had the sad privilege of inaugurating the French concentration camps; temporary encampments that were on the whole insufficient, sober and dirty ..."[26]

It raises the question of why the Spanish republicans in France at this time were not involved in commemorating these former internment centers. The publication of memoirs began soon after they had left the barbed-wire confines, though it is worth noting that the earliest accounts tended to be published outside of France in other parts of the Spanish republican diaspora.[27] Within France, although the Spanish republicans were active in attending and organizing commemorations in the years following the Second World War, they commonly engaged with other aspects of the recent past that corresponded to their contemporary predicament. In other words, their attention was firmly fixed on securing French and international support for overthrowing Franco's dictatorship in Spain. Consequently, their commemorative activities stressed the Spanish republicans' role in combating fascism and extreme right-wing authoritarianism through the Resistance and liberation of France. They essentially avoided reference to the camps for fear of unsettling the French authorities' sensibilities.[28]

French Jewish organizations followed the closure and neglect of the Gurs camp more closely. The secretary of the Consistoire Central in Paris, Georges Apeloig, intervened on March 1, 1946, to secure continued state funding of the Gurs cemetery following the end of the maintenance contract held by the Highways Agency (Ponts et Chaussées) just months after the camp's closure.[29] Maintenance was a particular problem since the climate and local topography meant that unattended land quickly became overgrown.[30] There followed a pattern of petitions to the French local authorities, who in turn contacted their superiors in Paris for financing the required work on the cemetery. Although funds were sometimes provided, maintenance remained sporadic, leaving the cemetery in a visibly and, for visitors, distressing state of neglect.

Local Jewish associations reacted to conditions at the cemetery by attempting to create a commemorative focus in November 1946. The local branches of the Alliance Anti-Raciste and the Fédération de sociétés juives de France also demanded national recognition of the burial ground and the removal of the remains of four German prisoners of war.[31] They drew up plans for a monument and obtained the necessary permissions. An inaugural commemoration also seems to have been discussed, but there are no further details in the archives whether such an event occurred. The monument, though, seems to have been erected by early 1948. It took the form of an obelisk bearing the Star of David and an inscription: "In memory of all Jews deported to the extermination camps and the 1,250 who lay here victims of Nazi barbarity."[32]

The monument was significant in several respects. First, it marked the earliest attempt to create a commemorative focus at a former concentration camp in France through the construction of a monument. Second, it was part of a growing trend of memorials to Jewish persecution from the Second World War. The few memorials were relatively modest and varied among localities. Some could be found in public spaces, such as the two plaques that were mounted in Paris during the late 1940s. At 43, quai d'Austerlitz the inscription designated a satellite to the Drancy camp where internees had to sort, clean, and pack furniture and possessions stolen from the apartments of Jewish owners.From 1942 to 1944, the German authorities had seized thirty-eight thousand properties and removed all the contents for onward transport to Germany in a plan called Furniture Operation.[33] The Confédération générale des anciens internés et déportés victimes de l'oppression et du racisme and the Fédération française de l'Union internationale contre le racisme organized the plaque.[34] The other plaque could be found on the Vélodrome d'Hiver because of the Alliance Anti-Raciste's initiative. The Jewish Consistory in Paris also facilitated memorials across France in mostly private spaces by supplying ashes from the crematoria of the Birkenau extermination camp. Thirty-one Jewish organizations across France requested ashes for memorials in mainly Jewish cemeteries and synagogues.[35]

The third issue to note about the Gurs monument concerns the inscription's wording and the framework established for future commemorative narratives at the site. The French state's involvement in either the death or deportation of the Jewish internees was not mentioned. This was not uncommon in France for a similar degree of elision could be found with the aforementioned plaques in Paris in addition to other localities. For example, the inscription on the stele that was placed in the Sedan Jewish cemetery in 1947 read: "To our martyrs, our heroes. Victims of Nazi barbarism, 1939–1945 ..."[36] What is significant about the emphasis on Nazi barbarity on the Gurs inscription is that it laid the foundations for both the German and French commemorative speeches in 1963. It facilitated both a nationally specific or (West) German basis for racial persecution while creating the discursive space for highlighting the opposition and resistance of French nationals. In this way, the inscription encouraged the obfuscation of the French state's responsibility for the Gurs camp and the deaths that occurred under the French state's jurisdiction.

While the Gurs monument created a potential commemorative focus for the cemetery, its presence was not sufficient to ensure adequate maintenance of the burial grounds by either the French state or the local municipal authorities. Throughout the late 1940s and most of the following decade, the French government had failed to provide a long-term solution to maintenance of the cemetery, citing a lack of funds and a lack of legislation governing cemeteries of former internment camps containing the bodies of non-French nationals.[37] The call for action that created the impetus for change was not, though, directed at France but at the German authorities. After visiting Gurs, German journalist Peter Canisius wrote an article on August 10, 1957, in the Baden newspaper *Badische Volkszeitung*. It was entitled "Have the Baden Jews been forgotten?" and expressed indignation at the dilapidation of the grounds and graves at Gurs.[38] Reaction in the Baden city of Karlsruhe was swift. In September, the Oberrat der Israeliten Badens/Baden Jewish Consistory contacted the French prefect in Pau.[39] Within months, representatives of the Oberrat and the Karlsruhe Town Hall visited France, met with the prefect, and visited the cemeteries of the Gurs and Noé camps to assess the renovation work needed.[40] The Noé camp was close to Toulouse and had been created by the French authorities in 1941 to receive sick and injured internees from other camps, the majority of whom were either Spanish republicans with war injuries or German Jews. It was a much smaller camp than Gurs, though the highest number of deaths also occurred among the German Jewish internee population.[41]

During the spring of 1958, the Karlsruhe planning department drew up plans and costs for the renovation of the two cemeteries but eventually decided to focus exclusively on Gurs and transform the cemetery into a place of remembrance for all German Jews who died in southern France. The Karlsruhe Town Hall raised the necessary funds of 335,000 deutsche marks through the mobilization of the municipal authorities from where Jews had been deported in October 1940. Both the Town Hall and the Oberrat corresponded with the French local and national authorities to obtain the necessary permissions.[42]

The speed with which the municipal authorities and the Oberrat had reacted to the 1957 newspaper article was impressive and represented the first example of German Jewish-inspired commemorative activity at a Second World War site of trauma in France. It was also a notable achievement given that the creation, control, and administration of the Gurs camp had always remained under French jurisdiction. As we will shortly see, the issue of sovereignty and control over the camp cemetery might well have compromised the future of the burial grounds. However, the persistence of the mayor of Karlsruhe, Günther Klotz, and the head of the Oberrat, Otto Nachmann, was decisive to the transformation of the Gurs cemetery into a site of transnational commemoration that reflected the shared and interconnected pasts of the Baden and Gurs localities.

During the Second World War, both Nachmann and Klotz had spent time in France. Nachmann had emigrated with his wife and at least one of his sons, Werner, to escape Nazi persecution. Werner spent some time at a Parisian school until they relocated to the Aix-en-Provence area in France's Southern Zone following the German invasion in the summer of 1940. When the German military formally occupied the Southern Zone in late 1942, the family was forced into hiding, and it appears that Werner Nachmann participated in the Resistance before returning to Germany as an officer in the French army.[43] Otto died in 1961 before the inaugural commemoration at Gurs but Werner succeeded him as the head of the Oberrat. The mayor of the Karlsruhe Town Hall had also spent some time in France from 1942, serving in the German military construction outfit, the Organization Todt (OT).[44] Given the OT's focus on the Channel and Atlantic Wall defense constructions, it is likely that Klotz would have been in one of the coastal OT centers in western or northern France.[45]

In the postwar decades, both the Nachmann family and Klotz, now a member of the Social Democratic Party, were involved in encouraging Jewish and non-Jewish conciliation in Baden. In 1954, the Karlsruhe municipal authorities repaired tombs in the old Jewish cemetery, and in 1963 they unveiled a plaque recalling the twentyfifth anniversary of the destruction of the city's synagogue. The following year, Klotz met with one thousand Jews in New York who had emigrated from Baden.[46] Accordingly, the renovations of the Gurs cemetery in France can be regarded as part of a wider process of addressing the persecution of Jews in the German Baden region.

The dynamism of the German authorities contrasted with a degree of reticence from the French state that caused a two-year delay to the start of renovation. Although the Gurs municipal council agreed to a lease on the Gurs cemetery to the Oberrat for a period of ninety-nine years, the necessary authorizations from Paris were not forthcoming.[47] According to German archives, the French government was reluctant to grant the right to care for the graves of people who had been stateless or without German citizenship and who would probably have rejected such support from the German authorities.[48] Previously, however, the question of sovereignty had been raised within the French government for more or less the opposite reason: to justify the lack of maintenance at Gurs. In November 1950, the French Ministry of the Interior had explained to his counterpart in the Ministry for Veterans and Victims of War that he was unable to grant credits for maintaining cemeteries such as Gurs because French legislation did not allow for the financing of former internment camp cemeteries containing the graves of non-French nationals.[49]

According to the French administration's logic, neither the French nor the German authorities could manage the burial grounds. The issue was therefore essentially political. French Ministries declined to accept financial responsibility for the graves of stateless persons but neither were those officials comfortable with allowing foreign and specifically German involvement. The French solution was for French Jewish organizations, more specifically the Consistoire Central Israélite de France and Solidarité des Réfugiés Israélites, to oversee the use and distribution of the German finances. The impasse was eventually resolved, though, when the French accepted the German proposition to give overall responsibility for the renovation to the German Jewish association: the Oberrat der Israeliten Badens.[50]

Photos taken for the Oberrat and Karlsruhe Town Hall depict the various stages of the cemetery's renovation.[51] They begin with the state of the cemetery before renovation works commenced in June 1961 and show the monument surrounded by thick overgrowth that obscures the graves and many of the grave markers whether they were lopsided wooden crosses or small plaques mounted on low concrete bases.[52] This is followed by a photo of a scaled-down model of the proposed renovation of the "Deportees' Cemetery" that was produced by the Karlsruhe town planning office. The ensuing photos then show the renovation in progress during 1961 and 1962 with rows of neatly aligned new headstones.[53]

Once the work had been completed, a new inscription written in French and German was placed at the cemetery's entrance that read:

> In memory of the German Jews who were deported in 1940 and who found their last resting place here. The Cemetery was renovated during 1961–1962 by the towns and districts of the Baden region of Germany, and in collaboration with the Baden (Jewish) Consistory under the leadership of Otto Nachmann (1945–1961).[54]

The entrance plaque and cemetery's name clearly evoked the expulsion of the Jews from Germany and the renovation of the grounds by the German and German Jewish organizations. Given the predominance of Jewish graves and financing of the cemetery, this was clearly understandable. But at the same time, it overlooked the diversity of the Gurs internee population and invariably reinforced the monument's inscription that referenced Nazi barbarity, thereby positioning the history of the Gurs camp and its cemetery more narrowly in relation to the Occupation of France. The question of French state responsibility was missing with no reference to the creation of the camp under the Third Republic to intern refugees from the Spanish

FIGURE 10: The Gurs camp cemetery and monument before renovation. Courtesy of the *Département des Pyrénées-Atlantiques. Archives départementales*, 110W 26.

Civil War; the Vichy administration's role in interning the German Jews; and the ensuing negligence that proved a major contributing factor to the high rate of Jewish deaths in the camp. Many of the elements of the French and German speeches were thus in place before the cemetery's inaugural commemoration.

The 1963 Commemoration of the Deportees' Cemetery

The ceremony was initially set for October 30, 1962. The date was chosen to mark the anniversary of the Jews' expulsion from Baden and their subsequent arrival at Gurs in October 1940, but the ceremony had to be postponed until the following year because of German local elections. The eventual date of March 26, 1963, seemed to align more with French wishes than with the Germans' request for the ceremony to coincide with France's Journée du Souvenir des Déportés of April 28.[55] Franco-German liaison was assured by André Chabrerie, a former diplomat who had been the French consul in the Palatinate region of Germany in the late 1930s, and who, by chance, had retired to the village of Gurs.[56] In addition to having represented the German and German-Jewish interests during the renovation, Chabrerie had also played a role in the selection and organization of the activities accompanying the commemorative ceremony. His background in diplomacy undoubtedly facilitated matters and contributed to the smooth running of an event that included a considerable number of participants.

The German delegation was composed of seventy people, including a representative of the German ambassador to France, the German consul from the Bordeaux consulate, the mayor of Karlsruhe, officials from diverse local authorities from the Baden region, the head of the Baden Jewish Consistory, and two Rabbis. Journalists from the German regional press, television, and radio also attended.[57] The French delegates included the prefect from Pau, his accompanying staff, and officials from the Bayonne and Oloron subprefectures. Three senators, four députés and a couple of other parliamentary staff were joined by councilors from nearby Oloron. A sizeable multifaith presence was ensured by the grand rabbi from Paris; the rabbi of Pau; the archbishops of Bayonne and Lescar; a couple of vicars; pastors from Pau and Oloron;

FIGURE 11. Model of the proposed renovation of the cemetery. Courtesy of the Département des Pyrénées-Atlantiques. Archives départementales, 110W 26.

the former pastor of the Gurs Camp (Pastor Charles Cadier); and another two Protestants from the CIMADE aid organization (Jeanne Merle d'Aubigné and Madame David). Finally, various associations representing the (French) Resistance and deportees had also been invited along with French journalists from the regional press.[58]

The morning of Tuesday, March 26, 1963, began with a military emphasis. At 9:15 a.m., Prefect Diebolt laid a wreath at the Gurs village war memorial. The German delegation was then welcomed and taken to the Deportees' Cemetery for an inspection of the First Company of the First Parachute Chasseurs Regiment. The Eleventh Light Intervention Division also performed the French and (West) German national anthems. The decision to include the French military was intriguing enough and potentially insensitive given the history of the camp, the German invasion of France in 1940, and the participation of the French armed forces in the postwar occupation of Germany. The specific choice of military attachments seems even more striking given that both had been in operations during the Algerian War and had only recently returned to France in the summer of 1961. At the same time, the military's participation at Gurs was consistent with commemorations at

FIGURE 12. Work in progress at the cemetery. Courtesy of the *Département des Pyrénées-Atlantiques. Archives départementales*, 110W 26.

the Memorial of the Unknown Jewish Martyr in Paris that had begun in 1956, and also represented a continuation of commemorative practices dating back to remembrance of the Great War in the 1920s.[59] There was also nothing untoward with the actual choice of military units which were present that day. It corresponded to geographical factors of proximity as the soldiers were garrisoned within the same *département*. Although the transnational commemoration of civilian deaths in a former internment center in France was a new phenomenon, the accompanying rituals followed existing conventions concerning the remembrance of military deaths.

The opening format of the commemoration reinforced the identification of the camp and its dead with war. This was emphasized further with the French and German speeches that were delivered at the cemetery's gates in front of a large audience. Monsieur Marcel Diebolt, the prefect and representative of the French government, began with a quote from Albert Camus' allegory of Nazi domination in the novel *La Peste*, "I was told that some deaths were necessary in order to create a world where we would no longer kill each other."[60] It served as an allusion to the deaths in the Gurs cemetery on one level, but deploying

Camus' allegory of Nazi dominance in France also pointed the finger of responsibility for the deaths at Gurs at the Nazi regime. After expressing thanks for the renovation work on the cemetery, Prefect Diebolt then set out a narrative that echoed national memorial narratives circulating in France during the early 1960s or, in other words, the Gaullist interpretation of France and the Second World War.

The history of the Gurs camp potentially disrupted the Gaullist myth of a French nation united in its resistance against tyranny. But this would not have been evident from the prefect's speech. The only eyewitness accounts and names cited were "the testimonies of French resisters and patriots."[61] More specifically, Dr. Gaucher was cited for his participation in a clandestine hospital for the camp's internees that also organized their escape from France. Grand Rabbi René Hirschler was also attributed with helping internees from Gurs to reach Switzerland and Palestine. The speech concluded with a call to the universal ideals of "Peace, Freedom and Dignity," albeit in the particular context of Franco-German friendship.

The next speech was by the Karlsruhe mayor, Günther Klotz. As a mayor, Klotz would not have been under the same level of obligation to reflect the prevailing memory narratives of his country, though he would have been mindful of the issues at stake given the attendance of representatives from the German embassy. He was also a member of the center-left Social Democratic Party that had started to publicly endorse solidarity with Jews in Germany at the end of the 1940s.[62] This might explain Klotz's dynamism in having heeded the German journalist's 1957 call for intervention at the Gurs cemetery, for a memorial action of this kind was very much an exception.[63] But at the same time, the mayor's speech was not entirely devoid of influence from the national narrative circulating in West Germany. During the 1940s and 1950s, this had placed great emphasis on German suffering and victimhood, and myth-making processes concerning the Resistance in Germany were also developing. From the start of the 1960s, a switch from a focus on victims to perpetrators started to occur alongside the coming of age of a new and more critical generation.[64] While these issues were certainly evoked in the mayor's speech, he also implicated other nations in the errors of the past.

FIGURE 13. Speeches at the gates of the Deportees' Cemetery. *Stadtarchiv Karlsruhe, 8/BA Schlesiger A10a/28/1/re.*

Klotz explained how the German journalist's work prompted the renovation.[65] He then envisaged the recent German past by combining elements of German culpability with the idea of wider shared responsibility. For instance, the first reference to shame and guilt was preceded by the qualification, "This chapter of the history of Germany or even, I must admit, of humanity, is also too dark and obscure." Events of the Hitler era and notably racial discrimination were cause for the shame of millions of men in Germany and elsewhere. But at the same time, the mayor also acknowledged German responsibility and referenced German youths as a generation who would be hard pushed to understand how their parents tolerated racial discrimination.

The next section of the speech reflected wider narratives of the war in West Germany that portrayed perpetrators of racial persecution as a minority from among millions of people. He frequently noted indifference to the atrocities (indifference was the most commonly repeated word of the speech), and the failure to prevent tyranny from arising was an issue that, according to Klotz, went beyond national limits. He

FIGURE 14. Wreaths laid at the memorial. Stadtarchiv Karlsruhe, 8/BA Schlesiger A10a/29/3/li.

lauded individuals who resisted in Germany, specifically, the Scholl (Hans and Sophie) siblings from Munich who had been executed for anti-Nazi activities. The other person named was the Austrian Jewish intellectual Stefan Zweig who committed suicide in exile out of despair from the rise of Nazism. It was within the framework of dying for one's country that the mayor evoked the Jews from Baden, and more specifically, the Jewish men who had fought for Germany during the First World War. After paying homage to those who survived the Second World War, Klotz ended his speech with a similar call for peace, freedom, and humanity and underscored the need to combat indifference as a hallmark of Franco-German friendship.

The final and least reported speech in the French press was by the head of the Baden Jewish Consistory, Werner Nachmann. His speech recounted the "barbarity of the Third Reich" in chasing Jews from their country, and he noted that all of the survivors from Baden personally knew some of those now buried in the Gurs cemetery. Nachmann also spoke about the international character of Jewish persecution by linking Gurs to a wider system of racial persecution when he referred to the memory of "the women, men, wives and husbands, the children, parents and friends whether they perished here in Gurs or in Dachau, Belsen, Auschwitz, Majdanek, Sachsenhausen, or Mauthausen [...] In Germany or in France, Poland, or Russia..."[66] Opposition to persecution was also cited in an international and multifaith context when he questioned whether enough had been done in the last twenty years to remember resisters from all countries: "French, Belgians, Polish, Christians, and Jews, and without also forgetting Germans in distress...." Although he ended the speech by stressing the importance of understanding the facts of this history, his closing remarks also thanked the local French population for doing everything possible to help the deportees. In doing so, his conclusion inadvertently reinforced the French prefect's emphasis on popular French concern for the Gurs internees.

The German and German Jewish speeches of March 1963 clearly aimed to acknowledge but also to deterritorialize racial discrimination and resistance. In this way, the content of the speeches reflected some of the specific circumstances that bound together Karlsruhe and the Gurs area. However, the reach of this undertaking was clearly limited and perhaps too nuanced to modify the trajectory of the French official's patriotic framing of the camp. Indeed, the emphasis on Nazi persecution inadvertently reinforced certain elements of the French commemorative narrative that depicted the Jewish deaths at the Gurs camp, and to some extent even the camp itself, as a result of Nazi evil. This also facilitated the French emphasis on Gurs as a site that potentially symbolized French opposition to Nazism.

At the 1970 commemoration, which marked the thirtieth anniversary of the German Jews' internment, Prefect Gabriel Gilly rehearsed an even stronger image of the French Resistance against "Nazi atrocities." Without any apparent irony, he concluded his speech with a quote from Alphonse de Lamartine's nineteenth-century poem, *La Marseillaise de la Paix*: "Can we see any borders in heaven?"[67] While the reference to mankind's errors is clear, another and less immediately obvious message can be taken from the history behind the verse. Lamartine penned his words in riposte to a German poem that was replete with bellicose nationalism. In the French official narrative of Gurs, all that was seemingly universal was essentially inflected with a patriotic framing of France, the war years, and its history of conflict with Germany.

Bibliography

Archival Collections
Archives départementales, Pyrénées-Atlantiques
   72W 53, cimetière: entretien, plan et cérémonies, 1945–1972.
   110W 26, cabinet du préfet.
Archives départementales, Pyrénées-Orientales
   1287W 1, camps provisoires d'hébergement.
Centre d'accueil et de recherché des Archives nationales (CARAN)
   F7 15104, dossier camp de Gurs.
Stadtarchiv Karlsruhe
   8/BA Schlesiger.

Newspapers
La Dépêche, February 2, 1939.
La République des Pyrénées, March 27, 1963.
Sud Ouest, March 27, 1963.

Books and Articles
Badia, Gilbert; Joly, Françoise; Joly, Jean-Baptiste; Laharie, Claude; Lederer, Ingrid; Mathieu, Jean-Philippe; Roussel, Hélène; Rovan, Joseph; and Vormeier, Barbara. *Les barbelés de l'exil*. Grenoble: Presses universitaires de Grenoble, 1979.
Barcellini, Serge and Wieviorka, Annette. *Passant, souviens-toi! Les lieux du souvenir de la Seconde Guerre mondiale en France*. Paris: Plon, 1995.
Caron, Vicki, *Uneasy Asylum: France and the Jewish Refugee Crises, 1933–1942*. Stanford, CA: Stanford University Press, 1999.
Cate-Arries, Francie, *Spanish Culture behind Barbed Wire: Memory and Representation of the French Concentration Camps, 1939–1945*. Lewisburg, PA: Bucknell University Press.
Chueca, Josu, *El campo vasco*. Tafalla: Txalaparta, 2nd ed. 2017.
Dreyfus, Jean–Marc. "Conflit de mémoires autour du cimetière de Bergen-Belsen," *Vingtième Siècle. Revue d'histoire* 2, no. 90 (April 2006): 73–87.
Dreyfus-Armand, Geneviève. *L'Exil des républicains espagnols en France. De la Guerre civile à la mort de Franco*. Paris: Albin Michel, 1999.
Fogg, Shannon L. *Stealing Home: Looting, Restitution, and Reconstructing Jewish Lives in France 1942–1947*. Oxford: Oxford University Press, 2017.

Gilbert, René. *Günther Klotz: Die politische Biographie eines badischen Kommunalpolitikers*. Karlsruhe: Info Verlag, 2014.

Hansen, Alise. "A *Lieu d'Histoire*, a *Lieu de Mémoire*, and a *Lieu de Vie*: The Multidirectional Potential of the Cité de la Muette," *French Historical Studies* 37, no. 1 (February 2014): 117–50.

Herf, Jeffrey. *Divided Memory: The Nazi Past in the Two Germanys*. Cambridge, MA: Harvard University Press, 1997.

Heuman, Johannes. *The Holocaust and French Historical Culture, 1945–65*. Basingstoke: Palgrave Macmillan, 2015.

Jackson, Julian. *France: The Dark Years 1940–1944*. Oxford: Oxford University Press, 2001.

Laharie, Claude. *Le Camp de Gurs, 1939–1945: Un aspect méconnu de l'histoire du Béarn*. Pau: J&D Editions, 1985.

Lebourg, Nicolas and Moumen, Abderahmen. *Rivesaltes: Le camp de la France 1939 à nos jours*. Perpignan: Éditions Trabucaire, 2015.

Ludwig, Max. *Das Tagebuch des Hans O. Dokumente und Berichte über die Deportation und den Untergang der Heidelberger Juden*. Heidelberg: Lambert Schneider, 1965.

Malo, Eric. "De Vichy à la Quatrième République: La Camp de Noé (1943–1945)," *Annales du Midi: revue de la France méridionale* 104, no. 199 (1992): 441–58.

———. "La Camp de Noé (Haute-Garonne) de 1941 à 1944," *Annales du Midi: revue de la France méridionale* 100, no. 183 (1988): 337–52.

Marcuse, Harold. "Memorializing Persecuted Jews in Dachau and Other West German Concentration Camp Memorial Sites," in *Memorialization in Germany since 1945*. Bill Niven and Chloe Paver, eds. Basingstoke: Palgrave Macmillan, 2010.

Maurel, Stéphane. *Aux Origines de la Fédération des Déportés et Internés Résistants et Patriotes (FNDIRP, 1944–1946)*. Paris: FNDIRP, 1993.

Nora, Pierre. *Les Lieux de Mémoire*. Vols. 1–3, Paris: Gallimard, 1997.

———. "Between memory and history: Les lieux de mémoire," *Representations* no. 26 (Spring 1989): 7–24.

Perego, Simon. "Les commémorations de la destruction des Juifs d'Europe au Mémorial du Martyr juif inconnu du milieu des années 1960," *Revue d'Histoire de la Shoah*, 193, no. 2 (2010): 471–507.

Peschanski, Denis. *La France des camps. L'internement 1938–1946*. Paris: Gallimard, 2002.

Schramm, Hannah and Vormeier, Barbara, *Vivre à Gurs: Un camp de concentration français 1940–1941*. Paris: François Maspero, 1979.

Schulze, Rainer. "Forgetting and Remembering: Memories and Memorialisation of Bergen-Belsen," *Holocaust Studies* 12, no. 1 (2006): 217–235.

Sharples, Caroline. *Postwar Germany and the Holocaust*. London: Bloomsbury, 2016.

Soo, Scott. "From international origins to transnational commemoration: the cemetery of the Gurs camp, 1939–1963," *French History* 34, no. 1 (October 2020): 82–104.

———. *The routes to exile: France and the Spanish Civil War refugees, 1939–2009.* Manchester: Manchester University Press, paperback ed. 2017.
Weill, Joseph. *Contribution à l'histoire des camps d'internement dans l'Anti-France.* Paris: Centre de Documentation Juive et Contemporaine, 1946.
Werner, Josef. *Hakenkreuz und Judenstern: das Schicksal der Karlsruher Juden im Dritten Reich.* Karlsruhe: Badenia Verlag, 1990.
Wieviorka, Annette. *Déportation et Génocide: Entre la Mémoire et l'Oubli.* Paris: Plon, 1992.
Zuccotti, Susan, *The Holocaust, The French, and the Jews.* Lincoln: University of Nebraska Press, 1999.

Notes

1. Speech by Günther Klotz, *La République des Pyrénées*, March 27, 1963. All translations are my own unless otherwise indicated.
2. "La journée franco-allemande à Gurs," *Sud-Ouest*, March 27, 1963.
3. Annette Wieviorka, *Déportation et Génocide: Entre la Mémoire et l'Oubli* (Paris: Plon, 1992), 391–92, 395–6.
4. Serge Barcellini and Annette Wieviorka, *Passant, souviens-toi! Les lieux du souvenir de la Seconde Guerre mondiale en France* (Paris: Plon, 1995).
5. Alise Hansen, "A *Lieu d'Histoire*, a *Lieu de Mémoire*, and a *Lieu de Vie*: The Multidirectional Potential of the Cité de la Muette," *French Historical Studies* 37, no. 1 (2014): 117–50; Nicolas Lebourg and Abderahmen Moumen, *Rivesaltes: Le camp de la France 1939 à nos jours* (Perpignan: Éditions Trabucaire, 2015); Scott Soo, "From international origins to transnational commemoration the cemetery of the Gurs camp, 1939–1963," *French History* 34, no. 1 (2020): 82–104.
6. Centre d'accueil et de recherché des Archives nationales (hereafter CARAN), F7 15104. État des personnes inhumées dans le cimetière de Gurs, February 9, 1945.
7. Barcellini and Wieviorka, *Passant, souviens-toi!*, 318–24.
8. Johannes Heuman, *The Holocaust and French Historical Culture, 1945–65* (Basingstoke, UK: Palgrave Macmillan, 2015), 16; Caroline Sharples, *Postwar Germany and the Holocaust* (London: Bloomsbury, 2016), 6–8.
9. Wieviorka, *Déportation et génocide*, 391; Barcellini and Wieviorka, *Passant, souviens-toi!*, 7–9.
10. Pierre Nora, *Les Lieux de Mémoire.* Vols. 1–3 (Paris: Gallimard, 1997).
11. Barcellini and Wieviorka, *Passant, souviens-toi*, 8.
12. Pierre Nora, "Between memory and history: Les lieux de mémoire," *Representations*, no. 26 (1989): 7.
13. Sharples, *Postwar Germany and the Holocaust*, 117–20.
14. Harold Marcuse, "Memorializing Persecuted Jews in Dachau and Other West German Concentration Camp Memorial Sites," in *Memorialization in Germany since 1945*, ed. Bill Niven and Chloe Paver (Basingstoke, UK: Palgrave Macmillan, 2010), 192–204.
15. Rainer Schulze, "Forgetting and Remembering: Memories and Memorialisation

of Bergen-Belsen," *Holocaust Studies* 12, no. 1 (2006): 217–35; Jean-Marc Dreyfus, "Conflit de mémoires autour du cimetière de Bergen-Belsen," *Vingtième Siècle. Revue d'histoire* 2, no. 90 (2006): 73–87.
16. Archives Départementales des Pyrénées-Orientales, 1287W 1. Instructions, May 3, 1938.
17. Geneviève Dreyfus-Armand, *L'Exil des républicains espagnols en France. De la Guerre civile à la mort de Franco* (Paris: Albin Michel, 1999), 59.
18. *La Dépêche*, February 2, 1939.
19. Vichy's rapid implementation of anti-Semitic legislation is discussed in Julian Jackson, *France: The Dark Years 1940–1944* (Oxford: Oxford University Press, 2001), 355–60.
20. Claude Laharie, *Le Camp de Gurs, 1939–1945: Un aspect méconnu de l'histoire du Béarn* (Pau: J&D Editions, 1985), 76. Laharie's book also contains information on the various groups and waves of internees. For further details on the Basque internees, see Josu Chueca, *Gurs: El campo vasco* (Tafalla: Txalaparta, 2nd ed., 2017). More information on the International Brigades can be found in: Barbara Vormeier, 'Les internés allemands et autrichiens en 1939–1940,' in *Les barbelés de l'exil*, Gilbert Badia et al. (Grenoble: Presses universitaires de Grenoble, 1979); Jean-Philippe Mathieu, 'Les communistes allemands et leur organisation (avril–août 1939), in Ibid.; and Denis Peschanski, *La France des camps. L'internement 1938–1946* (Paris: Gallimard, 2002), 52–62.
21. Vicki Caron, *Uneasy Asylum: France and the Jewish Refugee Crises, 1933–1942* (Stanford: Stanford University Press, 1999), 332–3; Susan Zuccotti, *The Holocaust, The French, and the Jews* (Lincoln: University of Nebraska Press, 1999), 65–7.
22. For a firsthand account from the head of the women's hospital in the camp, see Max Ludwig, *Das Tagebuch des Hans O. Dokumente und Berichte über die Deportation und den Untergang der Heidelberger Juden* (Heidelberg: Lambert Schneider, 1965), 16–19. See also Hannah Schramm and Barbara Vormeier, *Vivre à Gurs: Un camp de concentration français 1940–1941* (Paris: François Maspero, 1979), 71–98.
23. Laharie, *Le Camp de Gurs*, 228. The scale of death at the Gurs camp was staggering compared to the total of three thousand deaths in all of the French camps between the summers of 1940 and 1944: Peschanski, *La France des camps*, 146.
24. Laharie, *Le Camp de Gurs*, 228, 236.
25. CARAN, F7 15104. Ministre de l'Intérieur to Direction Générale des Camps.
26. Joseph Weill, *Contribution à l'histoire des camps d'internement dans l'Anti-France* (Paris: Centre de Documentation Juive et Contemporaine, 1946), 9.
27. An in-depth analysis of incarceration in the Spanish republicans' memoirs and other literary forms is the focus of Francie Cate-Arries, *Spanish Culture behind Barbed Wire: Memory and Representation of the French Concentration Camps, 1939–1945* (Lewisburg, PA: Bucknell University Press).
28. For further details of this proto-commemorative culture of exilic memory, see Scott Soo, *The Routes to Exile: France and the Spanish Civil War Refugees, 1939–2009*, paperback ed. (Manchester: Manchester University Press, 2017), 204–09.

29. CARAN, F7, 15104.
30. CARAN, F7, 15104. Rapport de l'Ingénieur, February 21, 1944.
31. CARAN, F715104. Président de l'Alliance Anti-Raciste, Comité directeur des Basses-Pyrénées to Préfet, November 4, 1946.
32. Archives Départementales des Pyrénées-Atlantiques (hereafter AD PA), 72W 53. Président de la Fédération des sociétés juives de France to souspréfet d'Oloron, June 16, 1947.
33. Shannon L. Fogg, *Stealing Home: Looting, Restitution, and Reconstructing Jewish Lives in France 1942–1947* (Oxford: Oxford University Press, 2017), 1.
34. The Confédération générale des anciens internés et déportés victimes de l'oppression et du racisme was mainly composed of former Drancy internees. Stéphane Maurel, *Aux Origines de la Fédération des Déportés et Internés Résistants et Patriotes (FNDIRP, 1944–1946)* (Paris: FNDIRP, 1993), 51.
35. Barcellini and Wieviorka, *Passant, souviens-toi!*, 381–2, 458–60.
36. Ibid., 456.
37. Soo, "From international origins," *French History*, 96.
38. René Gilbert, *Günther Klotz: Die politische Biographie eines badischen Kommunalpolitikers* (Karlsruhe: Info Verlag, 2014), 256.
39. CARAN, F715104. Oberrat to Préfet, October 24, 1957, and note from the Préfecture, November 23, 1957.
40. Gilbert, *Günther Klotz*, 257.
41. Before the deportations in the summer of 1942, the Noé camp population fluctuated from 1,200 to 1,500 internees, of whom approximately 300 died in the camp. Peschanski, *La France des camps*, 239; Eric Malo, "De Vichy à la Quatrième République: La Camp de Noé (1943–1945)," *Annales du Midi: revue de la France méridionale* 104, no. 199 (1992): 338; Eric Malo, "La Camp de Noé (Haute-Garonne) de 1941 à 1944," *Annales du Midi: revue de la France méridionale* 100, no. 183 (1988): 441.
42. Gilbert, *Günther Klotz*, 257.
43. Josef Werner, *Hakenkreuz und Judenstern: das Schicksal der Karlsruher Juden im Dritten Reich* (Karlsruhe: Badenia Verlag, 1990), 353.
44. I would like to thank James McSpadden for highlighting Klotz's participation in the Organization Todt.
45. Gilbert, *Günther Klotz*, 28.
46. Ibid., 262–3.
47. AD PA, 72W 53. Souspréfet to maire de Gurs, June 13, 1959, and correspondence between the Oberrat and souspréfet, August 4 and 20, 1959.
48. Gilbert, *Günther Klotz*, 259.
49. CARAN, F715104. Ministre de l'Intérieur to Ministre des Anciens Combattants et Victimes de la Guerre, November 24, 1950.
50. Gilbert, *Günther Klotz*, 260.
51. AD PA, 110W, 26.
52. AD PA, 110W, 26. Deportationsfriedhof in Gurs, Sudfrankreich, zustand vor 1961.

53. AD PA, 110W, 26. Neugestaltung 1961/62.
54. AD PA, 110W, 26.
55. AD PA, 72W 53, M. Chabrerie, Administration Provisoire du Cimetière des Déportés to Secrétaire Général de la souspréfecture d'Oloron-Ste-Marie, January 18, 1963.
56. AD PA, 72W 53. Monsieur Chabrerie's CV.
57. AD PA, 110W 26. Délégation Allemande.
58. Even though some Spanish republicans had been part of the Resistance in this region of France and had also suffered from deportation, they were not represented at the commemoration.
59. Simon Perego, "Les commémorations de la destruction des Juifs d'Europe au Mémorial du Martyr juif inconnu du milieu des années 1960," *Revue d'Histoire de la Shoah*, 193 (2010): 472.
60. AD PA, 72W 53. Transcript.
61. AD PA, 72W 53.
62. Jeffrey Herf, *Divided Memory: The Nazi Past in the Two Germanys* (Harvard: Harvard University Press, 1997), 253. Sharples, *Postwar Germany*, 39.
63. Marcuse, "Memorializing Persecuted Jews," 193.
64. Sharples, *Postwar Germany and the Holocaust*, 30.
65. AD PA, 72W 53. Transcript of the mayor's speech.
66. AD PA, 72W 53. Transcript of Werner Nachmann's speech.
67. AD PA, 72W 53. Transcript, October 25, 1970.

Contributors

SHANNON L. FOGG is professor of history in the Department of History and Political Science at Missouri University of Science and Technology. She is the author of *The Politics of Everyday Life in Vichy France: Foreigners, Undesirables, and Strangers* (Cambridge University Press, 2009) and *Stealing Home: Looting, Restitution, and Rebuilding Jewish Lives in France, 1942–1947* (Oxford University Press, 2017). She has held fellowships at the United States Holocaust Memorial Museum, the École des Hautes Études en Sciences Sociales, and the Paris Institute for Advanced Study. Her current projects examine the geography of looting and restitution in Paris and the humanitarian aid provided by the American Friends Service Committee in France during World War II.

BERTRAM (BERT) M. GORDON is professor emeritus of history at Mills College in Oakland, California. His most recent book is *War Tourism: Second World War France from Defeat and Occupation to the Creation of Heritage* (Cornell University Press, 2018). Among his numerous other publications, Gordon's groundbreaking study of *Collaborationism in France during the Second World War* (Cornell University Press, 1980) was based in part on interviews with former French supporters of Nazi Germany. With Erica J. Peters, he co-edited "Food and France: What Food Studies Can Teach Us about History" for French Historical Studies (2015), and has written on the history of chocolate, the 1968 revolts in France, and the history of Vichy as a spa town. Gordon is Associate Editor of the *Journal of Tourism History* and is general secretary of the International Commission for the History of Travel and Tourism. He is a core member of the Tourism Studies Working Group at the University of California, Berkeley, and with Shelley Baranowski has co-edited *H-Travel* since its inception in 2003.

ABIGAIL E. LEWIS is a George L. Mosse research fellow at the University of Wisconsin-Madison. She is writing a book, *Double Exposure: French Photography and Everyday Choices from Nazi Occupation to Liberation, 1940–1950*, about the history of photographs and photographers in German-occupied and Vichy France. Her work analyzes multivalences of photography to illuminate the complex realities of daily life in both the occupied and Vichy zones of France. She also shows how photographs were critical to French society's understanding of this contentious history after 1944. Her research has been supported by generous funding from the George L. Mosse Program, the Chateaubriand Dissertation Fellowship, the Société des Professeurs Français et Francophones d'Amérique, the Mellon Foundation, the United States Holocaust Memorial Museum, and the Hebrew University of Jerusalem, Israel. Lewis has written about photography, Jewish history, and resistance for *In geveb: A Journal of Yiddish Studies*, *Film and Fiction for Scholars of France*, and *H-Diplo*. She also has a forthcoming article in *French Politics, Culture & Society*.

SANDRA OTT is professor of Basque studies at the William A. Douglass Center for Basque Studies, University of Nevada, Reno. She received a master of letters and doctor of philosophy in social anthropology from the University of Oxford. Her works include *The Circle of Mountains: A Basque Shepherding Community* (Oxford: The Clarendon Press, 1981) and *War, Judgment, and Memory in the Basque Borderlands, 1914–1945* (Reno: University of Nevada Press, 2008). *Living with the Enemy: German Occupation, Collaboration and Justice in the Western Pyrenees, 1940–1948* appeared in 2017 (Cambridge: Cambridge University Press). She has held a fellowship at the École des Hautes Études en Sciences Sociales in Paris and received a summer stipend from the National Endowment of the Humanities. Her current book project explores the experiences of Jews in the Basses-Pyrénées during the Occupation and the spoliation of their property, as well as local complicity and strategies for protecting Jewish property from theft by the Vichy and Nazi regimes.

SCOTT SOO is an associate professor in European history and Director of the Centre for Transnational Studies at the University of Southampton. He has published on refugee history in France and is the author of *The Routes to Exile: France and the Spanish Civil War Refugees, 1939–2009* (Manchester: Manchester University Press, paperback ed. 2017). With Sharif Gemie, he co-edited *Coming Home? Vol. 1: Conflict and Return Migration in the Aftermath of Europe's Twentieth-Century Civil Wars* (Newcastle-upon-Tyne: Cambridge Scholars Publishing, 2013) and *Coming Home? Vol. 2: Conflict and Postcolonial Return Migration in the Context of France and North Africa, 1962–2009* (Newcastle-upon-Tyne: Cambridge Scholars Publishing, 2013). Soo is a member of the editorial committee of the journal *Diasporas: Circulations, migrations, histoire*. His current projects examine the mobilization of refugees for the Battle of France and the commemoration of France's internment camps in the postwar decades.

JULIA S. TORRIE holds an AM and PhD from Harvard University and is a professor of History at St. Thomas University (Canada). Her research focuses on the social and cultural history of wartime in twentieth-century Europe. She has written *German Soldiers and the Occupation of France* (Cambridge, 2018), which uses soldiers' diaries, letters, and amateur photographs to examine the occupation of France (1940-44) from below. A previous book, *"For Their Own Good": Civilian Evacuations in Germany and France, 1939-1945* (Berghahn, 2010), compared civilian evacuations in the two countries. Torrie has been a fellow of the Institute for Advanced Study, Nantes, and the Alexander von Humboldt Foundation. Her research has also been funded by the Social Sciences and Humanities Research Council of Canada and the German Academic Exchange Service. She has published articles and reviews on soldier tourism, photography, the German home front, and wartime food history, and is working on a book about German women's wartime roles as military auxiliaries.

EDWARD B. WESTERMANN received his doctorate from the University of North Carolina, Chapel Hill and is a Regents Professor of History at Texas A&M University, San Antonio. He has published extensively on the Holocaust and military history. He is the author of *Hitler's Ostkrieg and the Indian Wars: Comparing Genocide and Conquest* (University of Oklahoma Press, 2016), *Hitler's Police Battalions: Enforcing Racial War in the East* (University Press of Kansas, 2005), and *Flak: German Anti-Aircraft Defenses, 1914–1945* (University Press of Kansas, 2001). He is a former Fulbright Fellow at the Free University of Berlin, a J. B. and Maurice C. Shapiro Fellow at the United States Holocaust Memorial Museum, and a three-time fellow of the German Academic Exchange Service. Cornell University Press published his newest book, *Drunk on Genocide: Alcohol and Mass Murder in Nazi Germany,* in March 2021.

Index

A

Adenauer, Konrad 164
alcohol 8, 86-89, 91, 92, 93, 95, 96, 99, 110, 120, 121, 123, 125
Alliance Anti-Raciste 172, 173, 190
American Friends Service Committee 5, 41, 43, 49, 54-61, 193
anti-Semitism 15, 16, 17, 19, 42, 169, 170
Apeloig, Georges 172
Argelès-sur-Mer 170
Armenia 169
armistice 20, 44, 46, 47, 49, 68
Auschwitz 6, 9, 27, 40, 88, 100, 103, 116, 171, 185
Austria 2, 111, 147, 169

B

Baden-Baden 54, 60, 61
Basque Country 4, 9, 108, 114, 170
Bayonne ix, 114, 179
BdS (*Befehlshaber der Sicherheitsdienst*) 114, 115, 118
Béarn ix, 4, 9, 108, 164, 187, 189
Béarnais 108, 119, 120, 121, 123, 125
Beaune-La-Rolande 166
Benoist, Alain de 138, 154, 155, 156, 157, 163
Bergen-Belsen 168, 169, 186, 187, 189
Birkenau 173
Bordeaux 7, 114, 115, 116, 117, 118, 119, 120, 128, 130, 133, 134, 135, 179
Borrisow 96
Braque 141, 144
British Blockade 48, 59

C

Caen 97
Canisius, Peter 174
Chabrerie, André 179, 191
children 5, 6, 14, 22, 26, 27, 33, 35, 43, 44, 45, 47, 48, 49, 51, 53, 54, 56, 58, 59, 61, 63, 65, 67, 73, 74, 93, 94, 112, 114, 116, 117, 121, 127, 128, 133, 142, 171, 185
children's colonies 43, 44, 47, 51, 53, 54
Churchill, Winston 46
CIMADE 180
Cocteau, Jean 141, 144
collaboration ix, 3, 31, 42, 47, 128, 171, 177
colonial 63, 64, 65, 66, 72, 73, 74, 86, 87, 88, 95, 96, 98
colonialism 64, 65, 66, 73, 75
comradeship, Nazi notion of 69, 109, 129
concentration camps 9, 164, 168, 169, 170, 171, 173
Confédération générale des anciens internés et déportés victimes de l'oppression et du racisme 173, 190
Consistoire Central Israélite de France 176

D

Dachau 185, 187, 188
Daladier, Édouard 169
De Col, Jackie 93
de Gaulle, Charles 151, 164
deportation: of Jews 9, 27, 29, 40, 52, 53, 115, 116, 117, 118, 128, 130, 134, 173, 191
Diebolt, Marcel 180, 181, 182
Dimanche Illustré 21
Doberschütz, Otto v, viii, 7, 9, 108, 109, 110, 111, 112, 113, 114, 115, 116, 117, 118, 119, 120, 121, 122, 123, 124, 125, 126, 127, 128, 129, 131, 132, 133, 134, 135, 136
Dohse, Friedrich Wilhelm 114, 120
Dostoevsky, Fyoder 148, 150
Drancy 6, 27, 116, 165, 166, 167, 173, 190
drinking rituals 109, 123
Dudnik, Raisa 96

E

Eastern Front 62, 67, 101, 102, 103, 107, 110, 111, 142
Eberbach, Heinrich 97
Elmes, Mary 53, 55, 58, 61
emigration 115

F

Federal Republic of Germany 166, 168
Fédération de sociétés juives de France 172
Fellowship evenings: in Germany 110
female auxiliaries 8, 62, 64, 67, 77, 86
female labor 7, 63, 77
femininity 7, 8, 63, 70, 72, 73, 74, 77, 87, 109
flânerie 142
Fortunoff Video Archive 14, 18, 38, 40
Fourcade, Marie-Madeleine 119, 126, 129, 134, 135
Francs-tireurs et partisans-main d'oeuvre immigrée (FTP-MOI) 21
Frawley, Margaret 48, 58
Freiburg 102, 106, 164
friendship, German notion of viii, 7, 109, 129, 164, 182, 184
fundraising 45, 48

G

Galicia 95, 99, 106, 170
Garat, Pierre 115, 116, 117, 133
Gaucher, Dr. 182
gender roles 2, 63
German Democratic Republic 168
Germany v, vii, 2, 8, 9, 13, 41, 43, 44, 46, 49, 50, 54, 56, 57, 58, 65, 68, 72, 75, 78-82, 84, 88, 89, 91, 98, 100, 104, 106, 108, 109, 117, 121, 123, 127, 128, 131-134, 139, 140, 142-147, 149, 150, 152-155, 160, 161, 164-170, 173, 175, 177, 179, 180, 182-188, 191, 193, 195-196
gilets jaunes (Yellow Vests in France) 154
Gilly, Gabriel 185
Great War 11, 12, 43, 45, 55, 59, 79, 81, 181
Gurs v, vii, viii, ix, 8, 9, 58, 60, 164-182, 185-190

H

Hague Convention 46
Heydrich, Reinhard 93, 111, 113, 115, 130, 132
Higher SS and Police Leaders

(HSSPF) 91
Himmler, Heinrich 89, 100, 104, 111, 112, 127
Hirschler, René 182
Hitler, Adolf vii, 3, 7, 10, 13, 41, 57, 59, 72, 78, 79, 80, 82, 83, 85, 87, 90, 97, 99, 101, 102, 103, 105, 106, 107, 110, 112, 118, 129, 130, 131, 132, 144, 146, 149, 150, 151, 152, 153, 183, 196
Hoover, Herbert 43
Hörner, Helmut 98, 100, 107
Hôtel Bompard 6, 26, 28, 40
Hôtel Raphael 138
Hoth, Hermann 87
hypermasculinity 8, 91, 98, 109

I

Identitaire movement 138, 154
International Brigades 170, 189
internment camps (*also see* Beaune-la-Rolande, Gurs, Mauthausen, Mérignac, Noé, Pithiviers, Rivesaltes) 6, 9, 26, 27, 28, 30, 166, 176

J

Jewish Historical Institute 18, 24, 25, 29, 32, 37, 38, 39, 40
Jewish National Front 20
Jünger, Ernst v, 6, 7, 9, 10, 13, 137, 138, 139, 140, 141, 142, 143, 144, 145, 146, 147, 148, 149, 150, 151, 152, 153, 154, 155, 156, 157, 158, 159, 160, 161, 162, 163
Jünger, Gretha 146

K

Karlsruhe 9, 164, 165, 166, 168, 174, 175, 176, 177, 179, 182, 183, 184, 185, 186, 187, 188, 190
KdS (German security police and intelligence service, Kommando of the Sipo-SD) 114, 115, 118, 120, 125, 126
Kershner, Howard 49, 50, 56, 58, 59, 60
Kielce pogrom 6, 34
Kirchhorst (Saxon) 141, 142, 144, 147
Klotz, Günther 175, 176, 182, 183, 184, 187, 188, 190
Kohl, Helmut 150
Kolomädel 72, 73, 74, 77, 78
Koloniale Frauenschule 72, 73

L

Laborde, Jean (Basque double agent) viii, 7, 108, 109, 115, 118, 119, 120, 121, 122, 123, 124, 125, 126, 128, 129, 131
Les Milles Joint Distribution Committee (JDC) 26, 40
Loustaunau-Lacau, Georges 119, 135

M

Majdanek 185
manpower shortages 63
Marseille v, 5, 6, 9, 14, 15, 16, 19, 20, 21, 23, 24, 25, 29, 30, 31, 32, 33, 34, 35, 36, 37, 38, 40, 44, 49, 51, 53, 56, 58
masculinity, Nazi notion of 7, 8, 64, 87, 89, 90, 91, 94, 98, 99, 104, 109, 110, 118, 123, 124
maternalism 64, 75, 76
Mauthausen 185
MBF (Militärbefehlshaber in Frankreich) 3, 4, 94
Mérignac 116, 117, 130, 133, 134
Meyer, Kurt 97

Ministry of Economic Warfare 49, 52
Montmartre 145
Mont-Valérien, executions at 150
morale, and perception of troops as "soft" 63
motherhood 8, 63, 70, 74, 77, 78
mothers 7, 24, 46, 64, 65, 73, 74, 77, 78, 116

N

Nachmann, Otto 175, 177
Nachmann, Werner 175, 184, 191
Nachrichtenhelferinnen 62, 77, 80, 83
National Bolshevism 139, 154
Navarrenx 164
Nazi regime 8, 87, 151, 182
new woman 64, 77
Noé camp 129, 135, 174, 187, 190
Normandy 98, 143, 157, 160
nostalgia 143, 145
Nouvelle Droite (New Right in France) 154

O

Oberrat der Israeliten Badens 174, 177
Organization Todt 175, 190
Ostheer (Eastern Army) 95
Ostrausch (Intoxication of the East) 86

P

Palestine 18, 182
Papon, Maurice 115, 117, 118, 128, 129, 130, 131, 133, 134, 136
Paris v, 3, 6, 7, 10, 13, 35, 37-40, 44, 48, 49, 55, 58, 59, 61, 68, 69, 78, 82, 83, 84, 92, 93, 114, 115, 118, 129, 130, 132-138, 140-146, 148-154, 156-163, 172, 173, 176, 179, 181, 186-190, 193, 194
Pau, court of justice in viii, ix, 7, 108, 118-121, 123-126, 134-136, 174, 179, 187, 189
Perpignan 53, 187, 188
Pétain, Phillipe 37, 52, 151
Piaf, Edith 21, 22
Picasso, Pablo 141, 144
Pickett, Clarence 46, 48, 56, 58
Pirotte, Julia v, 5, 6, 9, 14-27, 29, 31-40
Pithiviers 166
Poinsot, Pierre 114, 118, 119, 120, 129, 135
Poland 6, 14-16, 19, 34, 35, 36, 37, 39, 48, 66, 68, 72, 73, 92, 99, 101, 106, 113, 115, 144, 185
Polish Communist Party 19
propaganda 47, 48, 118
Prussian Socialism 139

Q

Quakers (*See also* American Friends Service Committee) 5, 43-49, 51, 53-61

R

Radical Party 169
Rakovka ghetto 97
Ravoux, Sophie (aka Doctoresse, Charmille) 146, 153, 160
refugees 15, 20, 21, 43, 44, 50, 51, 55, 58, 144, 166, 169, 170, 171, 177, 188, 195
Rivesaltes 53, 61, 166, 187, 188
Roma and Sinti 96
Russia 96, 169, 185

S

Saarland 9, 170
Sachsenhausen 185

Sacré Cœur Cathedral 143
Sarraut, Albert 170
Scholl, Hans and Sophie 184
SD (Sicherheitsdienst, Nazi security and intelligence service) 106, 108, 110-115, 117, 118, 120-126, 129, 132
Security Police (Sipo) 93, 94, 106, 111, 113, 114
Six, Franz 111
Skarżysko labor camp 97
Slitinsky, Michel 117, 130, 133, 134
sociability, Basque importance of 2, 108, 109, 121, 125
Solidarité des Réfugiés Israélites 177
Sontag, Susan 17, 38, 39
Soviet Union 2, 68, 87, 94, 97, 101, 104, 142, 149
Spaak, Suzanne 14, 19, 38
Spanish Civil War 43, 166, 169, 170, 177, 188, 189, 195
Spanish republicans 172, 174, 189, 191
Stabshelferinnen 62, 68, 69, 71, 77, 81, 83, 84, 85
Stülpnagel, General Otto von 103, 149, 151
Switzerland 50, 182
"sword and shield" argument in France 151, 152

T

Tour d'Argent restaurant v, 6, 137, 141, 152, 153, 154, 158, 160
tourism 4, 144, 153, 163, 195
tourists 94

V

Vélodrome d'Hiver 173
Venus, altar of 143, 153
Vichy, and anti-Jewish statutes viii, ix, 1, 2, 3, 5, 6, 9-12, 16, 20, 37, 38, 40, 42, 46, 47, 49-61, 115, 119, 128, 130, 133, 134, 151, 152, 157, 158, 161, 162, 166, 169, 170, 171, 179, 187, 189, 190, 193, 194
Violence, Sexual v, 7, 86, 96, 100, 101, 102, 104, 105
Von Brauchitsch, Walther 92

W

Wagner-Bürckel-Aktion 170
Wehrmacht v, 7, 8, 40, 62, 63, 65, 70, 71, 72, 73, 74, 77, 80, 81, 82, 85, 90, 91, 92, 95, 96, 97, 99, 101, 102, 103, 104, 105, 106, 138, 140, 145, 151, 153, 157, 159, 162
Wilflingen, Jünger Museum 150, 156, 161
Witzenhausen Colonial School 72, 79, 85

Y

Ybarnegaray, Jean ix, 124
yellow star 7, 148, 151, 153

Z

Zweig, Stefan 184